The Art of Classic Quiltmaking

HARRIET HARGRAVE
& SHARYN CRAIG

C&T PUBLISHING

Editor: Annie Nelson
Technical Editor: Carolyn Aune
Copy Editor: Steven Cook
Book and Cover Design: Christina Jarumay
Design Direction: Diane Pedersen
Illustrations: Jay Richards with assistance from Claudia Boehm and Norman Remer © C&T Publishing
Photography: Harriet Hargrave's quilts, contributor quilts, process shots, photos taken at Harriet's home, and photo
of authors by Brian Birlauf; Sharyn Craig's quilts by Carina Woolrich; Sharyn's studio by Sharyn Craig.

Attention Teachers:
C&T Publishing, Inc. encourages you to use this book as a text for teaching. Contact us at
800-284-1114 or www.ctpub.com for more information about the C&T Teachers Program.

We take great care to ensure that the information included in this book is accurate and
presented in good faith, but no warranty is provided nor results guaranteed. Since we have no
control over the choice of materials or procedures used, neither the authors nor C&T Publishing,
Inc. shall have any liability to any person or entity with respect to any loss or damage caused directly or indi-
rectly by the information contained in this book.

Library of Congress Cataloging-in-Publication Data

Hargrave, Harriet.
 The art of classic quiltmaking / Harriet Hargrave and Sharyn Craig.
 p. cm.
 Includes bibliographical references and index.
 ISBN 1-57120-079-7
 ISBN 1-57120-070-3 (pbk.)
 1. Patchwork. 2. Strip quilting. I. Craig, Sharyn Squier.
II. Title.
TT835.H3379 2000
746.46--dc21   99-6823
                                   CIP

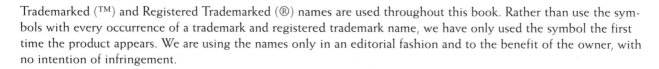

Trademarked (™) and Registered Trademarked (®) names are used throughout this book. Rather than use the sym-
bols with every occurrence of a trademark and registered trademark name, we have only used the symbol the first
time the product appears. We are using the names only in an editorial fashion and to the benefit of the owner, with
no intention of infringement.

Published by C&T Publishing, Inc.
P.O. Box 1456
Lafayette, California 94549

Printed in China
10 9 8 7 6 5 4 3 2 1

Dedication

We both feel strongly that the opportunity to write this book has been a privilege provided by C&T Publishing. We could never have written this book without the support of our students, families, and friends. We deeply appreciate all the quiltmakers responsible for so many of the techniques found in these pages. We recognize that we have been given a gift as competent teachers and a commission to pass it on. To that end, we dedicate *The Art of Classic Quiltmaking* to every quilter who is looking for "something more."

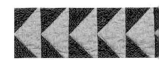

Acknowledgments

The writing of this material wouldn't have been possible if it weren't for the pioneers in our industry. It is not our intention to insinuate that we are directly responsible for the creation of the methods and techniques shared here. What we've attempted to do is present an accumulation of the methods we consider valid, long term, and worthwhile.

We would like to acknowledge Ernest Haight and Barbara Johannah. They are the true pioneers in the development of many of our efficient machine piecing and quilting techniques. We feel that it is unfortunate that these two innovators have not received their due credit for the multitude of contributions they are responsible for. They have definitely made an impact on our personal quilting skills.

Three quilters, who were inspired by the techniques of Ernest and Barbara, then expanded and shared them with all of us through their books and workshops, include Eleanor Burns, Mary Ellen Hopkins, and Blanche Young. There are many other people who have made incredible contributions to the world of quilting that we would like to mention, including Jinny Beyer, Judy Martin, Marti Michell, Jean Ray Laury, Bonnie Leman, and Nancy Crow. If it weren't for all of these people, we probably wouldn't be quilting today.

The quilts shown in this book would never have been possible were it not for all the thousands upon thousands of quilts made by our ancestors. These were the true pioneers who made quilts without the benefit of books, patterns, classes, speed methods, and tools. Without their quilts and the people of today who included photos of their quilts in books, magazines, calendars, and so forth, for our inspiration, we may never have been turned on to the beauty and wonder of quiltmaking.

We would also like to thank the following manufacturers who graciously donated much of the fabric and batting used in the creation of many of the quilts included in this book: Moda, Fasco, RJR, Marcus, Benartex, Northcott Monarch, P&B Textiles, Mountain Mist, and Hobbs.

Thank you to Omnigrid, Fiskar, John Flynn, and Lynn Graves for providing some of the supplies and notions used in the photography.

Finally, we would like to thank Bruce Fightmaster for allowing us to invade his private home to take pictures of some of our quilts deliciously displayed on his clothesline, front porch swing, and back fence. Thanks also to Galen Hasenpflug for his design expertise and assistance in setting up the photographs taken in Harriet's house.

Table of Contents

We thought you might enjoy hearing the story of how we got involved in this project. The concept of *The Art of Classic Quiltmaking* was to concentrate on antique quilts and their timeless appeal, while presenting in-depth information necessary to understanding the process of producing quality quilts.

Harriet's first task was to write an outline for the book. Once the outline was developed, she realized that in order to be able to do the best job, she needed help. In the spring of 1997, Harriet approached Sharyn about co-authoring this book.

Introduction

From the beginning, co-authoring was a natural because of our differences. We have always agreed to disagree, while at the same time respecting each other's right to be different. We have very different styles...not only in our quilts, but also in our homes, in the way we dress, in where we live, in the way we work, even in the way we think! We approach quilting from totally different directions. We have taken those differences and joined them to give you, the reader, the best of all worlds.

Through the years we have discovered how different we really are. One of our favorite stories is of a shopping trip to buy Harriet some new clothes for a lecture that she was giving. Sharyn kept pulling soft, drapey, "silky" garments for Harriet to try on, and then raved about how great they looked on her. Harriet fell for this and purchased a "beautiful" dress. That night during the lecture, a fabric lecture no less, she realized she felt almost naked in front of the group—a most unsettling feeling when you're standing in front of a room of strangers. That night on the way home in the car, we talked about the lecture and how we totally disagreed with each other on the subject of prewashing fabric. Sharyn always prewashes, and Harriet almost never prewashes her fabric. One of the reasons Sharyn prewashes is because she can't stand the feel of the stiff fabric. Harriet is just the opposite—the stiffer the better. As this conversation was evolving, we realized that this penchant for fabric texture followed right through with the clothes we like to wear. Sharyn likes silks, rayons, light, and loose cottons—anything soft and drapey.

Harriet, on the other hand, prefers denims and wools that are heavier and more tailored.

Even though we have these differences, we are constantly amazed at how similar we are. One morning, years later, as we met for breakfast, we were amazed to see that we looked like the Bobbsey Twins in form-fitting blue jeans and white long-sleeved tee shirts. However, Sharyn's tee shirt was very long, loose, and scooped-necked, while Harriet's was turtlenecked, tucked in, and fitted. We both just laughed! Another time we were to lecture together. We both showed up in black loafers, jeans, black jackets, and white shirts. However, Sharyn's jacket was a rayon caftan while Harriet's was a crisp linen tailored blazer. The point of all this is, through our differences, we have similar end results.

Our quilts are no different. The way we approach our quilting is no different. We both start by looking at pictures of antique quilts. Harriet's goal is to technically re-create the quilt using modern methods and equipment, attempting to have the new one look as old as the original. Sharyn, on the other hand, uses antique quilts as a platform. Her goal is to be inspired by the original quilt, but not to replicate it. She needs her quilts to be something different.

We have both developed reputations of being thorough, knowledgeable, understanding teachers who are willing to go the extra mile for our students. Our main concern is to make sure that our students learn as much as possible in the short time we have together. If we have a complaint about teaching, it's that our classes are never long enough to share everything we want to. We are teachers, first and foremost. It is with this mindset that we join our individual talents at this time to put in writing so much of the information we don't have an opportunity to share in the classroom on a day-to-day basis.

In this book we provide a foundation of much-needed basics. Knowing various techniques is crucial to being able to make wise choices. There is not only one solution that is possible; there are many. It won't be a case of right and wrong. Our goal is that you start to investigate your needs and discover what methods produce the best results for you.

Perhaps you've done recipe quilts in the past and now want to expand on what you've learned. Or maybe you want to be able to make your own decisions about your quilts without having to rely on what someone else has decided is the exact size, exact number of fabrics, or type of border for your quilt. You want control of your quilts, but perhaps you lack the confidence or skills necessary to have that control. We hope that you find inspiration and solutions within these pages.

What you'll find in this book will be two different styles of working and teaching. Harriet is known for her knowledge in the technical aspects of quilting, which include such topics as the care of fabric, workspace formulas, figuring yardage, and working through basic quilts. Sharyn's talents will take you into drafting, piecing, and the exploration of design options. We are not going to be imposing rules; we give you guidelines and suggestions. We want you to accept the responsibility for your choices. If you try all the exercises in each chapter, you'll be able to decide what methods and techniques work best for you. By using the book as a workbook and doing the various exercises, you'll become an informed, educated quilter, capable of making the right choice for yourself. You can't make informed decisions if you haven't explored all the options. You will probably discover that you'll use different methods depending on a given situation, and that's okay. What we are striving for is that you discover what gives you the best result for any project you choose. That won't always be the same technique because needs change. If you have all the options, you can make the choices. This strategy isn't only used for choosing a piecing technique; we want you to approach tool choices, fabric care options, workspace set up, working style, and design possibilities in the same way. It is our desire that through this book we can enable each of you to become more independent, responsible, and capable quilters. So now it's time to relax, have fun, and enjoy the process of making quilts!

Harriet & Sharyn

Selecting & Collecting Fabric

For a quiltmaker, color and fabric become a love affair. We buy fabric just to own a piece of a certain print we fall in love with. We buy yards and yards of fabric, then store it on shelves, stroke it, dream about the quilts it will become, and simply "possess" it. Quilters tend to buy fabric impulsively. There is something about the color, texture, and feel of fabric that lures us into this art in the first place. So building a collection is no problem for most quilters. But to have a great collection of fabric, one needs to have a wide variety of colors and prints.

So, how does one go about collecting fabric toward the goal of having a full-spectrum collection? Begin by reading through the following information about the different types of prints, as well as the discussion on color, value, and intensity. Later we will have you work with your own fabric collection to begin to identify where there are gaps.

Fabric Categories

If you're just beginning to quilt, walking into a quilt store for the first time can be an overwhelming experience. You will be greeted by hundreds of bolts of beautiful fabric. Tiny prints, stripes, plaids, vines, bold designs, oriental motifs, jungle prints, and old-fashioned calicos seem to jump off the shelves at you. The mixture of various types of prints needed for a quilt tends to

make us uncomfortable, as we would never select such a combination for the clothes we wear. Often our guidelines in the way we select clothing will hinder our ability to explore different combinations of color and pattern when it comes to putting fabrics together to make a quilt. Just keep telling yourself, "This will get easier. . . this will get easier." The selection of fabric for a quilt can be the most exciting, and yet the most intimidating and frustrating aspect in quiltmaking. We've yet to meet a quilter that does not agonize a bit when choosing the fabric for a particular project.

How in the world do you know where to start selecting fabric? If you realize that different fabrics fall into different categories, and that you need a combination of fabrics from these different areas, it will be much less intimidating. Understanding the types of fabrics will also help you determine whether or not your collection is truly balanced. Let's look at the categories that fabrics fall into and their effect on a quilt.

SOLID FABRICS
Solid fabrics have no design or markings. A contemporary look is easily achieved using solids. Traditional Amish quilts are famous for their imaginative use of solids. Solids define and offset one or more prints used in a design. Solids do, however, show every piecing flaw and uneven quilting stitch. If you

are a beginner, you might want to avoid working with a large amount of solids.

SMALL PRINTS
These are fabrics with a small, subtle print, usually a two-color contrast print. These fabrics tend to "read" as solid from a distance but add the texture that solids often lack. They make an excellent background choice.

Solids

Small prints

CALICOS

Calico fabrics have small prints with one color for the background and two or more other colors in the print design. Because of the various colors and sizes of the prints, be sure to stand back from the fabric and see which colors are predominant. In some calicos, the background will be the only color you see from a distance, while in others, one or more colors from the print will stand out. Because of the variety of color in these prints, you can often persuade a color to look different from what it actually is. An example is a peach flower that can be made to look pink with the addition of other predominantly pink fabrics. Our advice is to relax when trying to determine what color is really present in the original fabric. The more you experiment with this concept, the more you'll see how true it is.

DOTS

These are fabrics with a one-color background and a dot or a print that appears as a dot from a distance, such as apples or flowers. Your eyes tend to jump around when trying to focus on them. These fabrics add interest, but can become very busy. The fewer fabrics your quilt has, the more important it is to limit the use of this type of print.

VINEY PRINTS

These prints tend to be larger in scale than small prints, with meandering lines running throughout. They have one background color and at least one other contrasting color used in the print. These prints read as airy and light, and add a lot of interest to the patchwork.

LARGE PRINTS

These are prints with large patterns that can be splashy or subtle, and often use multiple colors. Large prints offer many possibilities. When

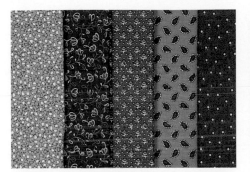
Calicos

Viney prints

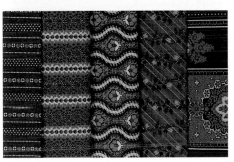
Stripes

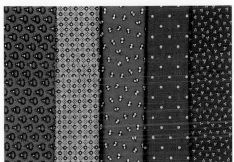
Dots

Large prints

Plaids

cut into pieces, a variety of color combinations and movement are created. Eighteenth and nineteenth century quilts used large prints and paisleys, giving a richly colored and elaborate look. Many of these prints are being reproduced today.

STRIPES

These are fabrics that contain bands of print or lines that most often run parallel to the selvage. These can be simple two-color stripes or multi-colored intricate patterned stripes. Stripes are exciting when used as borders or sashing. It's fun to cut them apart to use individual design elements, or to try cutting them into bands, mitering them together, and using them as frames around units in the piecework. You can get different uses from one

stripe by placing a template on the striped fabric in different directions.

PLAIDS

Plaids are fabrics with lines, either woven in or printed on the surface, running perpendicular to each other. Plaids have become very popular, especially with the interest in reproducing antique quilts. If it's important to have the lines of the plaid be straight with a pattern (i.e. borders, sashing, alternating blocks, etc.) then be advised that printed plaids are frequently printed off grain, making them very difficult to manage. It has become acceptable to use plaids that are not straight in pieced blocks to add more interest. A woven plaid is easy to straighten if necessary, and can be cut exactly on grain.

TONALS

Also known as tone-on-tone, these fabrics are printed within the same color family. An example would be a fabric that uses three different blues to create a floral or any other pattern.

Tonals

The next time you go to the fabric store, start looking at the fabrics to determine the category they belong to. Once you start to group those hundreds of bolts of fabric into categories, it will make it easier to "see" the fabrics. *Remember, your collection needs a variety of print types.*

Color

If you've made a quilt in colors that you liked, but haven't been happy with the end result, you might jump to the conclusion that you have trouble with color. The first thing you have to do is figure out what bothers you about the quilt. Perhaps it is too washed out, or the opposite, too high contrast, or maybe the prints are too busy. Not everyone likes the same kind of feeling in their quilts, so don't ask someone else how to fix the problem until you know what the problem is for you.

Color is simply a matter of personal taste. If you like a particular color combination, then it's okay to use it. If you went back to school and studied color, you would learn that all colors go together. In a nutshell, there are four basic color schemes:

1) Monochromatic (all one color)
2) Complimentary (across from one another on the color wheel)
3) Analogous (adjacent to each other on the color wheel)
4) Polychromatic (all colors)

Every possible combination of colors fits somewhere into one of these color schemes. So relax. Trust your instinct and personal taste when selecting various colors to put together.

Sharyn tends to like clearer, brighter colors and higher contrast of value in her quilts. Harriet is more drawn to the softer contrast and duller-value colors. This doesn't mean that we don't use both, nor does it mean that Sharyn never makes a low-contrast quilt or Harriet a high-contrast one. It means that knowing what we like best makes it easier to avoid mistakes when selecting fabrics for a quilt or our fabric collection.

Color wheel

Value

Value is the degree of light or dark a color has. We'll have you arrange your fabrics in a range from light to dark in just a bit. This will be to arrange the color by value. The pure color from the color wheel is made lighter by adding white, darker by adding black. Value is relative! The color, as well as the value of a fabric, will change according to the type of print, adjacent colors and objects, the light source, position of the light source, finish of the fabric, etc. All fabrics have their place on the light/dark scale. An example would be placing a medium blue between a pale yellow and pale pink.

Light to dark

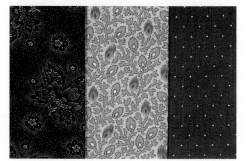

Fabrics of the same value

Value is relative

It would look quite dark in comparison. The same medium blue, on the other hand, would look quite light if placed between a dark navy and a burgundy.

Fabrics of the same value will combine and run together when placed next to each other.

An understanding of value will keep you from creating quilts with little depth and interest.

Range of color intensity

Value finder tools

Intensity

Intensity is the brightness factor. A color can range from very dull to very bright. The pure color from the color wheel is the most intense it can be. Changing the intensity of a color occurs when gray is added. The more gray you add, the duller it appears.

Value and intensity are difficult concepts for many people to grasp. An afternoon in a quilt store stacking up combinations of fabrics is the best way to start to understand how all this fits together. You might find it helpful to use a value finder (a red plastic report cover from the stationery store or a tool, such as the Ruby Beholder® available at quilt shops).

When you hold the value finder up to your eye and look at the stack of fabrics through the red, you should immediately have a sense of whether a fabric is lighter or darker than others in the stack. It doesn't matter whether the fabric is red, green, blue, or pink. What comes across is which of the fabrics is darker and which is lighter.

Now, all the color study in the world works fine to a point. That point is really challenged, however, when you start to work with prints, which most quilters do. If you work

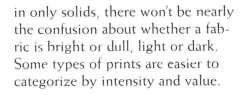
Categorizing by color intensity and value

Multi-colored fabrics

in only solids, there won't be nearly the confusion about whether a fabric is bright or dull, light or dark. Some types of prints are easier to categorize by intensity and value.

Tonals, for example, tend to be easier and safer to work with, which is probably why there is such an abundance of them. Once you begin mixing colors on a single piece of fabric, it's much more challenging to see how bright or dull, light or dark, it is. Is it a green, or is it a black? When both colors exist on a single piece of fabric just what exactly is it? We can't, and shouldn't, avoid these fabrics. They are the "glue" that often holds a quilt together. These multi-colored fabrics are sometimes referred to as "binder fabrics."

Sometimes it isn't important to know whether a certain piece of fabric is light or dark, dull or bright, unless this is what is causing your

quilts to "miss." So, think about it. What do you like? Next time you go to a quilt show we suggest that you take lots of pictures. Don't just take pictures of the quilts you like. Take pictures of the quilts that you don't like. Then, when you're in the privacy and quiet of your home, study those photos. You can't fix the problems in your own quilts until you fully understand what it is that you do or don't like about them.

Remember that color choice is a personal preference. You may love a combination of colors and prints, only to have a salesclerk or friend try to discourage you and replace your choices with their preferences. Remember, this is your quilt and it must suit your likes and tastes. The more quilts you make, the more you'll learn about your personal preferences.

Separate and Study the Fabrics You Already Own

If you've already begun to collect fabric, now is the time to get that fabric organized so you'll know what you have. One of the easiest ways to organize your fabric is by color. Separating the blues from the greens, from the reds, etc., will help tremendously when you are beginning to organize. Next, arrange all the fabrics in a value range from the very lightest to the very darkest shade of that color. If you can't tell where one fabric starts and the next leaves off, then you don't need any more fabric in that value. On the other hand, if you discover big gaps in your light to dark group, then those are the areas you might want to concentrate on when going into a fabric store.

Next, sort the piles into further divisions of bright, strong intensities and soft, dull intensities. If a certain fabric doesn't fit, remove it. You will probably find that you need to add a few fabrics and discard others.

Once you have done this, you may begin to see that you have more fabrics of one color as well as value or intensity than the others. Quilters tend to purchase more medium values than any other. If your piles are looking a bit flat, you may be missing the "zingers," as quilters call them. These are the "hot," "bright," or more intense colors that we often shy away from. Fuchsia, hot pink, turquoise, and yellow are some of these sparklers. If carefully blended into your colors, they can add the "zing" or life to an otherwise dull quilt. Remember, a little goes a long way, so tread lightly with these, but do not overlook them. If you only have these wild colors, you may need to calm things down a bit with softer and duller fabrics. Once you start to see what you have, you will need to go shopping. While there, concentrate on collecting by value, intensity, and print scale, not just color.

Once you've filled out your piles by value, you'll want to look at the color range. Do you have stacks of blue, but no red? Do you dislike rust or peach, so it's missing altogether? Now you're going to need to stretch your tastes and become aware of all the colors. For a great collection of fabric and one that is an endless source of inspiration, you need to fill out the color range.

Don't overlook your pile of blender fabrics. These are the neutral fabrics that can get lost in a pile of prints. They are the beiges, tans, creams, grays, browns, and blacks. These

 Tip Check a color wheel and identify where your gaps are. Perhaps you have a lot of purple and red, but no red-violet. Or you love reds and have lots of them, but they are all the same. Don't forget to add rusts, brick reds, reddish browns, burgundies, roses, all the way to pinks. Again, you need to go shopping for these colors in order to fill in the gaps. You might want to attach pieces of each of your fabrics, by color and value, onto notecards to take with you.

colors will not change other colors, but can add richness and compatibility to color schemes that seem to fight. You may be seriously lacking in these fabrics, as they are not the most exciting to buy. Quilts need these blenders, so start filling in this pile as you shop.

Don't overlook the back side of your fabrics. Remember that you own both sides, and that the back side is often the exact color and value needed for a particular spot. Many fabrics have an "aged" look on the back side.

Once at the store, select fabrics to bridge the gaps. Remember that the

Sort fabrics into lights, mediums, and darks

Further division of intensity

Back side of fabrics

colors available tend to follow those popular in ready-to-wear. To get the widest range, you must start buying now and never stop. Why? Because fabric colors change. Some years the yellow-toned colors, such as yellow-green, yellow-red, etc., are what the stores offer. The next year the blue tones may prevail. If you want to own a well-rounded collection, you need to start collecting immediately. You might not be able to find an olive green this year, or you might find a pumpkin orange that you really dislike. Make sure you buy a piece of it for the collection. You can be sure that when the color is no longer available and you do not have it, it will be the perfect color for one of your designs (trust us).

Ideas and Suggestions for Choosing Fabrics for a Quilt

Harriet loves antique quilts. She loves not only the overview of the color combinations, but also the exact type of fabrics that were used. That is why she has found so much satisfaction in the challenge of reproducing old quilts.

For Sharyn, the exact type of prints in a quilt never enters the decision making process. She goes more by the look one gets from ten feet away. Harriet would like to be six inches from the original quilt when selecting fabrics. Sharyn might borrow the color scheme from an 1870 Log Cabin quilt to make an Album quilt. It has taken both of us years to learn these characteristics about ourselves and the way we like to work, so don't be too hard on yourself.

Following is a list of hints and tips that will give you some tangible guidelines for choosing fabrics for a specific quilt. Initially, the quilts you make will probably have a limited

number of fabrics in them, but as you make more and more quilts and get a bigger and bigger fabric collection from which to work, you may want to try a scrap quilt.

■ **Start by falling in love with one fabric.** You might find it easier if this is a multi-colored print of a medium to large scale. Other fabrics can be chosen that have the colors used in the print of this one fabric. Make sure that if the large print is taken away, the other fabrics still work together and can stand on their own.

■ **Choose prints that vary in scale.** The use of many different types and scales of prints will make the quilt come to life! If only tiny prints are used, they will cancel each other out and the quilt will die. If you select all large prints, it can become extremely busy.

Different types of prints

■ **Use small prints and tiny dot-type fabrics instead of solids to create interest.**

■ **Use small prints and tonals as blenders.** These are dull fabrics that work as cement to hold the units together. They are most often used as background in quilts. These fabrics allow the more interesting ones to look their best and not compete. Blenders also allow the design or pattern to be dominant.

■ **Vary the theme of the print.** Too many paisleys, rosebuds, or leaves become monotonous.

■ **Choose the darker fabrics first, lighter fabrics last.** We tend to find that medium and dark fabrics are easier to select. In addition there are more of them available than there are lights.

■ **Satisfy the quilt before the room it is to live in.** Too many times we over coordinate a quilt to make it match wallpaper or carpeting exactly. Instead of the quilt being the showpiece of the room, it merely blends into everything else.

■ **Experiment with fabrics that may "clash" a bit.** Clash is not always bad. It keeps a quilt from being ho-hum. Instead of rust, try maroon. Instead of navy, try purple or mauve. Try a color that looks good with the whole quilt.

■ **Don't be afraid to throw in a little black.** Black will put life into color and give it spark.

■ **Think about what you like most.** Think about the colors you tend to prefer. Become aware of your environment. Things like advertisements, greeting cards, upholstery color schemes, flower gardens, and so forth, offer great inspiration. Clip out ideas and make notes of color combinations you see and like.

■ **Three to seven fabrics** are a good number to aim for when first beginning to make quilts. Scrap quilts are easier as you gather experience, but can definitely be overwhelming when you are first starting out.

■ **Stack the selected bolts, then step back 6 to 10 feet and squint at them.** This will help the colors stand out and you'll start to notice which colors are too similar, too bold, or blend too much. Squinting magnifies the difference between the fabrics by letting less light into your eyes, therefore reducing the influence of the color, making the lighter colors more visible. After some trial and error, you'll develop a combination that combines dark, light, medium, varying print scales, etc. If you squint and they live harmoniously together, you probably have a winner. This is where some quilters find red value finders really helpful.

■ **Lay the bolts on their sides** so that you're only seeing the edge of the bolt. Remember that you'll be cutting the fabric into small pieces. Seeing the fabrics in the relationship and proportion as they will appear in the block can prove quite helpful.

■ **Go with your instincts.** If you feel that it looks too busy, it probably is. If the colors make you nervous, don't use them. You need to like your fabric, but remember that trial and error and experimentation are the best ways to learn. Your tastes will change, but you must be willing to take a chance occasionally.

■ **Intense colors or contrasting colors can emphasize parts of a design.** Conversely, low-contrast combinations can give the eye a place to rest. Having some high-and some low-contrast blocks can be particularly important in scrap quilts.

■ **Be aware of one-way prints.** They have a distinct up and down direction and can appear upside down if not worked with carefully.

■ **Utilize the "view-a-patch" system.** Cut various template shapes and sizes from a sheet of frosted or white template plastic. Place it on the fabric to see what it will look like when cut up. There are precut templates like this that are commercially available.

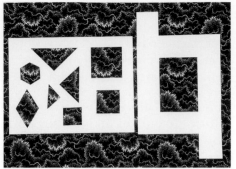

"View-a-patch" tools

■ **Think of:**
1) Type and scale of print
2) Value and intensity of each fabric
3) Color
Color is the least important of the three. If strong on color only, but weak on the other two, you can end up with a boring quilt.

■ **Try to look at the fabric in natural light.** Artificial lighting can distort colors and the way they relate to each other. When making a quilt for a specific place, we suggest that you also look at the fabrics in that environment to check for the way the colors work together.

■ **Pull the fabric off the shelf** and look at it alone. Other colors on the shelf can affect its color.

Block Mock-ups

Once you've chosen the fabrics you think will work, you might want to buy ⅛ yard of each to experiment with before buying large quantities. This can eliminate the possibility of purchasing yardage only to find that one or more of the fabrics really doesn't work as expected. Remember that fabric can sell out fast, so time can be of the essence here. There are different ways to experiment with your fabrics. You might find one of the following methods works better than another for you. Some quilters are okay with just cutting fabric and charging right into the project, while others like the security of seeing it first.

■ **Make a mock-up with the actual fabric of the block or blocks in the quilt to scale on graph paper.** By cutting small pieces of each fabric and positioning and gluing them onto the graph paper, you'll get a true idea of what the block will look like when pieced together in full size. This allows you to work out color placement and design ideas before committing to a particular fabric. It may seem time-consuming, but it can save you time and money in the long run. This step can also be helpful to beginners by letting them see how the pieces are going to fit together for the piecing.

■ **Coloring graph paper with colored pencils is another option** if a fabric mock-up is too much for you. You will need to be careful to simulate the value and texture of the fabric, as pencils can be deceiving.

■ **Utilize any of the quilting design programs available for your computer.** Many fabric libraries are now available so that you can actually design with currently available fabrics right on screen.

■ **Simulate the block with pieces of fabric.** Lay the chosen background fabric on the table. Fold it so that it's the approximate size of the block. Place other fabrics on top next to each other to get a feel for how they will work together. Adjust the fabrics until you feel comfortable with the result.

■ **When working with a collection of fabrics and blocks, distance from them is usually the best way to determine if they are "working."** Using a reducing glass, the viewfinder of a camera, or looking through the large end of binoculars makes items appear at a distance. This can give you a feel for the finished product.

Choosing Fabrics for Sashing and Borders

Sashing and borders act as frames around the blocks and the entire quilt. These fabrics need to enhance the overall quilt.

Think about the following ideas when planning your sashings and borders:

■ Because of their position and purpose, the color of the border and/or sashing fabrics can influence the color scheme of the entire quilt. The color used for the sashing or the border can be the same color as found in the blocks, or it can introduce a whole new color to the overall effect of the quilt. Often a combination of repeating a predominant color along with adding one or two new fabrics gives a striking result.

■ The fabrics used in the blocks can be repeated in the sashings and borders or totally different fabrics, perhaps a solid or stripe, can be introduced.

■ The use of a large scale print that contains the colors of the fabrics in the quilt top can have a dramatic effect and can pull all the colors together.

■ Border stripes create a coordinated look to the overall quilt. When mitering corners, the border becomes an elaborate frame but with very little effort.

■ Consider how you want to quilt the borders. Remember that a busy printed fabric will not let the quilting design show. A solid or small print fabric allows the quilting to be the focal point.

Tip When buying a border stripe, check to see how many repeats are across the width of the fabric. If there are four repeats, the yardage needed will be the length of the quilt. If there are only three, you'll need to buy double that amount.

Tip It's often easier to select sashing and border fabrics once all the blocks are done. Take the blocks to the quilt shop and "audition" them with a variety of fabrics. Stand back and study the effect different fabrics and even different colors can give. You'll start to see that the fabric you are choosing to work with can affect the width of each border. It's sometimes fun to ask a total stranger for an opinion. But again, remember that you make the final decision. It's your quilt, and you need to like it.

Scrap Quilts

Scrap quilts are very popular, but they require a much larger variety of fabrics. So far we've been talking about choosing fabrics that work together in a quilt that coordinates and follows a color scheme. This method of color selection is indicative of modern-day quilts. We tend to make quilts more for decorating purposes than for using up scraps and making bedding. Therefore it's necessary to be very selective about the colors chosen.

When you graduate into scrap quilts, you'll find that buying fabrics becomes a treasure hunt. You will begin buying more and more fat quarters, half yard pieces of every plaid and stripe you find, and constantly looking for those unusual fabrics.

Scrap quilts depend more on the effect created by the use of light, medium, and dark, as well as texture from the print, than they do on color. If you look at many old quilts, you'll find that more times than not the colors do not relate to one another, but the pattern emerges because of the value changes and surface (print) interest in the fabric.

Begin by sorting your fabrics, scraps and all, into three piles: light, medium, and dark. Keep large pieces of fabric folded so that they do not overpower the smaller pieces. If a fabric appears dark in the light pile or light in the dark pile, it's probably a medium. Mediums are the most apt to give you trouble. What you need to keep in mind is how they react to the other fabrics chosen for a particular project. As you sort through your fabrics, you may find that these piles are becoming stunning color combinations for a quilt. You almost can't have too many fabrics when making a scrap quilt—often the hardest part is deciding which ones to eliminate.

We often buy fabric because it's "pretty," ignoring the value and texture completely. If you were to examine old scrap quilts, you would find fabrics in them that you would not consider buying. There are even complete blocks that we don't care for when examined individually. However, when you look at the overall quilt, the effect is wonderful. If you're serious about making stunning scrap quilts, you need to make an effort to break out of buying only the pretty fabrics and start collecting some "dogs" and "uglies" so that your quilts will have life and depth.

Why Quilters Have to Collect Fabric

Quilters are constantly telling us that if they buy one more yard of fabric, their spouses will go off the deep end. As a result, they are always trying to justify their fabric purchases. We believe that we need to reassess our thinking and give ourselves permission to be involved in an art that requires working materials. A fabric collection is no different than a stamp collection or a collection of fishing tackle.

In order to keep our inspiration and have ease in working through our design ideas, it is imperative that we have our fabrics around us. In the case of quiltmaking, a complete palette of fabric is a necessary tool. You cannot rely on the store to have the colors you need when you want them. What is available at any one time may give you a very unbalanced use of color and value. In the case of scrap quilts, a collection gathered over the years produces the richest quilts.

How Much to Buy?

Without a doubt, the single question we are asked the most is "how much fabric do you buy when you see a print you like?" The answer to this goes back to knowing and understanding what kind of quilts we like to make.

When buying for the collection, buy in the amounts that you have room to store and can afford. Think about why you are buying the fabric. If it's for a project, always buy a little more than you think you're going to need, so that the leftovers can be added to your stash. If you do not know what the fabric will be used for, buy a small amount, up to one yard. And please, stop worrying about what you would do if you ran out of a particular fabric. The most interesting quilts are created from running out of a fabric and having to fill in with a new, different fabric. Both of us primarily make scrap quilts. When making scrap quilts it isn't important to have a lot of any one fabric. What is important is to have a large variety of fabrics, but not a large quantity of any one fabric. For us, $\frac{1}{2}$ yard of one fabric is usually enough to own.

There are certain types of fabrics that we do tend to buy in larger quantities. One example is to buy larger amounts of blenders that we can envision as a control background fabric. Even in our scrap quilts, we often like to control the background. Until recently, there has not been a large assortment of good background fabrics to choose from, so when we saw one that we really liked, then we bought between 3 and 5 yards of it. (Now there are so many available that smaller yardages are purchased and a mix and match attitude takes over.) How much to buy for backgrounds depends on how large a quilt we intend to make.

Another type of fabric we tend to buy more yardage of is one that "reads" border or backing. Now granted, this is risky for the impulse buyer. After all, who really knows how much of that piece will actually be needed when you finally get around to making a quilt that needs that particular fabric. But when a fabric feels like a border, Sharyn likes to buy $1\frac{1}{2}$ yards and Harriet 3 yards. Backings are between 4 and 6 yards for the impulse buy, and that amount only when we find it on sale at a price too good to leave in the store. More often than not, backings are not purchased until the quilt top is done. Then you know exactly how much you'll need. Determining what kinds of fabric you are going to like for borders and backings will come only with personal experience.

When first starting out it's advisable to buy fabrics used for backgrounds, sashings, borders, and filling blocks after the individual project is developed and specific yardage requirements are known. Eventually you get to the point where you can just relax and buy fabric for the thrill and enjoyment of having it!! You can justify your fabric purchases as being every bit as valid as sporting goods and toys.

Where to Shop for Fabric

Where to shop for fabric is governed by where you live and what is available. You are one of the lucky ones if you have even one full-service quilt shop within an hour of you. Really lucky quilters have more than one quilt shop, because that provides more choices. If you don't have a quilt shop, do you have a good-quality traditional fabric store with a good assortment of 100% cotton fabrics? If you lack either of these shopping solutions, consider mail order. There are several excellent mail-order sources. Check ads in quilt magazines for various mail-order companies that sell fabric. If you're connected to the Internet, there are a myriad of online opportunities to order both supplies and fabric. Check out these if you're so inclined.

Fabric Care & Consideration

If you're a new quilter, you are no doubt confused by all the do's and don'ts you are told when it comes to caring for your fabric. If you've been quilting for a while, you might find that you want a change in the finished look of the quilts you're making now as compared to the past. Our style and taste changes constantly. What we would like you to become comfortable with is your right to make a decision based on your preferences, needs, and desires as to how you'll treat your fabric. Harriet does not prewash; Sharyn does. There is no right or wrong—just different needs and preferences. However, before you decide which path you'll take, *please* read this chapter to gain the knowledge you need to make informed decisions. You might be interested to know that this chapter was the birthplace for Harriet's book *From Fiber To Fabric*. There was so little factual information on fabric care available to quilters that she got carried away and wrote a book instead of a chapter on the subject. This chapter introduces you to the basic considerations needed for making informed decisions, but we strongly advise that you study *From Fiber To Fabric* for an in-depth look at this subject.

Why Do Quilters Prefer Cotton Over Blends?

Careful consideration of fiber content in the fabrics we choose can affect our success in piecing a quilt top, as well as the durability of the finished quilt. The fiber of choice for quiltmakers is 100% cotton. Between the 1950s and the 1970s, polyester was the predominant fiber. It was next to impossible to purchase 100% cotton, and when you did find it, the selection was very limited.

When quiltmaking was revived in the mid-1970s, the demand for cotton fabric began to grow. The new generation of quiltmakers was soon to learn what the long-time quilters already knew: cotton was superior to polyester and cotton/polyester blends when piecing, appliquéing, and quilting. The following aspects added to the growing appreciation of using cotton in quilts as opposed to using polyester and cotton/poly blends:

■ **Cotton can retain its pressed form,** giving a sharp crispness to a seam or an appliqué edge. Tension pulls and little puckers can be worked out of a seam allowance with a good pressing because of cotton's flexibility. The seams in cotton fabrics will lie flat, which is needed for accurate piecing and machine quilting.

■ **Polyester blends are made to release wrinkles.** They naturally resist keeping the knife edge press needed for flat seam allowances, making them have a tendency to lift.

■ **Distortion is minimal** if only 100% cottons are used in patchwork.

■ **Sewing cottons and polyester blends together can result in mismatched seams with puffy seam allowances** in spite of careful sewing. If you have to combine different fabrics, stay clear of "wobbly," low thread count fabrics, and stretchy or slick fabrics. Try to make certain that the weights of the fabrics are compatible. A heavier, coarser fabric will weaken the lighter fabric that it's stitched to, causing the seam to wear out.

■ **Cotton is more opaque than polyester,** reducing the problem of seam allowances showing through the top layer of the quilt.

■ **Polyester is more transparent than cotton,** allowing the seam allowances to shadow through the top layer of the quilt.

■ **Bearding is less prevalent in 100% cottons** than in blends. Static electricity, as well as low thread count of the fabric, can cause the batting fibers to work through to the surface of the fabric. Because of the lack of static in cotton, this problem is less prevalent than in polyesters.

■ **Pilling is a feature of blends that is very undesirable.** This is when little fiber balls appear on the surface of poly-content blends that have been heavily used or abraded.

■ **Cotton is easy to quilt** because of the soft cotton yarns used to weave the fabric.

- **The hardness of polyester** fibers makes them harder to push a needle through.

- **Cotton sticks to itself** and prevents slipping while you are piecing small pieces together.

- **Blends are slippery.**

- **Cotton will tear on grain,** making it possible to find the true crosswise grain so that straightening is accurate.

- **Many blends shatter** when torn if they will tear at all.

Standards and Expectations

Quilters need to be aware that not all cotton fabrics are created equally. Price very often reflects quality, but a higher price alone does not always signify that a fabric is troublefree! When choosing fabrics for quiltmaking, thread count, shrinkage, lightfastness, crocking, and colorfastness to washing all need to be taken into consideration.

- **Are there really different qualities of the same print?**
Quiltmakers must become informed, conscientious consumers. Today, many manufacturers are producing beautiful, top-quality fabrics for quiltmaking, and, considering the price at which they are sold, we are extremely fortunate to have them available. The industry does, however, make different grades of fabrics for various end uses. If we do not know about the different qualities and how to tell them apart, we are likely to purchase some products that are not appropriate for quiltmaking. It is quite common to see the same print in various retail environments at substantially different prices. What you need to be aware of is that the print can be on different qualities of cloth (greige goods)

and that the quality of the dye and/or finish can also differ. Price is often a reflection of the quality discrepancy. It doesn't make sense to work with inferior products, and it need not happen if you take the time to learn about fabric testing.

- **Thread count** is one determinant of how many years a fabric can last, what chance the batting will have of coming through the fabric, what percentage of shrinkage there will be, and how high the print quality will be. You need to be aware that thread count (and dye and finish quality) can fluctuate within a brand, within a season, and within different types of retailers. Thread count is not stated on the bolt board. Try not to depend on brand or price for quality and consistency. For the most part, today's cottons targeted for the quilting market are woven 68 threads per square inch in both the filling (crosswise grain) and warp (lengthwise grain) directions. This is considered an even weave fabric, and is the easiest weave to work with when piecing and doing appliqué.

- **Did you know that cotton fibers themselves are relatively stable and do not stretch or shrink?** But isn't shrinkage one of our big concerns, causing us to automatically prewash? This fear is directly related to our dressmaking experiences. In garment making, large units of fabric are sewn together with various grainlines. There is no added stability to the fabric other than the seams. When washed, the residual shrinkage of the large pieces of cloth can be noticeable. In quiltmaking however, we cut small pieces and sew them together with other fabrics, stabilizing all edges. Then we layer these joined pieces onto a batting and backing, stitching through all the layers. No one small piece of fabric will shrink more than the batting or backing. In

fact, the batting is the strongest determinant of shrinkage in a quilt, not the individual fabrics in the piecing. Harriet ran a test once to prove this to herself. She made two identical small quilt tops from unwashed fabric. One top was quilted, one was not. When washed, the quilted top showed no signs of uneven shrinkage, just the overall look that the batting gave the quilt. The different fabrics in the unquilted top, on the other hand, did shrink unevenly.

- **Tumble dryers and dryer heat are large contributors to shrinkage in natural fibers.** Most shrinkage occurs when drying the last 25% of moisture out of the fabric. Dryer temperature should never exceed 160°F (140° is best). Consider drying cottons on a low setting and removing them from the dryer when they are still slightly damp. Air and line drying are two ways to avoid possible problems the dryer might cause.

- **Lightfastness** is the ability of a fabric to stand up to light. Dyed fabrics that are exposed to light can, in time, fade or change color. Both natural sunlight and artificial lights can cause damage to color. The damage caused to a fabric from light depends on the intensity of the light source and the amount of exposure, as well as the properties of the dyestuff. Serious consideration needs to be made when choosing fabrics for bed covers and wall quilts that will be exposed to light in a room for long periods of time.

- **Crocking** is the transference of color from abrasion. Dark shades are more likely to crock than light shades. Printed fabrics tend to crock more easily than dyed fabrics because most of the coloring agent of printed fabric is on the surface and not inside the fiber. How does this relate to quilting? If your chosen fabric crocks, the fabric will continually lose color in use and washing. Over time, the fabric will appear frosted or streaked, much like old worn denim jeans.

A Decision to Make —Prewash or Not?

The most voiced reason for prewashing is fear pertaining to colorfastness. The problem is that colorfastness comes in many forms: colorfastness to light, to friction or abrasion, to heat, to chemicals, and so forth. Colorfastness technically refers to a color's permanence or its ability to remain unchanged throughout the useful life of the article to which it has been applied. Some colors may have excellent fastness to laundering, but poor fastness to light. It is unfair to state that a color is simply fast or not, without qualifying what is causing it to be fast or fugitive (the loss of color). To prewash fabric thinking that you'll eliminate all of these possibilities is thinking in the wrong direction. Instead, we need to learn each fabric's characteristics based on the dyestuff used to color it, then decide how to treat it from there.

THINK ABOUT THIS:
■ **Did you know that the water temperature** you wash your cottons in can affect their ability to retain their color? Have you heard that some people recommend that you boil your fabric to make sure that they are safe, when in reality this is one of the things that can damage the color?
■ **Water temperature** is one of the easiest troublemakers to control. Chemists and professors of textiles all agree that cotton fabrics should be washed in "cold" water. This means between 80°F and 85°F. We suggest that you actually measure the temperature of the water with a sim-

ple kitchen thermometer, then feel the water with your finger so that you can finger test water temperature from now on. Fabric that will never run in cold water often runs in water warmer than 85°. Check your water temperature and always wash your cotton products in this range.
■ **Did you know that the chlorine** found in normal amounts in processed tap water can cause some dyes to release their color, but that you can control this problem?
■ **Did you know that detergents** can be very damaging to the binders that hold the pigments onto the surface of the cloth and can be harmful to some fiber-reactive dyes because of the chlorine content?
■ **Did you know that many fabrics** do not lose their color in water, but when sewn to another fabric can transfer color at the seam when wet?
■ **Did you know that prewashing** fabrics will not necessarily render them washfast? There are many things that we do *after* we prewash that can cause stress, fading, or bleeding in our fabrics.

Choosing Detergent

A general guideline for choosing a detergent is to look for a product with the least number of ingredients. The more ingredients, the harsher the product tends to be. The best cleaning agents are non-ionic and anionic detergents. Look for clear (hand dishwashing) liquid products that say "non-ionic surfactant" on the label. One example is Ultra Ivory® dishwashing liquid. Non-ionic types are most effective at low temperatures.

Another product that is loved by quilters is sodium lauryl sulfate, commonly known as Orvus Paste®. This is a synthetic detergent designed to duplicate the soapmaking ingredient in coconut oil—lauric

acid. As a synthetic, it eliminates the tendency of coconut oil-based soaps to form a curd, and it retains its cleaning power, even in the processed, acid-type water found in many of today's cities. It is especially effective on greasy soil. Both of these products leave both dyed and printed colors and the "hand" of the fabric unchanged.

Synthrapol is a chemical that is used for what is called "soaping off" of dyed fabrics. It is made to remove unbonded dye molecules from fabrics and is normally used to wash the excess dye out of fabric that has just been dyed. It is what commercial fabric houses and wise hand-dyers use to remove excess dye from their fabrics at the end of the dye process. Synthrapol can be used for trying to remove dye stains once they do occur.

Retayne is what you can use in order to "lock" color that has been improperly processed (commercial fabrics), so they will quit bleeding and retain their color. This product has been used successfully to set dye that continues to run and bleed in pre-testing. It's especially useful on reds, maroons, and metallics. Use one teaspoon of Retayne per yard of fabric to be washed.

Sometimes you need one, sometimes you need the other. For most quilters, Retayne is all you need. If you purchase a bleeder, use Retayne.

If you're hand dyeing or already have a problem, use Synthrapol. A product called Dye Magnet® is available in the laundry section of many grocery stores. This product claims to have "magnetic" properties that grab and hold any excess dye during the washing process, which helps prevent bleeding and fading. Dye Magnet can be an excellent product to use every time fabric is prewashed or the finished quilt is washed as an extra precaution against potential problems with water or detergents. However, it does not eliminate the need to understand the properties of each fabric we work with.

PREWASH OR NOT?

The big decision is whether to prewash all your fabrics as soon as you get them home or store them new and make the choice whether to wash them or not depending on the project. Like everything else, this can be a multi-faceted issue. It has to do with how you work, as well as the style of quilting you're involved in. Harriet and Sharyn have two totally different approaches.

Sharyn prewashes everything as it comes in the door. This fits her working style, needs, and personal preferences. She is an impulsive worker who would be out of the mood and time to sew if she had to stop and wash the small amounts of fabrics needed for a specific project. She does a lot of scrap projects, working from strips. Every time a fabric is on the cutting table for the first time, she cuts a 2" strip that gets filed for future quilt use. Another major consideration for Sharyn is that she dislikes the crisp hand of unwashed fabric. Once a fabric is prewashed it becomes softer. Harriet's fabric lecture has educated Sharyn to the perils of recklessly throwing fabric in with the family laundry using her normal laundry

detergents. She now washes fabric separately using a colorsafe product called Easy Wash®. She also removes the fabric from the dryer before it's totally dry, again as recommended by Harriet. Another reason she prefers to prewash her fabric is due to the way she designs quilts. She makes her blocks and then plays with them on a flannel wall. She finds that washed fabric has a tendency to cling to the design wall better than unwashed fabric. Since blocks can often be on the wall for weeks on end, it's important to her that they cling well.

Harriet takes a different approach. She doesn't have a firm conviction on what appearance she wants her quilts to have down the road, so she stores all her fabric unwashed. Harriet's thinking is that the appearance of future quilts can be affected by automatically taking the fabric home and prewashing it. She has found that tastes and popular styles of quilts being made often change. With more and more new battings becoming available and reproduction quilting being so popular, there are too many possibilities to explore to be locked into any one direction. She finds that she needs to have options available when planning a quilt. Here's an example: let's say that you want to make a 1930's reproduction quilt, and you want the true look of an old quilt. This is achieved by allowing the fabric and batting to shrink together and give the "puckers" so characteristic of older quilts. When going through your fabric stash, you find that all your fabrics have been pre-shrunk. This is not going to help you achieve the look you want, and you'll probably wind up purchasing new fabric for the project.

Now, let's say that all your fabric is stored unwashed. You decide to use a piece from some yardage you have

and use it unwashed. After testing for colorfastness, you make that quilt and still have the remaining original piece. The next quilt that you want to use that fabric in needs to be prewashed for whatever reason, and you do so. The next time you want to use the fabric, it's again used unwashed. See the pattern? You now have options available to you.

Note Each quilt determines how the fabric should be handled. You accommodate each quilt, but retain the option for next time with the remaining fabric. Your fabric stash becomes a working tool. If you know that you're always going to want your fabric prewashed and that you'll never change your need for a different look in your quilts down the road, then there is no problem with prewashing for convenience.

You can see that each scenario is different. Neither one of us believe that one is right and the other wrong in our preferences. We respect each other's decisions, and we enjoy each other's quilts, but we work differently. It's as simple as that. Now, *you* think about *your* preferences and work styles. Try working both ways if you're brand new to quilting, and then decide what works best for you. Start out by not automatically prewashing your fabrics when you get them home. If you find that over time you're constantly washing every piece, you will probably be a candidate to prewash as it comes in the door. If on the other hand you find that you need the choice of non-prewashed fabric for some of your projects, you may want to store all your fabric unwashed and wash it when it is called for. It's okay to question and experiment. The bottom line is you need to take responsibility for your decisions and make them based on fact, not guess work or because "someone told me I had to."

FABRIC GRAIN

Does fabric grain really make a difference in the outcome of your projects? Is grain placement important to a finished quilt? When and why should it be considered? As with everything else in this book, it is our goal that you understand the options available before making a decision as to when and where grainline position is important. Understanding what fabric grain is will help you decide how much importance you need to place on grainline for each project. The more novice a quilter you are, the more care you need to take in grain positioning. As you gain more experience, you'll be able to see where the trueness of grain impacts your finished quilts.

Woven fabrics are made by interlacing two sets of yarns at right angles to each other, the lengthwise (warp) yarns and the crosswise or widthwise (filling) yarns. The selvage runs along the lengthwise edge on both sides of the fabric. It is usually from $^1/_4$" to $^1/_2$" wide and is actually a self-edge. Its purpose is to ensure that the edge of the fabric will not tear when the cloth undergoes the stresses and strains of the finishing process.

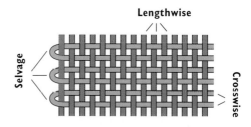

Lengthwise

Selvage

Crosswise

Fabric grain is the lengthwise and crosswise yarns that are woven into fabric. When the grain is parallel to either the warp or filling yarns the fabric is said to be "on-grain." Lengthwise grain, which runs parallel

to the selvage, has very little stretch. Crosswise grain, which runs perpendicular to the selvage, has more stretch. The most stretch is in the bias direction or 45° angle to both sets of yarns. This is because the yarns bend and shift from the pulling force being exerted.

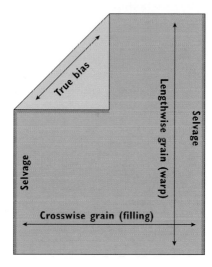

True bias

Selvage

Lengthwise grain (warp)

Selvage

Crosswise grain (filling)

Fabric that is on-grain drapes and sews well. Fabric that is off-grain does not drape properly and stretches when you sew it. This is because the yarns are not at right angles to each other. To check the grain on a bolt of fabric, make sure the warp yarn that runs along the length of the fold does not have more than $^3/_8$" variance. Crosswise grain can be checked by tearing the fabric across the width from selvage to selvage. The tear should align with itself and be perpendicular to the selvages. Fabrics with more than $^3/_8$" variance in 45"-wide fabric can be difficult to straighten and work with.

When checking the grain on the bolt, notice how the print aligns with the grain. You can tell if the print has been printed straight by examining the torn edge. A seemingly random print may be directional. The print actually takes on a diagonal stripe effect. If it's printed off-grain, you need to consider how you are using the fabric and whether this will affect the finished quilt. Too

often you don't notice this problem until the quilt is finished and hung and the off-grain fabric wavers.

CUTTING VS. TEARING

Although sometimes a fabric is off-grain, other times it's simply wrapped onto the bolt unevenly. Many of these fabrics can be straightened and put back on-grain, which brings us to the subject of tearing versus cutting fabric from the bolt. As with any issue, there are opinions on both sides—and both those who tear and those who cut fabric think they are right. You need to make your own decision and act accordingly.

If a fabric is cut at a perfect 90° angle to the selvage, you might think you have the exact amount of fabric you need. You must, however, consider whether the fabric is on-grain crosswise. You will need to look very closely to see how the filling yarns align with the warp yarns. Are they perfectly straight and even with the cut or running off the cut edge at an angle? If they are not perfectly straight and even, you'll need to straighten the fabric to get straight grain strips and pieces. To find the crosswise grain, tear a strip from the end of the fabric, on both sides. This can often add up to a large loss if the fabric is really off-grain. Once torn and straightened, you may find yourself short of the yardage needed for the project. If you detect this at the store, you'll need to purchase up to $^1/_4$ yard extra just for straightening.

On the other hand, if the fabric is torn from the bolt, you automatically know if the fabric is on-grain or not. You will have exactly the same usable length on each selvage edge, even though the ends do not line up. The biggest argument against tearing is the streaking that occurs when darker printed colors are torn. When tearing, some of the threads will turn over, exposing the backside that has not been saturated or printed with dye. This damaged area is generally added to the yardage you're buying at each end. Therefore, after straightening, this damaged area can be cut away, leaving you the exact yardage you purchased and needed for the project. If you find the torn edges of the fabric on the bolt are up to 3" off-grain, feel the hand of the fabric. If it has a stiff finish, it's unlikely you will be able to straighten the grain. If the fabric is soft and pliable, you'll most likely get the grain realigned with little effort. If the fabric is more than 3" off, reconsider buying it. Finishing standards find fabric that is 2" to 3" off-grain still acceptable. If it says on the bolt that the fabric is perma-press, it will be very difficult to straighten.

REALIGNING THE FABRIC GRAIN

Many people believe that by pulling the fabric bias opposite the direction it is off, they can straighten the fabric. But if you really examine a piece of fabric where this has been done, you'll see that the yarns are now misaligned and pulled out of square. An alternative way to realign the fabric grain is to press a new center fold into the fabric.

Realigning fabric grain

To press a new center fold, start by tearing each end of the yardage to find the crosswise grain. Next, dampen the fabric with a spray bottle. If you're prewashing or preshrinking the fabric, you can do this step while the fabric is damp.

The sizing must be damp in order to allow the yarns to move back to their original position. Fold the fabric in half lengthwise and pin each torn edge together evenly. Then pin the selvages together. Work in short yardages of about ½ yard when doing this. If you can work with a partner, it's helpful. If one holds the fabric at the selvage corners and the other pulls at each end at the center fold, the fabric will realign. Now press a new center fold, working from the torn edge and selvage down to the new fold. Once this is complete, turn the fabric over and press the other side, checking for folds and distortions. Then, fold the fabric in half lengthwise again. Check to see that the torn edges again align. If not, repeat the process. Up to a ³/₈" variance is acceptable here.

GRAINLINE AND PIECING

When referring to the traditional pieced patchwork block with small squares, triangles, rectangles, etc., grainline is a relatively insignificant problem. When there are lots of pieces being turned various directions, whether or not the grain is 100% straight or true will not be a major factor.

When working with strips, whether they be for strip piecing, sashings, or borders, the trueness of the grain can be a factor in how well your quilt top behaves. If grainline along the edge of your strip varies by more than a few threads, there is potential for stretching and distortion.

Knowing about grainline placement can avoid problems in quilt construction and give you more control of how the finished quilt will look. Squares and rectangles are cut with all four sides on grain. Other shapes such as triangles, diamonds, and curved pieces always have one or more sides cut on the bias. A general

rule is to position the template so as many sides as possible are on the straight grain.

There are two schools of thought when it comes to cutting diamonds. You can cut it so that two edges are on straight grain, which gives you two bias edges. But some feel that this shape should be cut with grainline running from point to point, which gives you the same amount of give on all four edges. You'll probably want to try some each way until you have experience to guide your decision. It is important that you look at the pieces as they are positioned in the finished block.

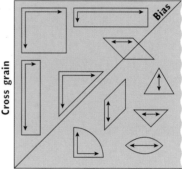

The goal is to end up with straight grain all the way around the outside edge of the block wherever possible. This gives the block the most stability.

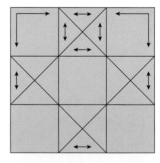

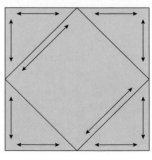

When cutting strips, it's very important to check that the crosswise grain is truly perpendicular to the selvage. If the grain is off when you cut crosswise strips, you could be cutting strips that are as much bias as straight. This will give you "rubber band" strips to sew, cut, and fit together with other rubber band pieces. Beginners can have a very difficult time achieving accurate piecing when the strips are off grain.

If the pieces are slightly off grain, there is generally no problem, but check your strips carefully to give yourself every advantage toward perfect piecing. Check the grain every so often to see that the grain is staying accurate. If not, stop and realign.

Remember to eliminate the selvage from all cut pieces. Do not include selvages in seam allowances, as they tend to shrink more than the rest of the fabric. This can result in puckered seams.

Because bias edges tend to stretch, sewing problems can be abundant. To help make the piecing go smoothly, consider the following hints:
■ Use tightly woven fabric. Loosely woven fabric has more stretch in all directions.
■ Check the placement of each pattern piece when considering grainline. Consider which edges will be sewn together before cutting each piece. All pieces that are on the outer edge of a block or quilt should be cut so the outside edges are on the straight grain.
■ If you have trouble when sewing a bias edge to a straight-grain edge you might try placing the bias piece on the bottom when sewing it to a straight piece by machine.
■ Be especially careful not to pull or stretch when sewing two bias pieces together.
■ Take extra care in pressing to avoid distortion. Be sure to read the section on pressing on pages 45-46.

When cutting long sections of the quilt, such as sashings and borders, remember that the lengthwise grain gives the least stretch. If a quilt or wallhanging is to hang on the wall, consider the grainline as the strength of the quilt.

If all four borders, or all of the sashing, are cut on the lengthwise grain, you'll have opposing grains— lengthwise grains at right angles to each other. When working with a border stripe, this is desirable.

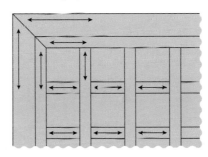

Borders and sashing on lengthwise grain

This may not be desirable if your fabric has a directional print or changes color as it changes position. If this is the case, cut the sashing or border according to its position in the quilt. Now the side borders will be on the lengthwise grain, the top and bottom borders will be crosswise.

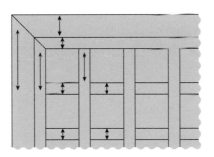

Directional print for borders and sashing

BACKING GRAINLINE
Another consideration of grainline is on the backing of the quilt. It is a general guideline to cut the backing fabric so that the length of the fabric runs the same direction as the length of the quilt. With larger quilts being made, this does not necessarily use the fabric efficiently.

For a king-sized quilt, you can save yardage by running the lengthwise grain across the width of the quilt. To save fabric by doing this depends on your opinion of the appearance of crosswise seams on the back. Another thing to keep in mind is if the quilt will be hanging on a wall. Because lengthwise grain is not at all stretchy, added strength will be gained if the grain runs the length of the quilt. Lengthwise grain helps the quilt to hang straight and hold its shape longer. If the quilt is on a bed, this is not a problem.

Harriet found years ago that when she was machine quilting, she needed to consider backing grainline. The least amount of movement between the three layers is in the lengthwise direction of the backing. After anchoring the layers together, stitch all lengthwise seams first. When you move on to the crosswise seams, they are secured and are not able to distort. Bias is saved until last, as it has the most stretch. Once the quilt is secured lengthwise and crosswise, the bias is totally under control and puckering and shifting is virtually eliminated. If the lengthwise grain of the backing is crosswise of the quilt top, anchor first, then quilt all crosswise seams, followed by lengthwise seams.

Beginners can benefit from taking time to learn about grainline and how it affects their efforts. If you're more experienced and are still seeing problems with tops that do not lay flat and quilts that are out of square, go back and examine the grainlines of the pieces in the quilt. Learn from your mistakes and take care next time.

Workspaces

Designing a Workspace

Designing and outfitting a workspace for quiltmaking can be almost as enjoyable as using it. We are firm believers that all quiltmakers deserve a studio to pursue their craft; however, not all are blessed with a house large enough to accommodate this desire. The information presented here gives you ideas for creating the most efficient use of the space you have, as well as guidelines for setting up work stations. A defined workspace tends to give importance to your work.

The Shakers had a saying that definitely applies to our smaller homes today: "A place for everything and everything in its place." Quilters are great accumulators of fabric, tools, books and magazines, and every sewing notion that comes along. All of these items need to be stored so that we can find them later. Organization is one of the key aspects to a functional workspace.

Before we start with solutions, let's first try to identify what you need and want in your space.
■ How much time do you anticipate spending on quilting?
■ How much space can you claim as yours? A whole room, a closet, the dining room table, a corner of the bedroom?
■ Will this space be shared?
■ Do you work best alone or do you like interaction with other people when working?

■ Is it important to have a television close by?
■ How much money can you spend on setting up this space?
■ Do you need to use this space for other hobbies?
■ Is it important that your stuff be organized, or can you work in clutter and chaos?

Next, look around and see what items you need to have readily available. These items need to be stored for convenience and accessibility. What do you want to have on display, and what items can be hidden from view? How many books do you have, and how many feet of shelving will it take to accommodate them? Go through the following list and decide which of these items you want to see or display, and which ones don't need to be seen. Also make note of which items you use constantly and want close at hand.

■ Fabrics
■ Threads
■ Notions: (cutting equipment, needles, drafting supplies, etc.)
■ Battings
■ Pressing equipment
■ Books, patterns, and magazines
■ Quilting frames and hoops
■ Quilts—new and antique
■ Idea files

Now you should have a better idea of what kind of enclosed storage you need, as well as what wall space, shelving, and display space will be required for items you want to remain visible.

When planning for storing your equipment and supplies, group things that are used together and try to store them as close as possible to where they will be used. If you start running out of storage space, think about which items can possibly be stored in another part of the house. For instance, if you have a collection of dressmaking fabrics, patterns, and books, but find yourself only quilting, these items could be stored in a closet in another room, still accessible, but not taking space needed for items being used all the time. Perhaps by combining different interests you can solve some of your problems. If you're a collector of baskets, think about using them for storing various quilting items. A pole suspended from the ceiling and S-hooks make a perfect place to hang the filled baskets and gain some space. Vinyl-covered grid systems for walls, found in container and storage system stores, are excellent ways to store notions on the wall. These grid systems come with various accessories such as hooks, baskets, and shelves. Pegboard is another system to consider. Pegboards can be attached to the wall so that a variety of small items can be close at hand. Tall slender baskets, stone jars, or antique churns can be used on the floor to hold longer rulers and yardsticks.

Think about flooring that will be low-maintenance and easy to move a chair around on. Carpeting is a magnet for pins and needles but warm if the room is cool. A low-nap, commercial carpeting may work well. Twelve-inch asphalt squares are extremely durable, as is vinyl sheet flooring.

ELECTRICAL NEEDS

When planning your workspace, don't overlook the electrical needs of your equipment. When sewing machines, irons, computers, task lights, televisions, and stereos are used simultaneously, they create a large power draw. Kitchens are wired for such power usage, but bedrooms, living rooms, family rooms, and basements generally aren't. Therefore, you need to check the amps available to the room you're planning to use. Kitchens generally combine four receptacles on one 20-amp circuit. This is sufficient to carry multiple appliances at one time. Bedrooms can combine lights and outlets on one less-powerful 15-amp circuit, often sharing this circuit with more than one room. Plug an iron into the outlet in one room and it can borrow power from the other rooms, causing lights to dim and motors to turn more slowly than they should. You may need to consider increasing the size of the wire and the capacity of the circuits or putting the lights on a different circuit.

You will need to start by determining the power requirements your workspace will need. Think about the activities you'll be performing at the same time in the room. We iron as we construct, leaving the iron on all day, as well as watch television or listen to the stereo while we work. Often a computer is part of the plan, and it's likely to be on while we work. How many lights will be on all at once, and will you need a space heater in the area? A little math allows you to find out what your needs are.

Find the wattage that each item requires and divide it by 120 (the average household outlet voltage). The resulting answer is the number of amps needed to run the item or to light the bulb. The iron is our biggest user of power. To see just how much is needed to run it continuously, try this example. The average iron is rated at 1200 watts. $1200 \div 120$ means that it takes 10 amps to run (and even more to heat it up). The average sewing machine requires one to two amps, as does a stereo, television, VCR, computer, or light. Add a printer, which can need up to 6 amps, and the power needs really add up. The standard 15-amp circuit will run five to seven 1- to 2-amp items. Add an iron on the same circuit and an overload can occur, which has the potential of damaging a computerized sewing machine.

Once you add up your needs, consider having two circuits for your sewing space: one 20-amp circuit for your iron and one 15-amp circuit for everything else. If you're putting in a new outlet for the iron, consider installing it where you'll be ironing and at a height that makes efficient use of the cord. If this is not possible, hire an electrician to examine your space and see if the electrical load can be re-balanced. If not, find out which outlets share a circuit

breaker or fuse, then use an extension cord to plug the iron into a different circuit in a different location. Be sure that the extension cord has molded plug and socket ends, is no longer than 25 feet, and is made of 16 gauge wire.

If you have a computer in your sewing space, remember that it requires consistent power but not much of it. It is vital that a surge protector be used to protect your computer. When purchasing a strip surge protector, check that it's rated at 15-amps minimum.

Another consideration is the use of only one motor per circuit. Avoid plugging your sewing machine into a circuit that another motorized piece of equipment is using. If this is unavoidable, do not operate both at the same time. By analyzing your power needs, you can predetermine what changes need to be made in your room's circuits before they cause you trouble.

Electrical outlets need to be readily available to eliminate the need for extension cords running across the floor. Strip outlets mounted on the wall are a possibility when additional plugs are needed in one area. Coiled, expandable extension cords, mounted from the ceiling using a drapery rod will allow an electrical item, such as an iron, to be plugged in and moved from place to place without worrying about where the cord is. If you're starting from scratch, don't overlook placing outlets in the floor.

ERGONOMICS

Ergonomics has become a household word in the past few years. You may already understand the concept of ergonomics, but if not, it means improving the fit between your body and any given activity. It is the science of coordinating the design of tools, equipment, and furniture with the capacities and requirements of the user. Adjust your workstations and choose tools so that they accommodate your body dimensions. This will result in increased comfort and efficiency.

Standing, sitting, and moving incorrectly all increase your chance of pain. Posture problems overwork your body and strain your muscles and tendons, adding stress to your joints. With a little adjustment you can correct most posture problems. Line up your ears, shoulders, and hips. Keep your head upright and relax while you do this. This is called a neutral position, and it places the least amount of stress on your body. Your shoulders should be level, with your arms near your sides.

Note Quilting requires us to perform repetitive tasks with a certain amount of force for extended periods of time. This can cause repetitive strain injuries: those conditions that we know by discomfort or persistent pain in muscles, tendons, and other soft tissues. These conditions are usually chronic and long-term. It is important to look at the whole picture—workspace, chairs, tools, heights, lighting, standing position, and the shoes you wear.

You'll probably find that improving your posture requires adjusting your work area, as well as your body position. This is because the way you do a task is affected by where you do it and the tools you use. That is what ergonomics is all about. Our cutting tables, sewing surfaces, chairs, and ironing boards all need to be looked at and adjusted to fit us properly.

Specific Needs of Quilters

CUTTING TABLES

The cutting table is one of the most important units of the room. We spend as much, if not more, time at the cutting table as we do at the sewing machine. Designing, cutting, planning, and developing each project is often done at the cutting table. This table needs to be customized to your height and space requirements. The ideal table should be accessible from all four sides, hard-surfaced, and high enough to avoid stooping or bending while working.

Below are some basic principles of ergonomics that apply specifically to cutting tables:

■ The ideal size for a cutting table is determined by the type of projects you undertake. Generally, a table 28" to 36" wide and 56" to 72" long is sufficient for quilting. Avoid leaning forward to reach your work. Your reach should be kept to within 14" to 18" of your body on the table surface. Reaching too far can be awkward. It also reduces your muscle power. Never lock a joint by extending it until it can't go any further. This table will also make an excellent layering table when the time comes to baste your new quilt top.

■ To help you find the proper height for the work surface you stand at, stand in the shoes you normally work in, bend your elbows at 90° angles, measure from the elbow to the floor, and subtract 2" to 3". Ideally you should be able to perform the task at hand without raising the hand above the elbow level and without stooping.

■ Placing a rubber or padded mat on the floor in front of the table to stand on when you stand for prolonged periods of time will reduce circulation problems and fatigue. This is especially important if you have a hard floor surface.

■ Glare can be eliminated if the tabletop surface is a matte finish. Sufficient lighting over the cutting table is also important.

■ Wear flat-soled shoes when standing for prolonged periods. This allows your body to stand with good posture. A small footstool can be set up to rest your foot when you stand for long periods. Alternate feet, first putting one foot up, then the other. This will help you keep your back straight.

A custom built table is a wonderful luxury, but to create a personal cutting table, consider any of the following ideas:

■ If using a folding banquet table, raise up the height by either extending the legs with precut lengths of metal or PVC pipe (a diameter that will just slip over the legs) from the hardware store, or by placing 4" x 4" x 18" blocks of wood under each end. (These dimensions are arbitrary and should be refigured to reach your desired height. Most major home improvement centers carry these large pieces of wood and will cut the lengths to your personal needs.) Nail a small can on each block of wood to keep the legs in place.

■ Two pull-out wire basket units, made to your proper height with Formica®-covered plywood serving as the top.

■ Formica-covered plywood attached to a base frame that will sit on top of a banquet table at the required height.

■ A door hung on the wall at one end and supported on the other end by a dresser or pre-made kitchen cabinet base unit. Or use a door for the top and pre-made cabinet sections on either end for the supports. The cabinets provide support and much needed storage.

■ Have the tabletop reversible, so that one side is laminate-covered for cutting, the other side padded for pressing large pieces.

■ At the cutting table, have your rulers, cutters, mats, scissors, and so forth within easy reach.

SEWING SURFACES

Where and how your machine is set up can affect your ability to work without strain. Is your machine in a cabinet or are you using it as a portable? If the machine is sitting on a tabletop as a portable, you're likely to be uncomfortable and experience back strain after a short period of sewing. The height of your chair and the table are critical to a comfortable work session. You may also experience difficulty in controlling the fabrics you're sewing unless the machine is level with the table surface. Open arms and small extension areas do not give enough support to larger pieces. Having the fabric or quilt supported while working can make your sewing more accurate and hassle free.

■ The standard height of sewing cabinets (from bed of the machine to floor) varies from 29" to 30". Sit behind different cabinets and find which height is most comfortable for you. You may find that you need a higher table to accommodate your body proportions. Your shoulders need to be relaxed, and you need to be sitting high enough above your work to see down the front of your machine and into the hole of the presser foot, where the needle enters the fabric. If you can see this clearly, you'll have less eyestrain and more control of your sewing.
■ Is the needle more than 7" from the edge of the table? Is the reach to the needle too far or too close to work with control and comfort? Can you lean forward and rest your forearms on the edge and relax your hands over the fabric, like when playing the piano?
■ Make sure that you're sitting directly in front of the needle, not in front of the machine. This will keep you centered with your work.

■ Make sure that you have enough leg room and that you're comfortable sitting in the area provided for your legs. Many cabinets do not give enough space in the front of the cabinet for someone with long legs to sit comfortably.
■ How close can you get to the machine with your chair? Could you sit there for four to six hours comfortably?
■ Is the surface smooth? Does fabric glide across it easily? Formica is an excellent sewing table surface.

Piecing does not require an extensive work area, but machine quilting does. If you're planning to machine quilt, plan out your room so that, when possible, you're facing out into the room instead of facing a wall or corner. This will give room for the quilt to expand as it goes through the machine. You can place tables in back of your machine for support of the quilt as you quilt it. You might want to consider attaching a piano hinge and a piece of plywood to the back side of your table or cabinet to expand the work area when needed. This would work like a drop leaf table.

Needles, machine accessories, scissors, pins, etc. should be readily available at the machine. Also consider a small ironing surface that will be to the side of the machine for quick pressing. This and a small travel iron will save hundreds of minutes and steps across the room to the ironing board

CHAIRS

The chair you choose to sit in while sewing can make the difference between a pleasant sewing session and backaches. It must be comfortable and provide firm support. If you do not already have one, go shopping for a good quality secretarial chair. This type of chair will support you at a height necessary for good vision.

FEATURES TO LOOK FOR

■ The seat of the chair should be adjusted low enough that your feet can rest flat on the floor, yet high enough that your forearms and hands are at the proper angle to the sewing surface. If you can't find a height that meets both of these goals, give priority to the position of your arms. You can always use a footrest to make up for any gap between the floor and your feet. Your thighs need to be horizontal (at a 90° angle), or nearly so, when you're sitting.
■ You may want to calculate your needed chair height like you would for a computer keyboard. When everything is adjusted correctly for keyboard work (when you bend your arms at the elbow and hold your forearms straight ahead and parallel to the floor), your elbows are at the same height as the keyboard. The line from your elbow to your hand is straight or has only a slight upward tilt of the wrist (a 90° angle, plus or minus 20°). These guidelines can nearly eliminate wrist stress when sewing. Try it and see.
■ Chairs need five casters or "feet" for good balance.

- Look for a center hydraulic lift system for adjusting height of the chair. Sit in the chair and make sure that it goes high enough to position you in front of your machine as needed.
- Make sure to have a seat that is proportional to your body size. If you're very small, a small chair will fit fine, but if you're larger, a small chair will not provide you with the needed size and support. Seat test many chairs and feel the difference in their comfort level.
- Check on the adjustability of the chair back. Does it pivot or slide in and out? If you need to sit on the edge of the chair or in the center of the seat, will the chair back come up to your back and support it as needed for long periods of sewing?
- Do you want arms on the chair? Do they adjust in height so that they are not in the way when not needed?
- Does the front of the seat have a forward tilt adjustment? This feature will take the pressure off the back of your legs.

Buy the very best chair that you can afford. Often you can find very high quality, inexpensive chairs at railroad salvage or used office equipment stores. Government auctions and surplus warehouses offer tremendous values. Don't buy based on price alone. That $69.95 chair may seem like a great deal, but how will it feel after six hours of quilting?

Lighting

Lighting is one item that must not be overlooked in your workspace. Without proper and sufficient light, eye fatigue can constantly plague you. Whether you prefer track, fluorescent, or overhead incandescent lighting, having sufficient wattage is the most important item. The type of lighting we need to create is "task" lighting, which is functional and localized for a particular activity. Task lighting is usually placed near the activity but aimed to avoid glare, and is distributed evenly over the working surface to minimize shadows. This type of lighting includes one or a combination of recessed lights; track-mounted fixtures; and shielded fluorescent tubes, either hanging or placed under shelves or cabinets.

TO PROVIDE SUFFICIENT LIGHT
- Don't over-shield the light source. Provide just enough shading to eliminate glare.
- Provide adequate, but not excessive, wattage bulbs in fixtures and lamps.
- Lighten colors used on ceilings, walls, floors, and furnishings to produce more light from the same wattage.
- Avoid glare. Direct and reflected glare causes eyestrain and discomfort.
- Avoid excessive contrasts. An excessive contrast in amounts of light results when one area of a room is darker than another. Correct by adding general lighting.
- Avoid shadows. For sewing, the source of light for a right-handed person should be on the left; for left-handed, on the right.

There are standard formulas used by interior designers to figure the amount of light needed for different activities. These formulas measure light in foot candles. A foot candle is equal to the amount of light a candle throws on an object one foot away.
Accepted light levels for sewing are:
- 20-50 foot candles for occasional machine sewing and high contrast fabrics.
- 50-100 foot candles for machine sewing on light to medium fabrics.
- 100-200 foot candles for machine sewing dark fabrics with low contrast.
- 100-200 foot candles for fine hand sewing.
- 500 foot candles for sewing black thread on black fabric.

A light source or a lamp of a certain wattage has a light output measured in lumens. The lumen is the unit of light that will deliver a level of one foot candle to a surface one foot square at a distance of one foot. Following is a list of lumen output for various types of lighting.

LUMEN OUTPUT
LUMENS PER WATT OUTPUT

Incandescent	20
Fluorescent	80
Mercury	50
HID (high intensity discharge)	85

It is possible to calculate the level of illumination (in foot candles) that a fixture and spacing will give. The same formula can, in reverse, suggest the number and spacing of fixtures needed to produce a desired level of illumination.

illumination (in foot candles) = lumens supplied (lumens per watt x wattage) ÷ area in square feet to be lighted

Using this formula, let's work through an example. If our room is 16' x 20', we have 320 square feet of space to light. If we choose fluorescent lighting, we will be getting 80 lumens per watt. Fluorescent tubes average 40 watts per tube. Multiply 80 (lumens per watt) by 40 (wattage of a tube) to get 3200 lumens. 3200 ÷ 320 square feet = 10 foot candles supplied. We know from the adjacent chart that we need an average of 50 to 100 foot candles for machine sewing. If 10 foot candles are supplied by one fluorescent tube, we will need 5 to 10 tubes to light the room sufficiently.

What if we reverse the formula? We know we need 50 to 100 foot candles of illumination for the task. Multiply this by the square footage of the room. 50 x 320 = 16000 lumens needed. Divide the lumens needed by the lumens per watt output.

16000 ÷ 80 = 200. This tells you how many watts are needed. Divide this by the wattage given by each tube (40) and you have how many tubes you need. 200 ÷ 40 = 5. What if you plan on track lighting and want to use 60 watt long-life or energy saving light bulbs? Each light bulb will give 800 to 820 lumens. Divide 820 by 320 square feet to get 3 foot candles of illumination. To get sufficient illumination of 50 to 70 foot candles, divide 70 by 3 = 24 light bulbs needed. If you use standard 60 watt light bulbs, the lumens would be 1200 per bulb. Using the same formula, you'll find you need 18 light bulbs. If using 75 watt bulbs, only 14 are needed. If using 100 watt bulbs, only 10.

These calculations are easy to figure and will help you check on your present lighting and determine how much additional lighting you may need to add. If the area is too bright and glaring for sewing, light can be taken away.

When purchasing light bulbs, look for translucent bulbs. Opaque bulbs can't be seen through, giving mood lighting. Transparent bulbs can be seen through and tend to cause harsh, glaring light, whereas translucent bulbs can only be partially seen through and give a softer light.

Other Helpful Measurements for Functional Lighting

■ When placing a study lamp or high intensity lamp beside and close to the machine, place it 1' to the side of the needle, 1' above the needle, and 6" behind the needle.
■ Floor lamps should be to the side (approximately 15") and slightly behind the user (approximately 26" from your lap) so light comes over the shoulder onto the project.
■ The bottom of table lampshades should be approximately 42" to 44" from the floor, or at eye level for the person seated next to it.

■ For reading and hand stitching, place the lamp in line with your shoulder and 20" from the center of the book or project.
■ When drafting or working at a desk, place a lamp 15" left of your work (or right if you're left-handed) and 12" toward the rear of the desk.

When reviewing your lighting requirements and space layout, consider natural lighting available to the space and how you can use it to your advantage. Natural light can be soft and illuminating or bright and glaring. Will you need window coverings to keep out glare or ones that can be opened fully during the day and closed at night for privacy and light retention?

Consider how you're storing your fabrics when choosing lighting fixtures. Incandescent bulbs can give off a yellow tint to colors but will not cause any fading. Fluorescent tubes are available in several types, including full-spectrum, which will keep colors true. Fluorescent tubes have been reported to cause fading, but filters can be installed that will eliminate the possibility of this happening. Track lighting can be directed to the areas you want lighted, but if sufficient wattage is not supplied, it will be spotty and create shadows in the room.

Design Walls and Portable Design Surfaces

We consider design walls (also called flannel walls) to be an integral part of quiltmaking. A design wall is a vertical surface for designing projects. It lets you audition fabrics for blocks, play with patterns, and work out block arrangements and spacing.

Design walls are covered with fabrics that tend to be fuzzy, allowing the

blocks and quilt tops to stick to the surface without pins. Cotton flannel is the most commonly used fabric for this purpose. It can be purchased by the yard in various widths and seamed together if necessary or purchased as a bed sheet to get one continuous large piece. Chamois cloth is heavier than flannel and is available in 60" widths. Other good design wall coverings are fleece interfacing and needle-punched cotton battings. The nap on these products tends to be thicker, making it easier to support larger pieces of fabric. Felt also works well. These materials can be attached directly to the wall. You can thumbtack it securely at the ceiling and floor to keep it from flapping. The tauter the surface, the better it will work.

Using a board that you can pin into can help when working with large pieces. If attached to the wall, the space you have available will dictate how big the design area can be. If you don't have a large wall that can be used, consider using a door. If a door isn't an option, you can always make a portable flannel surface. A clever idea is to take an artist's canvas with its stretcher bar frame and taut canvas and cover it with flannel. Using a staple gun to fix the flannel to the stretcher bars works great.

Many quilters like to use foamcore board. Foamcore comes in a wide variety of sizes all the way up to 4' x 8'. The ¼" board tends to curl, but the thicker boards are quite stable. Foamcore can be covered with flannel and leaned against any space or even secured to the wall surface. Foamcore makes it easy to pin, if necessary, such as when an entire quilt top is being positioned on the wall. Other options include ceiling tiles, Celotex® insulation board, white Styrofoam® insulation (which tends to be fragile), extruded polystyrene, and builders board (also known as Homasote®). The lighter-weight boards can be left free-standing and portable, but it is advisable that the heavier types be attached to the wall.

Even if you have a wall to be used as a design wall, you might also want to have a smaller, more portable design surface to work on when creating smaller projects. Compact, portable flannel surfaces are very handy right next to the sewing machine, especially if what you're sewing together is a more complicated design. A little 12" x 18" portable flannel surface can be ideal for working on one block at a time. These smaller surfaces can be foamcore, corrugated cardboard, Masonite®, etc. As long as the surface is sturdy enough to support the block, it will work great. They are also good for transporting blocks or units from the work wall to the sewing machine.

Storage and Set-Up Ideas

FABRIC STORAGE

Your sewing room situation will be an important factor in determining how you can store your fabric and how much you can store. If you've never organized your fabric or had a sewing space of your own, you may need to experiment with different systems to determine which might work best for you.

Storage of fabric is very much a matter of personal taste. For Harriet, open bookshelves are the ideal solution. Sharyn, on the other hand, finds that having all the fabric visible while she is working tends to overload her senses. She stores her fabric so it is completely out of sight while she is working, but totally accessible when she wants to find a certain color or fabric.

Harriet loves having all of her fabric stored so that she can see it all the time.

Sharyn prefers to store her fabric in closed file cabinets and large plastic totes on shelves.

Bolts of fabric can either be stored on shelves like books, standing upright and supporting each other, or stacked on top of one another. Measure the folded fabrics and determine the spacing of your shelves if you choose to store your fabric in this manner. If you think you would like to stack the fabric on shelves, you'll need shelves that are approximately 14" deep x 2' wide between supports. If the shelves are any deeper, the back part of the shelf is either wasted or inaccessible. If the space between supports is wider, the shelves tend to sag.

Avoid storing fabric on unfinished wood or particle board shelves, as the acids from the wood can discolor and weaken the fabric. This can be eliminated by painting or using a polyurethane to finish the wood. Another solution to protect your fabric from the wood dangers is to line the shelves with aluminum foil, which is an inert substance.

Try not to store fabric or quilts in plastic bags. Moisture gets trapped inside the bag, leading to mildew. Cotton fabric needs to breathe. Plastic totes have lids, but they don't seal so tight that the fabric can't breathe.

You might consider putting glass doors over the fronts of your shelves or attaching a blind or curtain to the top shelf that can be pulled down when you're not working. These treatments will keep dust and light from affecting your collection.

Another storage system is putting the fabrics up on end in drawers, like file folders. When you open the drawer you can see the top edge of every piece of fabric. It is easy to find the one you're looking for and be able to remove it without messing up the rest of the fabrics in the drawer.

Fabric stored in a drawer

Storage of pieces smaller than ¼ yard can require a different kind of solution. Depending upon the amount of fabric you're storing, you might find small baskets or clear plastic shoe boxes to place individual colors in. Another idea is to ask your local ice cream parlor for their empty 5-gallon cardboard containers and use them for small pieces of fabric.

If you can't see the fabric where it's stored, consider labeling the container. The label can be as simple as a peel and stick tag that you hand letter, or it can be computer generated. If you own a label maker, you might want to use it to create labels for drawers or bins.

For easy reference as to what fabrics are in your collection and how much you have of each, consider creating reference cards from your fabrics.

Harriet does this in her store for inventory purposes. Some find these cards to be a great help in controlling large collections of fabric at home. The system uses 3" x 5" index cards and a card file drawer. Cut a 3" x 5" piece of every fabric in your collection. If you do not want this large a sample, make it the size of your choice. Attach the fabric sample onto an index card. On the back of the card, make a note of the amount of this fabric that you have, as well as the brand name of the fabric and any other information you know about it.

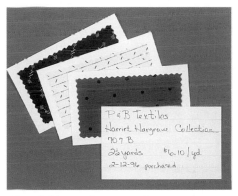
3" x 5" fabric reference cards

A spiral notebook is another item that is easy to keep clips of every fabric in and less time-consuming than the cards. Harriet often makes larger reference cards with poster board when she wants to keep a record of different collections of reproduction fabrics.

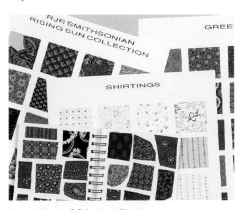
Recording of fabric collections

In the future, as you purchase fabric, it's a good idea to copy the information from the end of the bolt. This may seem like a lot of work, but there is good reasoning behind such record keeping. If you need more of the fabric, you can call around to various stores and ask for the fabric by name and number. Without this information, the store is looking for a needle in a haystack based on your description of the fabric. With computer networks as popular as they are, it's an excellent way to swap fabric over the wires. You'd be surprised how many quilters know all their fabrics by brand name.

Once you've attached all your fabrics to cards, sort them by color, then by value within each color. File them in this order. If you sort your fabrics in this same order on the shelf, you'll have no trouble finding them when needed. This is especially helpful if you store your fabrics in closed containers. You can develop a numbering system for the containers that gives you immediate access to a particular fabric. This system is particularly easy when you're a new quilter just starting to collect fabrics. If you do this as soon as you bring the fabric home, it's quite easy and manageable.

Book, Magazine, and Photo Storage

There are many options for storing magazines. Many of the quilt magazine publishers offer binders you can order to keep all the magazines together in one location. You will find both cardboard and plastic containers for magazine storage in container stores and mail order catalogs. This allows you to remove one magazine at a time. Photographs pose a huge problem once the collection gets large. Consider shoe boxes labeled by category; antique quilts, color ideas, design ideas, quilting ideas, quilts by specific quilters, and any other category that fits into why you took the picture.

Sharyn stores some of her books on a ledge under a desk.

Harriet's cutting table has built in shelves and cubbies for her books.

Inspiration and Idea Files

Ideas for quilts are abundant in magazines other than quilt specific magazines. Consider putting pages torn out of magazines into top loading page protectors and then into a loose-leaf notebook. Again, be sure to categorize and label the notebook for easy finding later. Some people prefer to file things in hanging manila folders. You can find small folder holders in office-supply stores to keep these hanging folders. Three possible ways of separating the pictures are to sort by style, color, or pattern.

Harriet has accumulated a collection of 5" x 9" loose-leaf notebooks of quilt pictures. She cuts the quilt from the page, leaving behind the room, which can confuse the issue. The pictures are categorized by topic—quilting ideas, color ideas, border and sashing ideas, and so forth. They are glued onto black construction paper (usually included with the page protector) and slipped into page protectors that fit the notebook. These notebooks are easy to use for inspiration.

Notion Storage

RULERS
Ideally, these need to be stored in close proximity to where you'll be cutting. If you have a wall nearby or a solid end on your cutting table, consider using a grid system, pegboard, or even a bulletin board. Rulers can hang from any of these systems and be easily accessible.

An idea for rulers that don't have holes in them is one of the numerous hanging folder systems. You can string any number of these folder holders together and place the rulers in the pockets. No wall to hang things from? How about using a heavy-duty vertical file folder sitting on the end of the cutting table or on a small chest nearby. Each slot can hold several rulers and keep them quite handy.

Ruler storage in a metal vertical file folder

CUTTING TOOLS
The same pegboard, grid system, or bulletin board that we used for rulers can be used to hang rotary cutters and scissors. Another simple solution is a mug that sits on the corner of the cutting table. If you are lucky enough to have a drawer as a part of your table, then you might want to put the cutters in the drawer. If you have children in your house, it is extremely important that you use caution when storing rotary cutters so that they are out of reach.

THREADS
The more techniques we learn, the more diverse our thread collection becomes. Many different commercially produced hanging racks and countertop stands are available. These are particularly nice for holding your most often used threads. Cabinets and drawers are great to keep seldom-used threads dust free. Cabinets can be hung on the wall where the beautiful colors and textures of threads can really show off. The ultimate in aesthetics is the antique spool chests. Some are large enough to be used as end tables.

Note Be sure to keep threads away from direct or bright sunlight. Sun causes degradation of the fibers.

In overly dry or damp climates, natural fiber threads are best kept in sealed zip-lock bags in the refrigerator. This is especially true of cotton machine embroidery threads. If the climate is dry, adding a spritz of moisture before sealing the bag will help maintain a good balance of moisture content in the bag. In damp climates, the moisture is controlled in the bag, preventing mildew.

Sharyn organizes her thread on thread racks

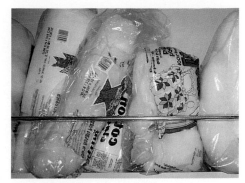
Batting stored on closet shelf

boxes, cardboard boxes, or plastic boxes. Container storage stores are full of wonderful treasures for this and other purposes. A clear plastic set of drawers about 8" x 8" x 8" is in Sharyn's sewing room for the purpose of holding her various templates. Each drawer is a different shape. Being clear, it's easy to see into them, but little labels on the front of the drawer make certain no time is wasted when looking for something specific.

Clear plastic boxes for storing templates

BOBBINS
Several different shaped and sized plastic boxes are made to hold bobbins. Magnetic bobbin holders are available if you have a machine that uses metal bobbins. Also consider the clips that keep the bobbin attached to the matching spool of thread. Ice cube trays, pill bottles, and embroidery floss organizers are other alternatives.

QUILTING STENCILS
Quilting stencils can often be a real challenge to store. Consider where you can keep them so that they are convenient when you want them, but out of the way the rest of the time. The really large and/or long ones are best hung. Do you have a closet door that you can hang them on the inside of? Pegboard or grid wall systems also work. How about using plastic totes on a shelf or in a drawer? The smaller ones can be stored in sheet protectors in a notebook by size.

TEMPLATES
Small boxes make perfect containers for storing templates. A separate box for half-square triangles, quarter-square triangles, squares, and rectangles makes it very easy for you to find what you're looking for later. These boxes can be stationary

If you make templates for one specific block, you can keep them in a box with the cutout fabric pieces while working on that particular quilt project. Another great storage system is a notebook filled with top loading page protectors. In these clear plastic pockets you can store not only the block diagrams and notes you take, but also the templates.

BATTING
Having extra batting on hand for when you're ready to layer a quilt is wonderful, but storing the extra packages of batting can be a challenge. It is another item that needs to be accessible but not in the way. One great idea is to use a closet shelf and anchor a tension curtain rod wall to wall in front of the battings to keep them from tumbling out.

Under stair closets are useful places to store batting, especially way deep inside where nothing else can be stored anyhow. Sharyn stores some batts under her cutting table, between the legs and the bookcase. They stay put and are very easy to access. Harriet keeps most of her battings in the attic of her studio, on shelves by size.

MARKING TOOLS
More plastic boxes are in order for holding all the various marking tools that you own. Or, how about one of those coffee mugs we're always collecting? Keep a specific mug designated only for fabric marking devices. Some quilters keep all the equipment needed for marking and layering a quilt together in one drawer or box, since these activities are often done at the same time.

HOOPS
Remember when everyone had swag lamp hooks hanging in their ceiling from which plants were hung? Has the plant died, leaving you with the hooks? Consider hanging baskets from these hooks. A lot can be kept in those baskets, including hoops. Another hoop storage solution is an inside closet wall. Nails in the wall can allow the hoop to be hung and easily found when you need it.

Harriet's studio combines function and comfort to ensure a productive work environment. She uses home furnishings to organize all of her quilting needs.

Equipment & Supplies

In this chapter we deal with some of the basic tools and equipment that you will need. We compare some different features for you to look at when deciding what to buy. Also in this chapter is "how-to-use" information that we hope you find helpful.

Sewing Machines

Questions constantly come up in the classroom about what to look for when shopping for a sewing machine. With the price tags reaching thousands of dollars, careful and smart shopping is necessary. The quality and condition of your equipment makes a big difference in its performance.

No one model or brand will combine all of the most desired and unique features of today's machines. Your questions and concerns need to ultimately lead you to a machine that delivers the various features relative to your style of sewing and quilting. When you go shopping for a sewing machine, have the demonstrations done on fabrics that apply to your type of sewing. The test cloth on which many demonstrations are done can show good quality stitches on any machine. You need to know how the stitch quality looks in real sewing situations on real fabric. Take a list of specific techniques that are necessary for the machine to do.

Shopping for a new sewing machine is just as big a decision as buying a new car. You are likely to spend as many, if not more hours behind it. Do not go solely by the opinions of friends and teachers. A sewing machine is a very personal tool, and it must feel right for you. Ask the dealer if you can borrow the machine over a weekend to sew on it in private, not while a salesperson is standing over you.

Following is a list of features to check out, ask about, and consider when looking at each machine:

■ Perfect tension adjustment no matter what combinations of threads are put into the machine.

■ Automatic needle stop. When you stop sewing, the needle stops instantly and does not coast, sewing more stitches.

■ Up-and-down needle position on command. Some machines allow for the needle to be down by pushing a needle-down button. This will make the needle stop down all the time. By pushing the button again, the needle will return to the up position all the time. Some machines give you the option of using the needle-down button or choosing which you want on demand by pressing your heel (or toe) on the foot control. If you tap once, the needle will go down. Tap it again, and it will go up. This gives you total control at all times.

■ The ability to sew for hours at high speed without overheating.

■ High-quality accessories that are made strictly for your brand. It's helpful to have a foot to make ¼" seam allowances. A straight stitch throat plate is also helpful in both piecing and quilting. If you are planning to machine quilt, you will also need a walking foot and a darning foot. An open toe appliqué foot comes in handy for piecing and appliqué.

■ How easy is it to change the feet?

■ If you need one, how easy is the needle threader to use?

■ How many yards of thread does the bobbin hold? 85 yards is the largest available—how does this machine compare?

■ How easy is it to get to the bobbin to change it? How easy is it to fill?

■ Is the bobbin tension adjustable?

■ How easy is it to drop the feed dogs? Can you get to that control feature readily?

■ Are there adjustable needle positions?

■ How much speed control does the machine allow you to have?

■ Does the machine have a good-sized working surface?

■ If you're looking at a computerized machine, can you override the computer on width and length selection of every stitch? Or does it adjust only within a pre-determined range?

■ How functional is the light on the machine?

■ Are classes available on your new machine so that you have a full understanding of its features and how to use them?

- Is there a nearby reputable dealer who will help with minor adjustments and who understands what you're trying to get the machine to do?
- Is there a nearby mechanic with a working knowledge of the atypical techniques and products quilters use on and with their machines?

MACHINE MAINTENANCE

Before starting a new project, be sure to clean and oil your machine. A well-maintained machine will give you many hours of pleasure.

Following are some guidelines for cleaning your machine:

- Thoroughly clean the bobbin area and the feed dog area with a lint brush. Often the smallest amount of lint or debris will cause the machine to skip stitches and have tension problems. Use brushes, cotton swabs, and/or pipe cleaners to remove lint from every reachable area. Tweezers can be used to remove caught threads, but otherwise avoid using metal tools to clean with, as they can create burrs that will cause thread breakage.
- Remove the needle plate and clean the lint from between the feed dogs. Scrub the feed dogs with a toothbrush. Use a small vacuum attachment meant for computers to suck away loose particles, then use a blower or canned air to blow out the tiny particles not removed by suction.
- Check the tension disks on the machine for any lint or residue. Clean between the tension disks with a pipe cleaner.
- Check the tension clip on the bobbin case (the clip that the thread goes under when threading the bobbin case). The tension clip on the bobbin case may contain lint or pieces of thread that can cause tensions to vary and cause poor stitches. Run a piece of thread under the clip, as though using dental floss, and dislodge any lint or threads.

Clean the inside of the bobbin case, as lint buildup can cause the bobbin to spin unevenly, which can also affect the quality of the stitches.
- Lightly oil the shuttle and race of the bobbin area every time you clean it. Use only high quality synthetic oil that has no detergents, purchased from your sewing machine dealer. Regular petroleum or household oils will eventually cause the mechanisms to lock up. Do not spray silicon or products such as WD40® into the machine because they over spray, and many parts need to be completely free of lubricant. Be sure to check with your mechanic for specifics relating to your particular machine.
- Once a month, if you're sewing a great deal or doing a lot of quilting, put a drop of oil on the needle bar (take the needle out before oiling). Let the machine run for two minutes after applying the oil, then let it sit for ten minutes so the excess oil can drain off. When not sewing, lower the needle into soft cotton fabric so that any excess oil can wick into the fabric.
- Clean the body of the machine and wax it with a high-quality car wax for enameled steel parts or a wax for plastic, such as a kitchen appliance wax for plastic body machines. Keep the machine covered when not in use to prevent accumulation of dust and dirt particles.

After you've oiled the machine, put in a new needle for the sewing technique you'll be doing. Check your manual to see if the flat side of the needle goes to the back or to the side. When inserting the needle, push it up until it hits the stop, then tighten the screw. Do not apply too much pressure on the needle clamp screw, as you can easily break off the point that holds the needle in place. Tighten until firm. If the needle is not inserted properly, the machine will skip stitches, if it will

sew at all. When sewing, listen to the sound of your machine. Any time that you hear a punching sound, stop and change the needle. A dull or bent needle can damage the machine.

TENSIONS

Once the machine is cleaned and oiled, it's time to adjust the tensions for a perfect stitch. Wind a bobbin with 50-weight, 3-ply mercerized cotton sewing thread. Do not use polyester or cotton-covered polyester to test tensions for quilting. When winding the bobbin, be sure that it is winding smoothly and evenly, and that the thread is being wound tight. Begin the winding process by putting the tail end of the thread through the hole in the side of the bobbin. Hold this end tightly until the thread has wrapped a couple of times up and down in the bobbin. Then snip it off even with the bobbin. Never let the thread wrap over the edge of the bobbin. This can cause the bobbin to feed unevenly.

Loose, unevenly wound bobbins cause poor stitch quality. When placing the bobbin in the bobbin case, be sure that it unwinds according to your manual. Most machines have bobbins that unwind clockwise when you look at the bobbin in the case, but there are a few that unwind counterclockwise, so be sure to check. This small item has a big impact on stitch quality. Thread the top of the machine with the same thread used to wind the bobbin.

Identify the tension adjustment dial on your machine. When getting to know your machine, you'll find it necessary to have a full understanding of its tension system. There is no magic about thread tension, and many service calls can be eliminated if you have a thorough understanding of how tension works.

Use a size 80/12 needle and 50/3 cotton thread. Sew a row of stitches in two layers of cotton fabric. Correct tension is evident when both threads are linked together in the center of the layered fabrics (Figure 4.1). Figure 4.2 shows the bottom thread being pulled tight. This can indicate that the top thread is too loose or the bobbin thread is too tight. Figure 4.3 shows the top thread being pulled tight. This can indicate that the top thread is too tight or the bobbin thread is too loose.

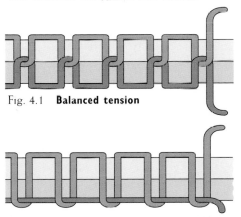

Fig. 4.1   **Balanced tension**

Fig. 4.2   **Top tension too loose or bobbin too tight**

Fig. 4.3   **Top tension too tight or bobbin too loose**

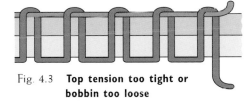

> **Tip**   If you're not happy with your stitch quality, start troubleshooting for possible problems, such as the following:
> • Is the needle the proper size for the thread it is carrying?
> • Is the top thread in between the tension disks?
> • Is the bobbin in the case properly?
> • Is there any lint in the feed dog area?
> • Do the top and bottom threads match in size and weight?

If all of these things check out, you may need to adjust your bobbin case to the thread you're using. With the high speed and long duration of sewing times quilters put their machine through, bobbin tension can fluctuate. Knowing how to check and adjust it can save a lot of time and irritation.

A general test for normal tension is done by letting the bobbin case hang down freely by the thread. It must not slide down by its own weight, but when you jerk your hand lightly upward, yo-yo style, it should gently fall. If it doesn't move at all, the tension is possibly too tight. If it falls easily, it's generally too loose. This doesn't tell you if the tension is exactly right, but gives you a good indication if you're in the ballpark.

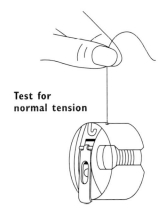

Test for normal tension

If needed, adjust the tension by turning the large screw on the tension clip. Adjust in very small increments until the tension is correct. Read the screw like a clock, and move only one hour at a time. Test this with different sizes and types of thread. You will find that the proper setting of the tension will be different for different threads.

HINT: Before turning a screw, make a note to yourself where it is positioned before you start, reading the screw like a clock face. This will allow you to return to the original

setting if need be. Turn the screw to the right to tighten, and to the left to loosen. If you can remember this old saying: "righty tighty, lefty loosey" you'll always know how a screw works.

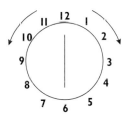

Close-up of screw

Incorrect tension is why your machine does not always sew properly. Polyester threads have more thread drag than cottons, requiring the tensions to be looser. The tension also needs to be loosened when heavier threads are used. If you find that your tensions fluctuate or you need to change the tension of the bobbin case often for different threads, consider purchasing another bobbin case. This bobbin case can be changed whenever you need anything other than normal tension, and the original case is set for your favorite thread and normal sewing.

NEEDLES

Needles are critical in obtaining a smooth stitch. Use only high quality needles and start each new project with a new needle. Check your manual for the size, type, and brand of needle recommended for your machine to prevent poor quality or skipped stitches. This information is often found imprinted in the bobbin area of the machine.

Many people who use machines have little knowledge of needles. See Figure 4.4, on page 38, of a needle and terms used to describe it. Hold a large sewing machine needle and examine it. Notice that the needle is flat on one side of the shank and has a long groove on the opposite side.

Run your fingernail down the long thread groove. This groove allows the thread to be protected within the needle while penetrating the material. The thread slides through the grooved side and the eye. Because it's pinched from behind, it creates a loop behind the needle as the needle rises. This loop and the scarf (the hollowed out area on the back of the needle) allow the hook point of the shuttle to pass between the thread and the needle, locking the stitch.

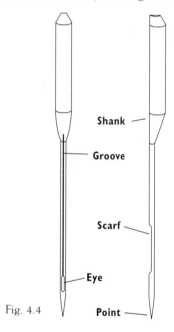

Fig. 4.4

Needle sizes are determined by measuring the width of the needle blade. The European system is widely accepted, but for reference, the U.S. equivalents are shown at right.

There are many sizes and varieties of needles. Most textiles are sewn with round point needles. Needles with cutting points are only used for sewing leather and similar materials. Use the chart at right for suggested uses of today's machine needles. The choice of the most suitable round point needle depends on the characteristics of the fabric to be sewn, such as woven or knitted; its fiber content, such as natural, blended, or synthetic; and the desired strength and appearance of the seam.

Almost all sewing machine needles are now considered semi-ballpoint or ballpoint, both being round-point needles. The type of round needle point has little influence on the resistance of the fabric to the penetration of the needle. Ballpoint needles do not pierce the yarns of the material but penetrate the gaps between the yarns. The coarser the fabric yarns, the more the point must be rounded.

Most fabrics can be sewn satisfactorily with a needle having a slightly rounded point (a semi-ball-point needle). This needle is known as the Universal point and is manufactured with a light rounding of the point for normal sewing of woven fabrics. This needle separates the yarns of the fabric and does not pierce the individual yarns, which may damage the fabric. The 705H Universal needle is the most versatile, as it is suitable for knits or wovens and is available in sizes 60-120.

The embroidery needle (H-E) has a larger eye to accommodate heavier embroidery threads. The scarf helps reduce skipped stitches and the thread groove is deeper to protect delicate threads like rayon from shredding. The denim needle (H-J) has a sharp point that sews a very straight line in woven fabrics. The quilting needle is designed for working with thick layers at seam intersections. The needle (H-Q) is slimmer than others to accommodate the thick layers encountered in piecing and quilting. Microtex or Metalfil are names of needles that have a special finish that helps control heat, as well as a specialized eye and scarf that helps eliminate stripping and splitting, so common with metallic threads. Sharp needles are once again available for sewing woven fabrics.

Most sewing machine manufacturers recommend Schmetz® needles for best results. They are produced

Needle Size Equivalents									
	Lightweight fabrics				Medium-weight fabrics			Heavyweight fabrics	
European	60	65	70	75	80	90	100	110	120
U.S.	8	9	10	11	12	14	16	18	20

Suggested Uses for Various Needle Types		
Fabric	Needle Size	Point Code
Quilting weight cottons	75/11	H-J for piecing
	80/12	H-Q for quilting
		H- for piecing & quilting
Heavier cottons	80/12	H-J for piecing
Flannels	90/14	H-Q for quilting
Silks, satins, delicate fabrics	70/10	H-M for piecing
Any fabric where you are	80/12	H-M
using metallic or heavy	90/14	H-M
machine emb. threads		
Any fabric where you are	75/11	H-E
using rayon threads	90/14	H-E

under very strict conditions to insure quality. Singer® sewing machines can be the exception.

The Singer hook-needle clearance is different, therefore warranting the use of Singer needles in their machines.

Hint: The top of the Schmetz needle package is magnified, making the needle sizes imprinted on the needle shank easier to read.

OTHER SPECIALTY NEEDLES
Embroidery (H-E)
Sharp (H-M)
Denim (H-J)
Quilting (H-Q)

THREADS

With the introduction of polyester fabric, polyester threads were needed for strength and stretchability. This thread overtook the market, making 100% cotton thread very difficult to obtain. Now with the increasing demand for natural fibers, cotton thread is again in demand and is more readily available. Why should quilters be concerned about which thread they piece and quilt their quilts with? It has to do with thread strength and fiber compatibility.

There are two guidelines to keep in mind when deciding on thread for a project.

■ Threads and fabrics need to be of like fibers, i.e., natural fabrics sewn with natural threads, synthetics with synthetics.

■ The thread needs to be weaker than the fabric. Thread that is too strong will cut and weaken the fabric in the seam, causing the fabric to "break." If a thread breaks in a seam, it can be mended; if a fabric breaks, it cannot.

Important Factors in Thread Selection

Thread size should be as fine as possible, consistent with the strength requirements of the seam. Finer threads tend to become buried below the surface of the fabric and are subjected to less abrasion than seams with heavier thread, which are on top of the fabric. Finer threads also require smaller needles, producing less fabric distortion than heavier needles do. The preferred thread size for sewing cotton quilting fabrics is 50/3. The "50" designates the yarn count of the thread or the weight and diameter. The "3" indicates the number of plys twisted together. The higher the first number, the finer the thread. The more plys, the stronger the thread.

Thread strength should be less than that of the fabric that has been sewn. Authorities agree that the seam should be about 60% of the fabric strength. The reason for this is if excessive stress is placed on a seam, the seam will break instead of the fabric. Cotton thread is weaker than the cotton fabric that we use, polyester thread is not. Polyester thread has tiny, abrasive edges that work as saw blades against the soft cotton fibers and cut through the seams over time. Mercerized thread is treated cotton thread that is stronger, more lustrous, and more stable than unmercerized cotton thread.

When purchasing cotton threads, unroll a length and check for quality. A fuzzy thread is made from short fibers, rendering it weak and giving it poor sewing properties. A thread with few fuzzy ends showing is made from long fibers. When twisted, the ends are secured, giving a much stronger thread. This thread will sew a nicer seam and last longer in the finished item.

When sewing, the relationship between the needle and thread is critical. If the needle eye is too small for the thread to pass through, the thread will fray and break, and stitches will be skipped. If the thread is too fine for the needle, the hole made by the needle will not be filled by the thread, leaving a weak and unsightly seam. Below is a chart that gives corresponding needle and thread sizes. This will assist you in choosing a needle for the thread size and fabric weight you are sewing.

Another thread consideration is when paper piecing. Because the paper tears away easiest when a tiny short stitch is used, regular 50/3 sewing thread can build up quite a bit in the seam. If using a very short stitch length, you might want to try using 60/2 embroidery thread in a size 70 needle. The short stitches give the strength, but the thread is small enough to lay very flat in the fabric.

Needle/Thread Reference								
Thread Size				Needle Size				
	60	65	70	75	80	90	100	110
Ultra fine 80/2	•	•						
Nylon monofilament	•	•	•	•	•			
Fine machine embroidery 60/2			•	•	•			
DMC® machine embroidery thread 50/2			•	•	•			
Embroidery thread 30/2				•	•			
Merc. cotton sewing thread 50/3					•	•		
Synthetic sewing thread (spun)					•	•		
Cotton-wrapped polyester						•		
Cotton 40/3						•	•	
Buttonhole (cordonnet)							•	•

THROAT PLATES

The throat plate is the metal piece that surrounds the feed dog. The standard throat plate on today's machines has an oval opening to accommodate a zigzag stitch. The oval hole allows the needle to push fabric down with it, and the stitch is not made cleanly. Another problem with a zigzag plate is keeping the ends of strips straight and even while sewing. Strips have a tendency to want to veer away from the edge as you approach the end. A straight stitch plate will help to eliminate this. Another major benefit of a straight stitch throat plate is that it can help keep the points from being "eaten" when starting or stopping a seam. A straight stitch plate opening is too small to allow the fabric to enter with the needle. Straight-stitch machines make perfect stitches, and many quilters still prefer to piece on their old straight-stitch machines because of the stitch quality.

  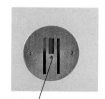

Zigzag plate   **Straight stitch plate**

PRESSER FEET

The regular presser feet available on machines were not designed for ¼" seams used in patchwork. In the past few years, we have seen feet developed just for piecing the ¼" seams. The first of these is the Little Foot®, developed by Lynn Graves. This foot was designed to be a perfect ¼" on the right side of the needle. The foot is marked with ¼" markings on the side, to indicate the needle position; ¼" behind the needle, for starting the seam; ¼" in from the edge, and ¼" in front of the needle, to indicate when to stop ¼" from the edge. The foot is available in several shank sizes to adapt to most machines.

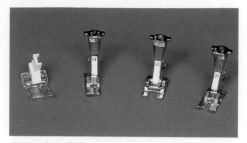

Examples of feet used for piecing

Sewing machine companies have started to make ¼" feet, but there is still much disagreement as to the total accuracy of the feet. The theory is that it's exactly ¼" from the needle position to the right-hand edge of the presser foot. We recommend that you actually check that measurement for yourself by placing the ruler under the presser foot, carefully lowering the needle until it just contacts the ruler on the ¼" guide line, and determining whether that actually is the edge of the foot.

If there is a discrepancy, first double-check the accuracy of your ruler, and then check the position of the needle. Occasionally the needle can become misaligned. This is a condition that can be corrected by your sewing machine mechanic.

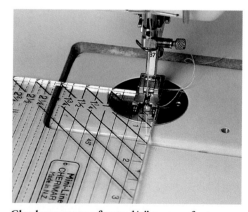

Check accuracy of your ¼" presser foot

Be sure to sew sample seams and measure for accuracy. When sewing to the edge of the foot, it's very important that your body be directly positioned in front of the presser foot. If you're angled with regards to the presser foot, your perception of the edge of the fabric and the edge of the foot will be incorrect, which can definitely affect the accuracy of your piecing. The time of day and the position of the light around your work will also affect the accuracy of the ¼". If you start piecing in the morning with natural light on your right side, then finish up at night with artificial light above you, your eyes are apt to see the edge of the foot differently. Keep the light consistent at all times if possible. Some ¼" feet have an open space between the toes so that you can see ahead of you and view the needle when needed. Measure different sections of your feet to see if these measurements are automatically built into the foot. You will be surprised by these types of hidden features.

Not all machine piecers like using a ¼" foot. Sharyn prefers the straight-stitch foot. A straight-stitch foot has a very narrow toe on the right side and a wider one on the left. You may remember this same foot on straight-stitch machines of years gone by, such as Singer Featherweights.

Another foot that many quilters enjoy using is the open toe appliqué foot. This foot is completely open, up to the needle, and allows you to see exactly where you are when sewing and where you are going as you sew. If you cannot find this foot, take your plastic embroidery or satin-stitch foot and clip away the plastic between the toes. File smooth and you will have a great patchwork and appliqué foot.

SEAM GUIDES

Once you've selected the presser foot you want to work with for piecing, you may want to use a seam guide beside it to ensure even seams. There are a variety of great gauges and attachments on the market for this purpose.

Various seam guides

Magnetic guides are available from different manufacturers. If you have a computerized machine, check with your dealer to make sure that the magnetic guide can be used. If you have a plastic bobbin cover or a plastic housing on the machine, this guide may not stick. Also, be aware that with use the vibration can distort the 1/4" distance. Two-piece guides that screw into the bed of the machine have long been available. This is a wonderfully accurate system, as it never moves with vibration.

Molefoam, an adhesive padding for pressure points on feet, is a commonly used seam guide. Use a rotary cutter (use an old blade) and ruler and cut the foam sheet into 1/4"-wide, 2"-long strips. Expose the adhesive and position on the bed of the machine. The only drawback to molefoam is that the sides will slowly wear away. Keep an eye on this or your piecing can become inaccurate.

Another adhesive guide can be made by building up layers of adhesive tape and placing them on the machine bed. This gives a very firm edge to use as a guide, but can leave a sticky residue on the machine.

Another seam guide, and a personal favorite of Sharyn's, is to use the quilting bar guide in combination with the straight-stitch foot. The quilting-bar guide is an attachment that comes with most new sewing machines. It is designed to allow machine quilters to quilt parallel lines by lining up the bar guide with the previous line quilted. Sharyn has the quilting bar guide positioned exactly 1/4" from the needle. If there is a space between the edge of the foot and the seam guide, you can tell by glancing occasionally when the edge of the fabric is making contact with the edge of the guide. If the guide lines up exactly with the edge of the foot, you may have trouble determining if the fabric is indeed clear out to the edge. You do know that you can't sew a seam greater than the 1/4" with the seam guide on, but there is nothing to stop you from sewing less than 1/4". This guide used with the straight-stitch throat plate is a great combination.

Straight-stitch foot with quilting bar guide

HINT: If you cut off the extra bar that is extending to the left of the presser foot, it makes a very compact, usable foot. The bar extension won't hurt anything, but it's cumbersome.

How to Position the Seam Guide: Addressing the Seam Allowance Challenge

As discussed in the thread section (page 39), consideration must be given to the accuracy of the sewn units, not just to the seam allowance size. Experimentation with the position of the seam guide is necessary to achieve your personal position. Start by placing a ruler over the feed dog, under the presser foot, and slowly lower the needle so it is just a hair to the right of the 1/4" line on your ruler. Lower the foot to hold the ruler in place. Keep the edge of the ruler parallel with the lines on the throat plate. The edge of the ruler is your starting point for positioning the seam gauge of your choice.

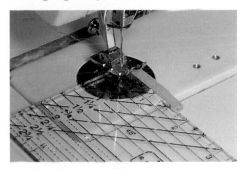

Position the seam guide

To check the accuracy of your guide, perform the following simple test.
- Sew two 2 1/2" squares of fabric together using your guide.
- Press the seam allowance toward one of the two squares.
- Measure the pressed unit. How close to 4 1/2", edge to edge, does your sewn unit measure?

Several things factor into the accuracy of your test. We are assuming that you cut the original squares correctly, but you might want to start by checking that. Did you realize that the thickness of the thread and the bend of the fabric, when pressing a seam to one side, also need to be taken into consideration? The diameter of the thread affects the 1/4" you're measuring. A thinner thread will lay flatter to the fabric, taking less space in the seam. A thicker thread takes more space. Our recommendation was for a 50 weight, 3-ply cotton thread (the closest to the size of the yarns weaving the cloth). And sewing it with either a size 75/11 or an 80/12 needle. This allows the thread to become a part of the cloth, taking a minimum amount of space. This may seem nit-picky, but think about it. If the thread accounts for $1/32$" difference in the seam width, then the more seams you sew, the more size distortion is occurring. If one seam is off by $1/32$", and there are four seams across the block, you could be off by as much as $1/8$"! If there are two different blocks in the same quilt, and each has a different number of seam allowance, then each block could finish a different size.

Another thing you need to consider when it comes to accuracy of your seam allowance, is the act of pressing the seam. The act of directionally pressing the seam allowance to one side forms a ridge, or bump on the seam. The fabric that has to fold over the bump will finish just slightly smaller than the other side. Consider that it takes about two yarns in the weave of the fabric to bend the fabric over on itself. Add to that a thicker thread, and the height of the thread sitting on top of the fabric in the seam, which takes up even more on the fabric. By the time the whole quilt is put together with all the seam allowances, the difference can be quite a bit more than you expected just because of the size of your thread and the way you press.

So, before you are ready to sew your first real block or quilt, make sure that you have the correct combination of things working for you. When you performed the test at the beginning of the section, how close were you? Was your seam guide positioned correctly? Did you have the right size thread and needle? How about your pressing? If you were off, make whatever corrections you need and repeat the test until you get the correct result. Maintaining the same combination of these factors will go a long way toward consistently giving you accurate piecing.

STITCH LENGTH

The stitch sizes on metric machines have always confused sewers. What do these numbers mean when we are talking about stitches per inch? Well, this is how it works. The stitch length is measured in millimeters (mm). The number on the machine indicates the length of each stitch when sewn on two layers of medium-weight cotton fabric. A setting of 1.0 is equal to 1 mm of length. A setting of 2.0 is equal to 2 mm in length. Just remember that 6 mm is about $1/4$". Following is a chart on how this translates to stitches per inch (spi).

MM Coverted to SPI	
MM	SPI
.5	50
1	25
1.5	16
2	12
2.5	10
3	8
3.5	7
4	6
4.5 - 5	5

For most machine piecing we recommend a 12-14 stitches per inch (1.75 to 2) setting on your machine. Harriet makes her stitch length no longer or shorter than the width of her seam ripper blade. An exception to this will be if you decide to try paper foundation piecing. Most quilters feel that shortening the stitch length to 20 stitches per inch (1.25) for paper piecing truly facilitates the removal of the paper afterwards.

PINNING

You are going to have to experiment with whether or not pins work for you. We both really dislike pinning unless there is no other way to line pieces up. When it's possible to use alternating, butted seams, and finger matching, we feel we get a much more accurate join and match. Conversely, there is no way to join

a long border strip to a quilt without using pins. Many quilters skip pins here, feeling it's just long strips being sewn together, even though they might pin every 2" on small sections of patchwork. The longer the section that you're seaming together, the more important the use of pins becomes. The natural action of the sewing machine has a tendency to feed the bottom layer of fabric through the machine faster than the piece on top. If you're seaming long strips together, such as a border to a quilt, then you often end up with ruffles, rather than flat border strips, unless you pin.

When you do need to pin, the pins you choose to work with can make a big impact on the piecing. Pins sold as "quilter's" pins are too large in diameter and create a bump at the seams. The extra-large head does not lay flat and can cause inaccurate stitching because the fabric is not allowed to lay flat against the throat plate of the machine. We highly recommend the IBC Fine Silk Pins® (#5004) by Clotilde®; the Iris Silk pins, either in the blue tin or the orange plaid box by Gingham Square™; and the Clover® Patchwork Pins and Silk Pins. If you prefer a pin with a head, the #5003 IBC Fine Silk Pins have the smallest glass head, but are the same length and diameter as the ones above.

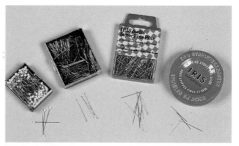

Various pins

If you do prefer the security of using pins, it is suggested that you pin perpendicular to the edge of the pieces being sewn.

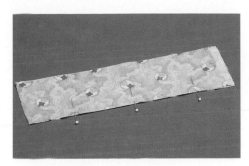
Pin perpendicular to the edge

It is also recommended that you remove the pins rather than sew over them. Even though our machines are supposed to be able to handle sewing over pins, it's still not a good idea. Too often you hit a pin and break a needle, and if you're using any kind of a barrier guide for your ¹/₄", the pins can't pass through.

Pressing Equipment

IRONS
A quality iron in good working condition is a valuable asset to quilters, however, not all irons are created equally. Quilters have specific needs when it comes to irons. The two most important questions to ask yourself are:
1. Can I leave the iron on all day?
2. Will it produce plenty of steam for years to come?

If your current iron doesn't meet these criteria or you want to purchase a new one, here are some features to consider and compare.

STEAM
■ Check the size of the tank and the ease of filling it. Make sure that the water it requires is not a problem. See if the control dials are easy to reach and read.

CORD
■ Make sure its location won't interfere with the ironing and pressing process. Check that it's long enough to reach every corner of your ironing surface.

■ If you're left-handed, check that the cord pivots to accommodate your needs.

AUTOMATIC SHUT-OFF
■ If you are constantly concerned that you've left the iron on, this is a feature you'll really appreciate. Hardcore quilters generally do not care for this option, especially if it beeps.

COST
■ Irons are categorized as household (averaging $90.00 or less, with a built-in water reservoir), semi-professional (more than $90.00, with a built-in water reservoir but made to be left on for hours at a time), and professional (costing $200.00 or more, with an external water system that produces a lot of steam and is meant to be left on all day).

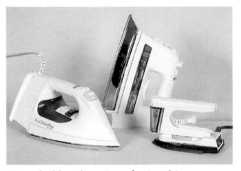
Household and semi-professional irons

STEAM PRODUCTION
Don't be fooled into thinking that more holes in the soleplate will produce more steam. The iron is limited in how much steam it can produce. The more holes, the more the steam is dissipated. Fewer holes mean that the steam is focused in a smaller area. Steam irons work by allowing steam to saturate the fibers and soften them; as the heat of the soleplate dries the steam, it removes any wrinkles. The more holes in the soleplate, the less contact the soleplate has with the damp fibers, so you must move the iron back and forth more to dry the fabric.

Household irons produce the least amount of steam. Steam is generated by water from the reservoir dripping onto the hot soleplate. If the iron is too cool when you start to press and hit the steam button, then the dripping water may pool on the soleplate and drip onto the fabric. Different brands of household irons can vary as much as 20° at the same setting.

Many iron manufacturers recommend using distilled water in your iron, especially if you live in an area of the country with hard water containing a lot of minerals. You may be one of the quilters who has sworn off steam because of problems with spitting and rust staining. Ask yourself what has caused this to occur. The right tools and supplies can make a world of difference.

Professional irons are made visibly different by their external water reservoirs. They are designed to be left on all day and to make steam available continuously, using gravity feed or a pump to deliver the water to the iron. These irons can produce up to 20-60 grams of steam per minute. You work much less with these irons. Because the holes are in the front point of the soleplate, the fibers are dampened, then dried by the solid back end of the soleplate. One pass does the job.

Professional irons

In a steam generator system, the steam is formed underneath the iron's base in a cylinder. It uses tap water and takes an average of five minutes to heat. The steam maintains a constant temperature.

Gravity-feed professional irons use a hanging water reservoir that is attached to the iron by a plastic tube. The steam is generated as in a household iron, but it has more propulsion because of the gravity feed system. These irons are less portable and carry higher repair costs. Many dislike the plastic tubing, feeling that it gets in the way and is often melted if the iron comes in contact with it.

WEIGHT
Although you may think that you need a light iron to make your job easier, the opposite is true. The heavier the iron, the more work the weight does to press the fibers. The lighter the iron, the more work you have to do by applying pressure. Look for household irons in the 3 to 4 pound range.

LONGEVITY
■ The normal life of a household iron is about five years. These irons are not designed for the rigors of quilting and sewing. They are designed based on an average use of two hours a week.
■ Semi-professional irons are better suited for daily use. Although the water tank is still an interior system, they tend to produce more steam than the average household iron. Shot-of-steam is often an option on these irons. Special coatings on the soleplates protect the surface from pin scratches and from fusing agents sticking.

In summary, buy the heaviest iron you can find and afford, and be sure to check your electrical supply (see Chapter 3, page 25) to be sure that your wiring is adequate to run all of your equipment.

PRESSES
Home-sized presses are a wonderful luxury. These pieces of equipment are fashioned after the old mangle concept, where heat and pressure are applied to the fabric without motion. The home models are referred to as "hot-head" presses because the top half is hot. The bottom half is foam-padded wood with a fitted muslin cover. They close with almost 100 pounds of pressure and give the fabric a very pressed look with no sideways distortion. Newer models are now available with optional steam settings.

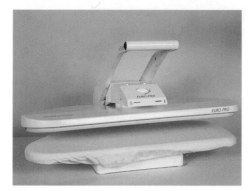

Home-sized press

Presses can be excellent for setting seams and squaring unruly blocks without the distortion that is often caused by an iron. If you happen to have a press, pull it out and use it in your quiltmaking. You will be surprised how adept you can become at perfect pressing by just lowering the handle.

Ironing Surfaces

THINGS TO LOOK FOR WHEN PURCHASING AN IRONING BOARD
■ Be sure that it is heavy, stable, and not warped.
■ Make sure it has sufficient cotton padding.
■ Consider purchasing one of the covers that are measured off in inches. This is a real help in keeping seams straight and blocks square.

MAKING AN IRONING BOARD
A piece of plywood can be covered with an old army blanket then covered again with pillow ticking to create an ironing surface any size you want or need. You might want to consider making an ironing surface to go on top of your cutting table, perhaps the same size. A very versatile ironing surface might measure 30" x 60". This would make the pressing of borders, backings, etc. much easier than fighting on a narrow, wobbly ironing board.

Ironing surfaces

You can make a small, portable ironing board to sit on the right side of the sewing machine. Sharyn has found that the empty cardboard from a bolt of fabric works great for this purpose. Harriet started with a piece of 14" x 14" plywood. She covered it with layers of wool blanketing and heavy pillow ticking. These small boards can be a real time and step saver. They are compact enough to take little space, but large enough to press pieces as they are being assembled. They are also great for taking to workshops.

STARCHES AND SIZINGS
Starches and sizings are a wonderful way to add body and stiffness to a fabric that is difficult to work with, as well as to make it easier for some quilters to cut and piece more accurately. Many quilters have found that by adding starch to a prewashed fabric, they get the body and firmness of a new fabric, but the preshrunk properties of a prewashed fabric.

Aerosol sizings will give a light starch effect. Sizings do not tend to leave the flaky residue that canned starches do. For a heavier starch effect, try liquid or dry starch. Liquid starch can be diluted with water and put in a spray bottle, then sprayed directly onto the fabric. Use purified water, and store any unused solution in the refrigerator to prevent souring. Use a mixture of 25% liquid starch to 75% water for a light starch. Heavy starch is 50% starch, 50% water.

Harriet prefers to use the old-fashioned dry starches still available in many grocery stores under the brand names of Faultless® and Argo®. When using a dry starch, a solution of three tablespoons dry starch in a quart of cold water works well. Stir, then pour into a spray bottle. This solution will continually settle to the bottom, so shake it before each use. This starch gives a very nice crisp finish. Spray the fabric piece with the starch solution. Wait a few seconds to let the starch saturate the fabric fibers, then press until dry with a cotton setting iron. If large pieces need to be starched, either submerge the fabric into the starch mixture, spin out the excess, and hang to dry, or spray the starch mixture onto the yardage until saturated, then let it air dry. Steam press the yardage.

USING YOUR IRON TO PRESS
There seems to be controversy over whether or not to use steam. Each quilter needs to experiment and find which method gives her the best results. The arguments against steam are that it causes distortion, stretching, and sometimes shrinkage, and that it is not needed for the seam to lie flat. The other side feels that the steam makes the seam behave better and a firmer press is obtained. One thing that is seldom discussed is the humidity factor where each quilter lives, as well as her experience in

using an iron. Many people do not know the difference between pressing and ironing, and the use of steam with a heavy hand can be deadly to a quilt block.

How to Press

If you treat your patchwork pieces with the vigorous approach that you do a shirt, your quilt could be in trouble. If done correctly, pressing can truly enhance your piecework. If done incorrectly, it can stretch, distort, and heat-set the pieces into a real mess.

We recommend pressing the sewn pieces first in the closed position. This sets the stitches and helps to prevent stretching and distortion. When you take two sewn pieces to the ironing board, consider which direction you're planning to direct the seam allowance. Normally we position the seam allowance toward the darker fabric. Experience (or a sample block) will help you know whether or not this is going to work in a particular situation. Unless our specific directions indicate otherwise, direct the seam allowances toward the darker fabric. When we do make an exception to this, we will try to tell you why we are doing so.

Set the two pieces on the ironing board with seam allowance away from you and the darker fabric (or whichever piece is the one the seam allowances will be directed toward) on top. Press in the closed position to set the stitches.

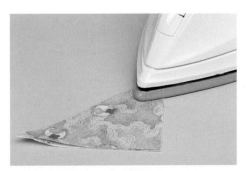
Press in the closed position

Open the piece on top and glide the iron gently across (against) the seam allowance. If you set the iron down on top of the opened pieces without first directing the seam allowance, you run the risk of pressing in glitches, pleats, and puckers.

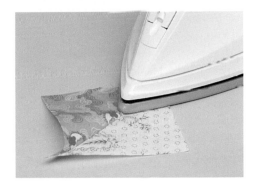
Press opened pieces

When strip sewing for a quilt project, the only way to get the strips to open and lay flat is to use an iron. You need to think about the direction the seam allowance will be pressed. Some sewn strip rows will alternate the seam allowances, always toward the dark fabric. In the case of a 9-patch strip row, you'll have two sets of dark-light-dark strips and one set of light-dark-light strips. It is often easier to sew two strips together and press, then add the third strip and press. Setting the stitches with the strips in the closed position prior to opening and pressing can be quite instrumental in preventing rainbow-shaped strip rows.

Many quilters (Harriet for example) press with the iron all the way through construction of the block. Harriet sews a seam and sprays lightly with starch before pressing. (Be careful not to saturate the fabric. If it gets too wet, stretching is more likely to occur when the iron hits it.) Refer to starches and sizings on pages 44-45. When another seam is sewn, it also is sprayed, then pressed. Every seam of the block is handled this way, giving the fabric the ability to stay in place and sew straight in the machine—no stretching or distortion. The finished block is very straight and square and has a crisp, firm hand. Blocks that have been starched will definitely machine quilt more easily and help prevent the fabric from shifting during machine quilting.

Sharyn—like many quilters—prefers to finger-press during block construction; she saves the iron for the completed block. When she presses the finished block, she does it from the wrong side first, letting the steam guide the seam allowances. The iron doesn't actually put any weight on the block; just the steam is working. Next she turns the block right side up and firmly presses the block. A light coat of spray sizing (rather than starch) is her stabilizer of choice. It doesn't give the block as firm a hand, but it does make your block smoother and flatter, and helps to prevent slipping during assembly and machine quilting.

Below are some guidelines for pressing seam allowances when piecing:

■ If the seam allowance was pressed in the wrong direction, don't just flip it over and run the iron over it. Fold the two pieces together again and re-set the seam, then open it and re-press.

■ Try to avoid pulling on the seam as you press.

■ Try to keep all of the quilt top on the surface you're pressing. If it hangs over the edge, drag occurs and can cause distortion.

■ If a dark seam allowance shadows beyond the edge of the seam allowance into the piece, grade (trim) the darker layer slightly to eliminate the problem.

■ To avoid undue bulk, consider pressing seam allowances to the lighter side if necessary. "Always press to the darker side" is not a hard and fast rule.

If you're interested in more specific pressing ideas, an excellent book is

Press For Success, Secrets for Precise and Speedy Quiltmaking by Myrna Giesbrecht.

Just like everything else in this book, you're going to have to experiment and make choices with the various methods. You should never make your decisions based on one teacher's particular favorite method. Most quilters find that they use different methods depending on what the circumstances of the individual project call for. Guidelines are much easier to live with than rules. Flexibility and the ability to try things before making up your mind is definitely going to work to your advantage.

USING FINGER-PRESSING TOOLS
Many quilters prefer to finger-press their patchwork blocks during construction, as opposed to using an iron. Finger-pressing can be just as effective as ironing if done carefully and correctly. It is possible to obtain as sharp a crease with your fingernail as you can with an iron, and you don't run the risk of stretching, distorting, and heat setting the little pieces.

The most convenient way to finger-press is to use the underneath edge of your thumbnail. One major advantage of using a thumbnail for finger-pressing is that you always know where it is. No time is ever spent looking for where you last set it down.

If you don't have a thumbnail, or if using your thumbnail causes you discomfort, there are many devices you can find on the notions wall of many quilt shops and fabric stores designed specifically to use for finger-pressing. Some of these devices include a Hera® manufactured by Clover®, which is a point turner and edge creaser, and The Little Wooden Iron®, which is a specially shaped piece of wood available in either left- or right-handed models.

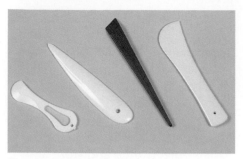
Finger-pressing tools

It is important that you find something that comfortably fits into your hand and gives the desired sharp crease. Look for a sharp angled edge with no rough spots that might tear your fabric. You might look around your home for other things that can also be used for finger-pressing. How about trying the edge of a spoon? Even a piece of sturdy cardboard can do the trick.

When properly finger-pressed, fabric pieces will lay open and absolutely flat. Sharyn uses the underneath part of her thumbnail and firmly draws it along the ridge from the right side of the two pieces. Working on a hard surface, such as a table, can increase the sharpness of the crease.

Proper finger-pressing

The important thing is to experiment and try different tools and methods. A device that works for one quilter doesn't always work for another. Having lots of gadgets can be fun, but is not always necessary. Think about your work styles as you consider whether or not to buy something, make do with something around the house, or even use those well attached thumbnails you already own!

Cutting Tools

SCISSORS

Quality scissors give you control of the cutting shape no matter how complicated the pattern cut. When buying scissors, buy the best money can buy, and buy the types, sizes, and styles that meet your cutting needs. Sewing is much more enjoyable with good scissors that perform perfectly for each job. Correct size selection is determined, in part, by the type and length of cut desired. Longer cuts are smoother if using long scissors. Cutting long lines with small scissors can give choppy results.

Excellent cutting performance means that the blades don't trap the fabric and that they don't tear things apart, but instead give a clean cut. One way of testing quality scissors is to cut a layer of fabric with the scissors' tip, the weakest point. The cut should be clean; the tips should not split apart. The ability to cut many layers of fabric does not indicate the sharpness, only the strength.

The fit of the handles in the hand is a primary consideration. The handle size is increased as the length increases. Therefore, a person with a small hand can handle a 6" shear more easily than an 8" shear. A person with large hands will prefer an 8" shear.

Smooth cutting action is a sign of quality. With scissors all the way open, both parts should move freely, not restricted by the nut or screw. When closing scissors, you should feel a gradual increase in pressure until the blades meet, ideally in the area where the blade begins, behind the nut or screw. The same pressure should then prevail all the way to the tip. Any change in the pressure indicates a possible nick in the blade area.

The tips of the blades have to meet at one point at the same time that the handles meet. Handles and shanks have to be at the same level with each other and the blades to make a perfect, clean cut.

Scissors are very sensitive to the wrong cutting material and can easily be destroyed if misused. Using embroidery scissors to cut wire or pry out staples is a very effective way to ruin a good cutting tool. The same philosophy applies to cutting cardboard with shears. Not only is the cutting edge being nicked, bent, or damaged, the scissors construction itself—the delicate balance between pressure and counterpressure of the blades—is destroyed. The practice will eventually result in two loosely-connected pieces of steel.

Never set a pair of scissors down in the open position. The tension where the blades edges meet can cause the sharp edge to be dented each time the scissors is jarred. A thin knife-edge will dull much faster than one with strong support. This is the leading cause of making the scissors dull and unable to cut.

FABRIC SCISSORS

There are many different types and brands of scissors on the market to cut fabric. Many are not suitable for cottons. A perfectly sharpened knife edge shear is best for cutting cottons. Many quilters like a finely serrated blade for more control. Before making a purchase, take some fabric to the store and try out several different sizes and types of scissors. Cut all the way to the point.
- Are they heavy in the hand or very comfortable?
- How do your fingers fit in the handle openings?
- How much control do you have when cutting around tight curves?
- How straight do they cut?
- Do they slip as they cut?

Little known fact: You will not damage your scissors by cutting paper! We're talking regular paper here—not cardboard, posterboard, etc. Paper is made of cellulose, which is also a component of fabric. Ages ago, when paper contained tiny particles of sand and grit, it would damage a knife edge on scissors. As paper no longer contains these elements, it's safe. This information is provided so that you don't panic if you cut freezer paper or pattern paper with your good sewing scissors.

THREAD SCISSORS

These are generally shorter and have more pointed tips than fabric scissors. Some brands are available with large eyes for larger fingers. Thread snips are very handy for machine work. They are spring-loaded so that they are open all the time. Hold the snips in the palm of your hand and place the third finger down into the finger hole.

UTILITY SCISSORS

These scissors are used to cut anything except fabric. If you end up cutting template plastic or sandpaper for piecing or appliqué templates, these scissors will be particularly handy. The ones your kids use are not going to work well for you. Look for thin blades, rather than thick, clunky ones. Thin-angled blades can do a better job of cutting accurately, because you can clearly see what you're doing.

ROTARY CUTTER

A rotary cutter is a tool made up of a round razor blade attached to a plastic handle, making it a rolling razor blade. They are available in 28mm, 45mm, 60mm, and 65mm. Recently, wave and pinking blades have been added for versatility. There are several different brands of rotary cutters, each with slightly different features.

Each cutter has its pros and cons, and each quilter will have a personal favorite. Generally speaking we recommend starting with the 45mm size. It is easy to cut with and not as intimidating as the 60mm and 65mm. As you gain confidence, you might find that the larger cutters cut more smoothly and easily through more layers. The 28mm size is great for specialty cutting, such as curves, or when working with templates and very small pieces.

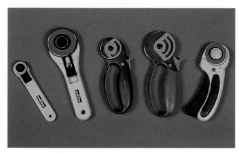

Various rotary cutters

Since rotary cutters were first introduced in the early 1980s, there have been many improvements and changes to the cutters, including the shape of the handle. Most of the newer cutters have thicker, fatter handles that have been proven to reduce stress and fatigue to the hand when doing a lot of cutting. Some of today's cutters have curved handles that are often beneficial to people with arthritis or who suffer from carpal tunnel syndrome. Quilters who prefer to cut sitting down often find the curved handle cutters are easier to work with.

Note If using a curved handle cutter, make sure that the blade is positioned correctly. It must be seated on the side that will be closest to the ruler during cutting. All curved handle cutters provide this option to accommodate the right- or left-handed user.

We strongly suggest that you go to the store and "test drive" every rotary cutter available, in every size, before purchasing one. So many criteria make up your ability to use the cutter safely and accurately, that it would be very hard to know which one was best for you until you try them all.

How to Use Your Rotary Cutter

It is critical to follow safety measures and be very cautious when using any type of cutter. Make it a habit to close your cutter every time you lay it down. Cutters can do major damage to fingers and toes! Never leave a cutter lying around, open or closed, where small children can get ahold of it. Educate your family about what they are and what they are for. Proper information can go a long way toward eliminating accidents.

Let's talk a minute about the proper way to hold your cutter. The handle of the cutter should rest comfortably in the palm of your hand. Your index finger should extend forward, resting on the grooved space at the top edge of the handle. Your thumb should be on one side of the handle and the other three fingers should curl softly around the other side.

How to hold a rotary cutter

The cutting motion should always be away from your body, never toward your body. Think about this. Why would we tell you to cut away from yourself? Number one, it's

safer. This is a sharp blade. If you're pulling toward yourself, what might happen if you slip? Number two, you have more strength in your pushing ability than you do in your pulling muscles. If you don't believe us, try moving a refrigerator.

It's a really good idea to practice with your cutter on the mat with no fabric first. Get accustomed to the way the cutter feels and the blade rolls. Remember that the blade should be rolling freely and easily. You should definitely not be pushing hard in order to feel the blade rotating.

CARING FOR A ROTARY CUTTER
Always store your rotary cutter in a closed blade position and keep it out of children's reach. Make sure your mat is free of hard objects, such as pins, to avoid damaging the blade with nicks. Note: Be sure to keep and refer to the care and maintenance instructions that come with your rotary cutter.

To maximize the longevity of your rotary blade, periodically remove the blade and carefully wipe the lint and residue from both the cutter and blade.

If there are any rust spots on your blade, use very fine sandpaper to remove the spots and keep the blade well oiled to avoid deterioration. Be sure to remove any spots where lint has dried and hardened onto the blade or the black plastic shield. Saturate a small piece of fabric with sewing machine oil to clean the blade. If you can't remove a particle, use a little acetone on a piece of cloth. Check that the pivot (screw) that fits in the center hole is not worn where the blade makes contact. Once you've cleaned everything, you are ready to reassemble the cutter as described on the packaging.

ROTARY CUTTER BLADES

A rotary cutter blade is finely polished and razor sharp. A blade should last through hundreds of cuts. However, its lifespan depends on a number of factors. Even though the blade is deadly sharp when new, it does eventually get dull. A dull tool requires more force than a sharp tool to do the same work. The duller the tool, the faster it continues to dull. Cutting synthetic and blended fiber content fabrics will dull the edge more quickly. The fibers are harder and more abrasive than the soft fibers of cotton fabric. The quality of the blade depends on two factors: how hard the steel is, and how sharp it is when you put it in your holder. There are at least ten brands of blades on the market, not all of the same quality. Some companies have more stringent quality control and material standards than others. Olfa® is known as one of the finest blades available. The standard flat blades are all interchangeable. It is not always so with the pinking and ruffled edge blades. Be brand consistent in this case.

Blades are very easily damaged. A slight tap against the edge of your ruler, dropping the cutter, or going over a pin or a small bump against a hard surface, can all deform the edge of the blade and cause a skip in the cut at that area.

ROTARY CUTTING SURFACES

Equally as important is the cutting surface you use. Rotary cutter mats

Various cutting mats

come in several different sizes and materials, so you'll need to think about your needs. There are basically three different types of mats: soft plastic, three layers of plastic pressed together, and hard plastic.

Soft plastic mats are usually translucent, white solid plastic with a textured side and a smooth side. Both sides can be used for cutting. The cutter may leave marks on the surface, but these can generally be smoothed with emery cloth or very fine sandpaper.

Three-layer mats are made of three layers, with the center layer being softer than the outer layers, and are "self healing," in that the cuts do not remain in the surface. Mats made of this material must be kept flat and out of heat, as they will buckle and distort if exposed to a heat source or left in a hot car.

The only hard plastic mat that claims to be weatherproof will not warp, crack, or peel is June Tailor®. This mat is made of a single thickness of hard plastic. It does repel cuts better than the soft plastic, but is not considered self-healing.

Most mats have a one-inch grid printed on one side. Quarter-inch markings are along the outside edges. These grids tend to wear off the soft plastic mats the fastest. The grids are more useful for squaring up fabric or blocks than for measuring when cutting.

Choosing the right mat for your needs is based on sizes needed, size of your cutting surface, storage considerations, portability, and budget. We recommend that you purchase the largest mat you can afford and have room for to do most of your cutting. Also consider smaller mats to have at the ironing board for trimming or cutting apart chain-sewn pieces. The June Tailor Cut 'n Press™

mat fits over an open drawer and is firm enough to support the pressure of an iron or cutter without flexing.

ROTARY CUTTING RULERS

Along with rotary cutters and cutting mats, rulers make up the foundation of the rotary revolution. A clear, accurate ruler is as important to guiding the cutter as a sharp blade is to cutting. There are many different rulers available, for both general and specialty use. Rotary rulers are made of thick, clear acrylic and have lines and numbers evenly spaced across them. The number of lines and their spacing vary between the various brands, as does the color and thickness of the lines. Some rulers have few lines, while others have lines every ⅛". You can find rulers that have numbers running in both directions, making it easy for both right- and left-handed quilters to use. Some of the brands that we suggest you try before buying are Quilter's Rule™, Omnigrid®, Judy Martin's Ultimate Rotary Tools™, and Cottage Tools™, just to name a few. Be sure that you place the rulers on top of both dark and light fabrics to make sure that the color of the lines shows enough for you to work with the ruler easily and accurately.

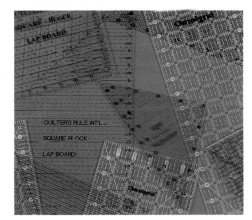

Various rulers

Common on most of the rectangular rulers is a 45° angle line, and many have 30° and 60° angles. Some rulers measure in full measurements, for

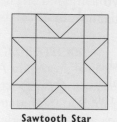

Sawtooth Star

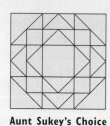

Aunt Sukey's Choice

Base grid is a 4-patch with four equal divisions (units).

1½" per unit = 4 x 1½" = 6" finished block
pattern pieces needed are 1½"△ 1½"□ △ 3"□
                                        3"

2" per unit = 4 x 2" = 8" finished block
pattern pieces needed are 2"△ 2"□ △ 4"□
                                     4"

Base grid is a 9-patch with six equal divisions (units).

1½" per unit = 6 x 1½" = 9" finished block
pattern pieces needed are
1½"△ 3"△ △ 3"□ 1½"□
          3"

2" per unit = 6 x 2" = 12" finished block
pattern pieces needed are 2"△ 4"△ △ 4"□ 2"□
                                    4"

Recapping the Four Simple Steps
- Determine the Base Grid
- Determine the Finished Block Size
- Determine the Pattern Pieces Needed
- Determine the Finished Size of the Pattern Pieces

EIGHT-POINTED STARS
There is another category of blocks known as eight-pointed stars. These blocks are based not on the equal division of a square into a grid, but instead on the division of a circle into eight equal pie-shaped wedges.

The simplest eight-pointed star block is the LeMoyne Star. Unlike grid stars, the sides of these blocks cannot be equally divided. However, the distance from point to point is equal.

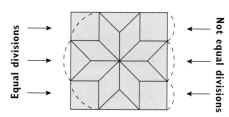

Three pattern pieces are required for this star block: a square (with its four equal sides), a 45°-angle diamond (also four equal sides) and a triangle (equal to half the size of the corner square). If we know the size of the corner square, then we can determine the size of the diamond and the triangle, because, as you can see, everything matches and fits together.

Grid Star vs. Eight-Pointed Star
If you were working with a grid star and wanted to know the measurement of the corner square, you would decide on the block size and divide the number of equal divisions into the size of the block to determine the size of the square.

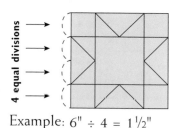

Example: 6" ÷ 4 = 1½"

The pattern pieces needed for a 6" block would be a 1½" square, a 1½" half-square triangle, a 3" square, and a 3" quarter-square triangle.

The LeMoyne Star is not a grid star, yet the divisions along the sides do have a relationship to one another. That relationship is based on a simplification of the Pythagorean Theorem. (Stay with us, we promise to make this understandable!) The Pythagorean Theorem is used to find the diagonal of a square (or the long side of a half-square triangle). $a^2 + b^2 = c^2$ Using the Pythagorean Theorem and our diagram:

If a = 1" and b = 1", then the formula would work like this:
$(1 \times 1) + (1 \times 1) = c^2$
$1 + 1 = c^2$
$2 = c^2$
The square root of 2 = c
c = 1.414

Okay, let's look at this information in layman's terms and how this relates to quilters. The diagonal of a square is always 1.414 times longer than its side. Always, always, always. There is no exception to this relationship.

Determining the LeMoyne Star Pattern Piece Size

So, how does this relate to eight-pointed stars? Look at our LeMoyne Star diagram again, keeping that 1.414 number in mind.

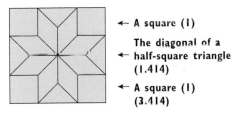

← A square (1)

The diagonal of a
← half-square triangle
(1.414)

← A square (1)
(3.414)

This makes the sum of parts along the edge equal to 3.414. To determine the actual size of the square, take the block size and divide by 3.414. The answer to the equation is the size of the square. Since we have already determined that once we knew what size the square was, we would automatically know the size both of the diamond and the triangle, we're done. One simple calculation on the calculator and you know the size of the pattern pieces. What could be easier?

Note You may not care about Pythagorus and his theorem. No problem. If you can remember the magic number "1.414", and that it is the relationship between the side of the square and its diagonal (or the side of the half-square triangle and its long edge), you'll be able to determine pattern pieces for any of the eight-pointed star blocks you ever want to make.

6" LeMoyne Star.
6 ÷ 3.414 = 1.75"
The actual size of the square, diamond, and half-square triangle is $1^3/4$".

How about a 12" LeMoyne Star?
12" ÷ 3.414 = $3^1/2$"
The actual size of the square, diamond, and half-square triangle is $3^1/2$".

(Remember that these are the finished numbers. You need to add seam allowances to the pattern pieces or to the numbers if cutting without templates.) It doesn't matter what size LeMoyne Star block you want to make. The sum of the parts is always the same.

Using a Calculator to Do the Calculations

It's helpful to use a calculator to do the long division. Calculators will, of course, always give you a decimal response. The decimal must be converted to a fraction for use with graph paper. (See the Decimal Equivalent Chart on page 68 to assist you in converting a decimal to a workable fraction.)

Sometimes, you'll run into a number that needs to be adjusted slightly to be a quilter-friendly number. It is important to be very careful when doing this. We tend to think that the amount we are adding or subtracting from the decimal is so minute that it "can't hurt," when in truth it can.

Example: 8" LeMoyne Star

8" ÷ 3.414 = 2.34
If you drop the "4" and use $2^3/_{10}$" as your fraction, then the resulting block would be.
2.3" x 3.414 = 7.843"
This number is smaller than the 8" block by almost $1/5$".

On the other hand, if you were to use $2^1/3$" as your fraction, the block would be 2.33" x 3.414 = 7.945". Now you're less than 5/1000 of an inch smaller. Not many of us can be that accurate in our piecing. This is why it's important to have a variety of graph paper grids available for making templates.

It's possible to make LeMoyne Stars by assigning a "nice" number to the square, diamond, and triangle pattern pieces. You can make stars with 2" pattern pieces. The finished block will be 2" x 3.414 = 6.828". This is not a block size one would normally choose to work with, but if all the blocks in the quilt are this same size, what possible difference can it make?

Understanding this 1.414 relationship between the edge and diagonal of the square and half-square triangle will enable you to draft any of the more complex eight-pointed star blocks, such as the Snow Crystal.

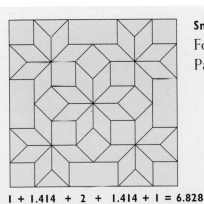

Snow Crystal
For a 12" block: 12" ÷ 6.828 = 1.75"
Pattern pieces needed:

$1^3/4$"

$1^3/4$"

$1^3/4$"

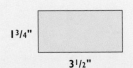
$1^3/4$"

$3^1/2$"

1 + 1.414 + 2 + 1.414 + 1 = 6.828

To Use or Not to Use Templates

If you decide to work with templates then the next step is to create those pattern pieces. If you decide to work without templates then you need to take the finished pattern numbers and convert them into numbers that reflect the addition of seam allowances so that they can be rotary cut without templates. It's possible to use a combination working with and without templates to cut the pieces for a block. The more you understand about your options, the better prepared you'll be to make choices.

First we will look at the conversion of finished numbers to cutting numbers when working without templates. In giving you this information, we are only going to provide the numbers for the basic shapes where the math involved is relatively simple. Some shapes—for example, squares on point—are, in our opinion, not worth the math computations, and are perfect examples of the situation that call for a combination of cutting some shapes with and some without templates.

Squares = finished size + $\frac{1}{2}$"

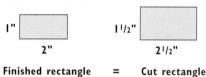

2"   Finished square   =   2$\frac{1}{2}$"   Cut square

Rectangles = finished size + $\frac{1}{2}$" both directions

1"   2"   1$\frac{1}{2}$"   2$\frac{1}{2}$"

Finished rectangle   =   Cut rectangle

Half-Square Triangles = finished size of the side plus $\frac{7}{8}$", cut a square and slice once diagonally, corner to corner.

2$\frac{7}{8}$" → → 2"

**2" finished half-square triangle = 2$\frac{7}{8}$"
square, slice once corner to corner**

Quarter-Square Triangles = finished size of the base plus 1$\frac{1}{4}$", cut a square and slice twice diagonally, corner to corner.

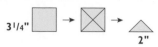

3$\frac{1}{4}$" → → 2"

**2" finished quarter-square triangle = 3$\frac{1}{4}$"
square, slice twice corner to corner**

Diamond = finished length of the side ÷ 1.414 + $\frac{1}{2}$" = width of the strip to cut. Next, establish a 45° angle, measure from this cut edge the strip width, and slice.

1$\frac{3}{4}$" diamond = 1.75" ÷ 1.414 = 1.23" + .5" = 1$\frac{3}{4}$" strip

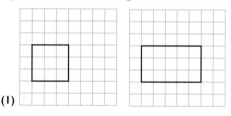

Cut 1$\frac{3}{4}$" strip

Establish 45° angle   45°

Measure over 1$\frac{3}{4}$" from angle and slice   1$\frac{3}{4}$"   1$\frac{3}{4}$"

For methods on creating other shapes, see Recommended Reading on page 234.

> **Note** Some diamond sizes do not have easy-to-use numbers when working without templates. Example: A 2" diamond means cutting a 1.9" strip; 1.9" is not an easy size to cut without a template.

Creating Pattern Pieces for Templates

Here is where you need accurate graph paper. The graph paper grid you select is dependent upon the size pattern piece you need to create. Whenever possible, it's recommended that you use 4-to-the-inch graph paper. But, if you need a 2$\frac{2}{3}$"

square, as discussed earlier, then you'll need graph paper that can accommodate creating that size. Six-to-the-inch graph paper is not easy to find, but is what you need to create a 2$\frac{2}{3}$" pattern piece. (See Resources on page 234 for more information on where to find odd sizes of graph paper.)

You always want to draw the finished size of the pattern piece first, then draw around the shape to add the $\frac{1}{4}$" seam allowance. Having both sets of lines will serve as a constant reminder that the template is complete with seam allowance. Many who choose to hand piece prefer templates without seam allowances so they can draw the stitching line directly onto the fabric by tracing around the finished template. Always label the pattern piece with its finished size so you don't accidentally pick up the wrong template.

Squares and Rectangles

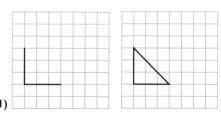

(1)

(1) To create a square or rectangle, follow the lines of the graph paper and draw the size you need, as shown.

Half-square Triangle

(1)

(1) In a half-square triangle, the perpendicular sides are of equal length. Draw the perpendicular sides on the graph paper lines, then draw the diagonal line on the third side, by connecting the endpoints, as shown.

Quarter-square Triangle

In a quarter-square triangle, it's the baseline measurement you know.

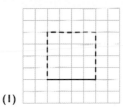

(1)

(1) Begin by drawing the baseline on graph paper.

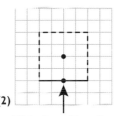

(2)

Midpoint of baseline

(2) Mark the midpoint of the baseline. To find the top point of the triangle, measure up from the midpoint the same distance as from the midpoint to the end of the baseline. Mark this point with a dot.

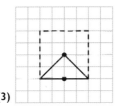

(3)

(3) Connect it to each end of the baseline, as shown, to complete the triangle.

Square on Point

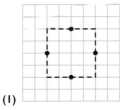

(1)

(1) To draft a square on point, picture it fitting into a second square where the lines do follow graphpaper lines. If the distance tip-to-tip is 4", you can draw a 4" square on the graph paper. Mark the midpoints of each side of the original square.

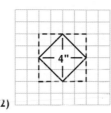

(2)

(2) Connect the dots, and what you now have is the square on point. Erase the outside 4" square and you're set. That was easy enough!

45° Angle Diamond

A 45° angle diamond has four equal sides. Opposite angles are equal as well.

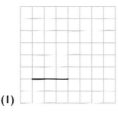

(1)

(1) On a piece of graph paper, draw a line the length of one side.

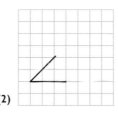

(2)

(2) Lay a ruler at one end of this line, angling it diagonally across the squares of the graph paper. Draw a second line equal in length to the original line.

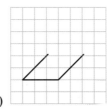

(3)

(3) Follow these same steps at the other end of the first line.

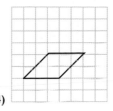

(4)

(4) Connect the ends of lines 2 and 3. You now have the finished diamond.

An "etceteras" shape can be drafted in the same manner as the square on point. Starting with the measurements you know, mark key points with dots and connect these dots.

ADDING SEAM ALLOWANCES

Seam allowances are added after drawing the finished size pattern piece. If your graph paper has 4 or 8 squares per inch, the grid lines on the paper can be followed when adding seam allowances to horizontal and vertical pattern lines. Add these seam allowances first, as shown.

If the number of squares on the paper is not 4 or 8 per inch, or if the seam allowances do not fall on grid lines, you must use a ruler to add seam allowances. First, lay the ruler over the pattern piece so that the ¼" ruler line exactly matches one of the finished lines on the pattern piece. Then back the ruler up just enough to allow for the width of the pencil line and draw as shown.

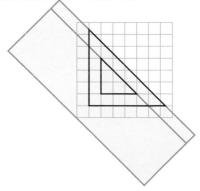

TRIMMING POINTS

You may wish to trim the long points on triangles or other pointed pattern pieces. This will not only make it easier to align pieces for sewing, but also can make the piecing easier, as the sewing machine has a tendency to "eat" the long, skinny points. There are many different schools of thought about where to blunt points. One method of trimming points uses a graph-paper line that is exactly ¼" from the finished point to draw the blunted edge. Another method blunts at a 90° angle to each intersecting line.

Being consistent about the way you blunt will make your life much easier. Try different methods to determine what works best for you.

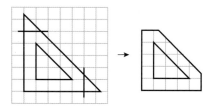

Trim points exactly ¼" from finished point

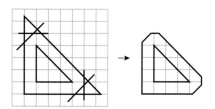

Trim points at 90° angle to each intersecting line

Turning Pattern Pieces into Templates

A pattern piece is the shape drawn on graph paper. A template is a sturdy, durable shape that can be used with the rotary cutter to cut fabric. Our goal is to be able to use these templates with rotary cutters for expediency and accuracy.

One way to do that is to make a template sandwich with heavyweight template plastic and sandpaper. Glue template plastic on the top side of the graph paper. Glue the sandpaper, rough side out, to the underside of the graph paper. Allow the three layers to dry before cutting out the template. This method is only going to be as successful as the weight of the template plastic and sandpaper. You need them to be quite stiff, but light enough to allow you to cut through the layers with scissors. If your materials are too flimsy, you may find that you slice them with your rotary cutter. Not a good idea!

Sharyn prefers the "John Flynn Cut Your Own Template" material. This material is a special-weight laminate that has been treated on the wrong side with a substance that clings to the fabric, allowing you to push against the template with your rotary cutter without it slipping and sliding. You cannot cut this laminate material with a rotary cutter. A template kit comes with a special cutter for cutting the laminate.

Cut your pattern piece out of graph paper, then glue it to the top side of the laminate. Using the special cutters and following the directions included with the kit, carefully cut the template out. You now have a durable template that can be used for years to cut your fabric shapes.

There are plexi-glass template sets that can be purchased to use in cutting your fabric. Once you understand the concept of drafting your own blocks, it's easy to know how and when to use these supplies. Keep in mind that these generic sets will not include all templates you might need but will often include the basic pieces. Again, a combination of templates may provide the best working solution.

CHAPTER 6

Cutting Techniques

In this chapter we concentrate on giving you some guidance on cutting fabric successfully. We deal with the manipulation of your fabric, cutting plain strips, and cutting patchwork shapes (both with and without templates). We give you different methods wherever possible, so that you can experiment with various ways of cutting to see which techniques work best for you.

There are four things you need to address before you actually cut fabric.
■ First, make sure your fabric is well pressed. Take a minute to iron your fabric and eliminate sharp creases where the fabric has been folded. Pressing your fabric carefully at this point makes it easier to cut now and to sew later.
■ Second, make sure that your cutting mat is on a firm, sturdy surface that allows plenty of room to support your fabric and tools. (You may want to reread page 26 in Chapter 3, which addresses cutting tables and recommended heights of cutting surfaces).
■ Third, look at the way you hold your cutter in relationship to the fabric. You want to position the cutter at the edge of the fabric closest to you. It should be not on the fabric but on the mat at the edge of the fabric. Your arm should be extended comfortably at an approximate 45° angle to your body. Hold the cutter with the blade toward the ruler. You should be able to make one clean cutting action across the fabric,

applying enough pressure to go through all layers, but not so much that you're cutting into the mat. You do not want to saw back and forth on the fabric; this will result in a rough, choppy edge.
■ Fourth, know how to fold your fabric. Fold it wrong sides together so that the selvage edges match up.

> **Note** If you're working with a very large piece of fabric, you probably won't be able to match for the entire length. If you're only going to be cutting one strip, then you only need to have the edges match for that amount of fabric. If you're going to be cutting multiple strips from the same piece of fabric, then you might want to stop and refold every 18" or so. It's far better to lose a bit of fabric through refolding than it is to get bends in the strips.

Fold fabric for cutting

Fold the fabric a second time so that the fold matches up with the selvages. The fabric is now 11" wide.

Once your fabric is folded, you will probably notice that the top and bottom edges are very uneven. Before you can cut accurate strips from this piece of fabric, you must even up, or straighten, these edges.

> **Note** Many quilters prefer not to make the second fold, but instead like to work with the fabric folded once, selvage to selvage, making the fabric 22" wide. This may eliminate some of the problems with bends in the fabric strips, but you're more apt to have the ruler slip as you cut such a long length. We suggest that you try both ways and determine for yourself which one feels the most comfortable and gives you accurate results.

METHOD ONE:
STRAIGHTENING EDGES

Right-handed people position the fabric so that it extends to the right.

Right-handed position: Method One

Left-handed people position the fabric so that it extends to the left.

Left-handed position: Method One

Position the fold edge of the fabric on a horizontal line of the mat. Place the ruler on a vertical line of the mat on top of the fabric you're cutting away. If your fold edge is on a horizontal line and your ruler is on a vertical line, you'll get a straight piece with no bends.

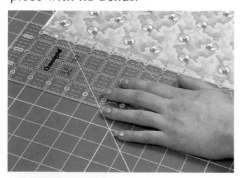

Use grid lines on mat

METHOD TWO:
STRAIGHTENING EDGES

A second method for assuring straight edges is to work with only the ruler, ignoring the mat lines. Right-handed people should position the fabric so that it extends to the left.

Right-handed position: Method Two

Left-handed people should position the fabric so that it extends to the right.

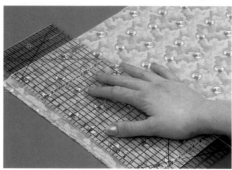

Left-handed position: Method Two

Align one of the cross lines on your ruler exactly with the fold on the fabric. Keep the edge of the ruler close to the edge of the fabric. This aligns the ruler at both the fold and the edge to be cut.

Align cross lines on ruler

Once you've trimmed the edges, the fabric and mat will now have to be turned 180° so that the bulk of the fabric is on the same side as the hand you cut with. Turn both the mat and the fabric at the same time to avoid disturbing the newly aligned edges.

> **Tips** Place the ring finger of the hand holding the ruler against the outside edge of the ruler. This serves as a brace so that the ruler doesn't slip while cutting. While cutting, you can walk your hand up the length of the ruler to keep it straight and accurate, keeping your finger against the edge of the ruler.

Brace edge of ruler

Cutting Strips

To cut strips, position the ruler on top of the fabric, measuring in from the cut edge. Align the line of the measurement you desire with the cut edge, extending the ruler that amount into the body of the fabric. Make sure that the horizontal lines of the ruler align with the fold of the fabric perfectly and that the vertical measurement line is running exactly along the cut edge.

It's a good idea to unfold the first fabric strip and check the fold. If it's straight, your fabric strip is straight. If it has a "V" at the fold, your strips will continue to be bent. If your ruler is not aligned perfectly with both the fold and the cut edge, you'll get "Vs" in every strip.

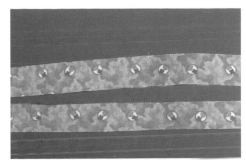

"V" strip and straight strip

Squares

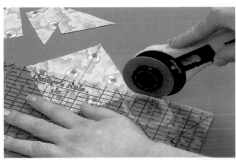

Quarter-square triangles

Rectangles

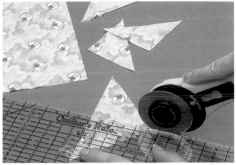

Alternate cutting method for quarter-square triangles

Half-square triangles

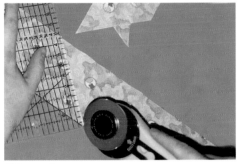

Diamonds

After cutting three or four strips, check again for straightness. If there is any "V" to the strips, realign the fabric piece and square it up again. The importance of this step cannot be overstressed. Too often we assume that everything is okay, only to find after cutting, that the strips are bent and much more difficult to work with.

Cutting Strips Into Patchwork Shapes Without Templates

Begin by cutting strips as described on page 60. Next, cut the strips into the desired shapes. When working without templates, leave the fabric strip folded. Work from the end of the strip, continuing to cut the strip into squares, triangles, diamonds, and so forth.

SQUARES: To cut squares, begin at the open end of the strip and eliminate the selvage-fold edge. This cut not only removes the selvage, but also squares up the ends. Place the ruler on top of the strip, measuring in the same distance as the strip is wide. The ruler lines need to align perfectly along both long edges and the end of the strip. Cut the first square and proceed in the same manner until the strip length is used up. The measurement for cutting squares is finished size plus $1/2$".

RECTANGLES: When cutting rectangles, you need to square up the end of the strip. Align the edge or a horizontal line of the ruler along one long side of the strip. Measure in the needed measurement for the rectangle, and make sure that the measurement line aligns exactly parallel to the end of the strip. The measurement for cutting rectangles is finished size each direction plus $1/2$" each direction.

HALF-SQUARE TRIANGLES: Half-square triangles are cut from squares that are the finished size of the side of the triangle plus $7/8$". Cut a strip, cut squares, and slice once corner to corner.

QUARTER-SQUARE TRIANGLES: Quarter-square triangles are cut from a square that is the finished length of the base of the triangle plus $1 1/4$"; cut a strip, cut squares, and slice twice, corner to corner.

HINT: You may find that the triangles slip a bit when positioning the ruler the second time. If you have trouble with this, try cutting one triangle in half at a time, positioning the ruler so the side runs directly through the point, and the end is aligned evenly with the bias edge of the triangle.

DIAMONDS: To cut a diamond without a template, determine the width of the strip to cut by dividing the finished size of the diamond by 1.414 and adding $1/2$". Cut a strip and establish a 45° angle with your rotary ruler. Measure from that cut edge the same amount as the width of the strip you cut. Slice.

Below and on the following pages are photos and illustrations of various quilts that utilize linking blocks. Can you identify the design blocks? Are the blocks sharing corners? Are more than two blocks involved? Has an overall new pattern developed? What would a color change do to the design?

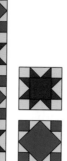

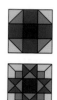

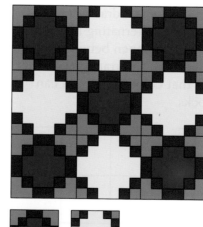

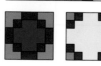

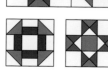

Cu
Sh
Te

Onc
strip
How
cut t
quilt
in m
grain
men
folde
shou
temp
strip
of yo
new
the s
plate

Cuttin

Co
Te

CUT
Octa
zoid
shap
accu
need
Snov
sashi
page
great
inste
the l
you a
othe
nam

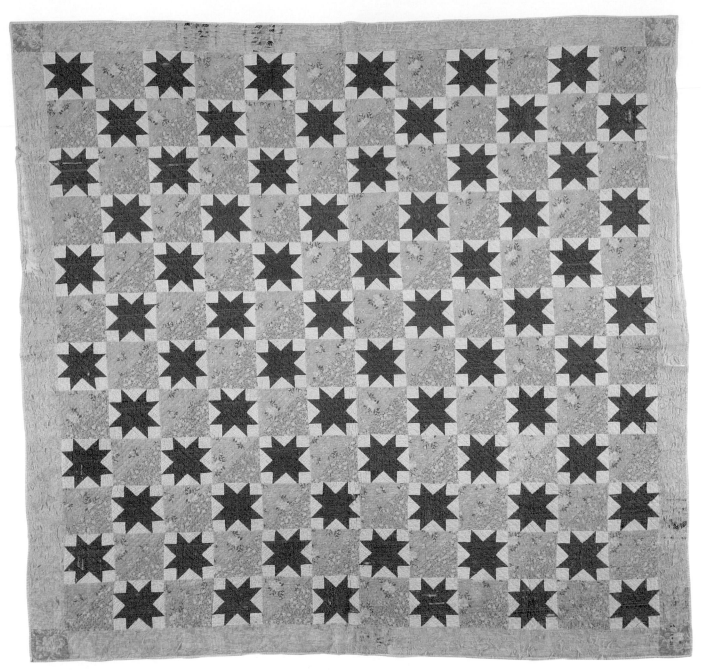

Antique Variable Star, late 1880s, 72" x 72". Collection of Harriet Hargrave.

9-patch and Connector Block, 1994, 60" x 72".
Pieced and quilted by Harriet Hargrave.

Sage Tracks, 1994, 79" x 100".
Designed and pieced by Sharyn
Craig. Quilted by Laurie
Daniells and Sharyn Craig.

SNOWBALL BLOCK

The Snowball block is probably the most used linking block of them all. This block can transform a quilt in many ways, as the following illustrations show.

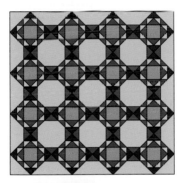

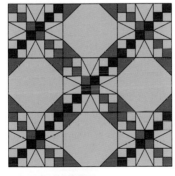

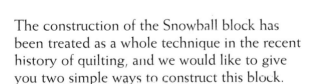

The construction of the Snowball block has been treated as a whole technique in the recent history of quilting, and we would like to give you two simple ways to construct this block.

One technique is known as "cheater corners," "folded square corners," and several other names. Start by completing your design blocks. Turn one block over to the back side and measure raw edge to raw edge of the unit you want your triangle corner to line up with.

Cut a strip from the fabric for the corner the same width as this measurement. Cut the strip into squares. These will become your triangle corners.

Either fold in half diagonally and press in a crease line, or lightly draw a diagonal line corner to opposite corner on the wrong side of the square.

Fold in half   **Draw line**

Cut squares for the connector block from the background fabric the same size as the design block. Place the small squares on each corner, making sure that the diagonal lines form a circle.

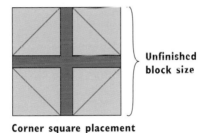

Unfinished block size

Corner square placement

Sew on the fold or the line of each square. You can do this efficiently by turning the block for each corner without cutting the threads.

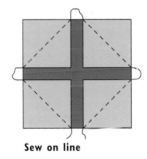

Sew on line

Tip If you have trouble with the line curving, or staying in place while sewing, put a tape guide on the bed of the sewing machine, which allows you to line up the corner of the square during sewing. Find details for this procedure on page 166.

Trim away the outside corners of each square ¹/₄"
beyond the stitching. Do not cut away the background corner. When the triangle is turned back and
pressed, make sure that the corners are the same and
the block is square. Once this is done, the background corner can be cut away if you choose.

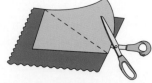

Trim square ¹/₄" from stitching

We hope you enjoy playing with the concept of linking blocks. The possibilities are endless, and the
more you play, the more you'll see that wonderfully
intricate quilts can often be achieved by simple
pieced blocks and strategic color placement.

Fold over

Blocks sewn in vertical rows

Note Corner Cutters is an optional technique to construct these corners.
Instructions can be found in Chapter 6 on page 62.

DIVIDING THE ALTERNATE BLOCKS

A very simple and striking effect arises if you make the alternating blocks
from two half-square triangles instead of one solid block. You will need to
plan your quilt so that you have an odd number of design blocks across the
top row, ensuring that the finished design is balanced in color. This setting
looks good either diagonal or straight. See page 73 for a quilt made with a
straight setting and split squares.

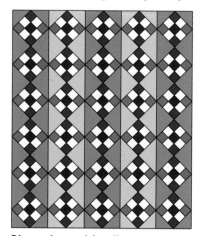

Diagonal set with split square

Straight set with split square

Blocks sewn in diagonal rows

If using the diagonal setting for this configuration, there are two possible methods for
piecing the top together. The triangles can
be pieced together into squares, making the
alternating block. You will need quarter-
square triangles made into half blocks for
the top and bottom edges of the quilt.

(Remember to sew the bias edges together
so that all the outside edges are straight
grain.) The blocks are sewn in diagonal
rows as illustrated to the left. Be careful in
your planning and placement of the pieced

alternate blocks to make sure that
the color changes are in the
needed position. Setting triangles
have straight grain on outside
edges of quilt.

Another method used to construct
this design is to treat each vertical
row of design blocks as a section of
the quilt. Insert colored triangles
(diagonally) to each side of the
block to form the straight sides for
the row of blocks.

Referring to the illustration below,
notice that the short side of a half-
square triangle is sewn to the upper
left and the lower right sides of each
block. The top and bottom blocks of
each row will need a quarter-square
triangle added to both outside edges
to finish the row. Again, watch the
placement of bias when working

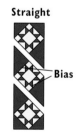

Straight

Bias

with these triangles.
The bias edge needs
to be attached to the
block so that the
straight edges of the
triangles are on the
outside, giving stability
to each row.

The same color is used for all the
triangles within a row, with colors
alternating in every other row. After
assembling the rows, sew them
together. Refer to the information
about diagonal sets starting on page
66 if you're confused about grainline
in triangles.

Simple Sashing

Simple sashing is another way to change the look of a straight or diagonal set. Sashing is strips of fabric that separate the blocks and join one to the other. It can be used to create a bold or subtle look, depending on the print, color, and/or value of the fabric chosen. When the sashing color matches the background of the blocks, they appear to "float." Contrasting fabrics can create separation, as well as adding a unifying element to blocks that don't blend well next to one another.

As a general guideline, the finished size of the sashing strip is one-fourth the size of the finished block. Using this guideline, a 6" block would work well with a 1½" finished sashing strip; a 3" sashing strip is often used with 12" blocks. Remember, this is a guideline, not a rule. This is definitely another instance of learning to trust your instincts about what feels right.

The addition of sashing adds more steps to construction of the quilt top, but with careful measuring, sewing, and pressing, your quilt top should be straight and even.

For simple sashing, start by cutting the sashing into short strips the same length as the block. Join the blocks of each row, adding a sashing strip between each.

Press the seam allowance toward the sashing. Once the rows are constructed, carefully measure the length of each row, including the seam allowance needed at the top and bottom, and cut sashing strips this length. You might want to consider cutting the strip from the lengthwise grain. You are more likely to get the strip in one piece, thereby eliminating the need for piecing, and the strip is less likely to stretch when sewn along the long length.

Simple sashing with straight set

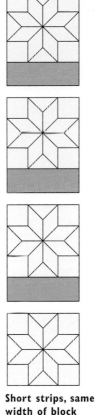

Sashing is length of row

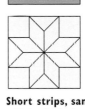

Short strips, same width of block

Marking for sashing placement

¼" — Finished size of quilt block — Sashing — Quilt block — Finished size of sashing — Quilt block — Sashing — Quilt block — ¼"

It is often helpful to mark placement guides in the seam allowance of the vertical sashing. Beginning at one end on one sash, measure the finished size of the block plus ¼" on one end (for the outer edge seam allowance). Mark in both seam allowances or make a firm crease with an iron. Next, measure the finished width of the sashing and mark this distance beyond the first mark on both edges. Measure the finished block again and mark. Continue down the length of the strip, ending with the finished size of a block plus ¼" on the end for the outer edge seam allowance. Repeat this process with all vertical sashing strips.

These strips will now be sewn in between the rows. Pin the strip to the right side of row one, matching the marks to the seam lines of blocks and sashing in the row. Make any adjustments to the row that are necessary for a perfect fit. Stitch the sashing onto the row of blocks. Press carefully, seam allowance toward the sashing. Next, position the opposite side of the sashing to the left side of row two, again be careful to match the marks and seams. Stitch and press. Continue with each row until all the rows are joined.

Once all the rows are sewn together, add sashing to the sides of the quilt top. Next add them to the top and bottom to completely frame the blocks.

Setting Triangles for Diagonal Sets with Sashing

If you use sashing with your diagonally set blocks, your setting triangles will need to be refigured based on the new measurements.

The triangles are no longer equal in length to the side of the block. Now the side triangles are equal to the block plus the finished sashing measurement. The base of the corner triangle is equal to the block plus two sashing widths. We'll use a 6" finished block as our example. We'll assume a 1½" finished sashing.

Diagonal set with sashing

SIDE TRIANGLES
METHOD ONE: (exact sizes)
6" + 1.5" = 7.5" x 1.414 = 10.6" + 1.25" = 11.85", or, in quilter's language, 11⅞" square, which we slice twice corner to corner.

METHOD TWO: (floating sizes)
8.5" + 1.5" + 3" = 13" square, sliced twice corner to corner.

CORNER TRIANGLES
METHOD ONE: (exact sizes)
6" + 3" (two sashes) = 9" ÷ 1.414 = 6.36" + .875" = 7.24" or 7¼"square sliced once corner to corner.

METHOD TWO: (floating sizes)
6" + 3" (two sashes) + 2" = 11" square sliced once corner to corner. We've put together two handy reference charts for you, one with the exact sizes and one with the floating sizes for some standard block sizes.

If you don't like to do the math for cutting these triangles, remember that you always have the option of making templates. If you do opt for templates, be sure to watch grainline when positioning the template on the fabric. You still want straight grain on the long edge for the side triangles and the two short sides for corner triangles.

Because diagonal sets are harder to visualize than straight sets, refer to the chart on page 68 to help you determine the number of blocks needed for the inside and outside rows, as well as the number of side triangles for different sizes of quilts. Remember that you always need four corners, so they have not been added to the chart.

Sizes for Exact Corner and Side Triangles

Original Block Measurement	Size to Cut Side Setting Triangle	Size to Cut Corner Setting Triangle
6"	9¾"	5⅛"
7"	11⅛"	5⅞"
8"	12½"	6½"
9"	14"	7¼"
10"	15⅜"	7⅞"
11"	16¾"	8⅔"
12"	18⅛"	9⅜"

Sizes for Floating Corner and Side Triangles

Original Block Measurement	Diagonal Measurement	Size to Cut for Side Triangles	Size to Cut for Corner Triangles
6"	8½"	11½"	8"
7"	10"	13"	9"
8"	11½"	14½"	10"
9"	12¾"	15¾"	11"
10"	14¼"	17¼"	12"
11"	15½"	18½"	13"
12"	17"	20"	14"

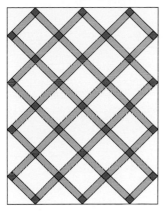

Sashing with cornerstones in a straight set

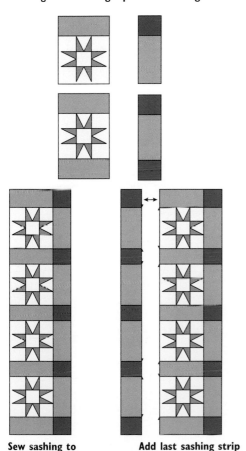

Sashing with setting squares in a diagonal set

Sashing with Setting Squares (Cornerstones)

Using setting squares where sashing strips intersect adds a new dimension to simple sashing. Many of the techniques for measuring, cutting, and piecing will be the same as for simple sashing, but the sewing is actually easier, due to the cornerstones, and no marking is needed. Each sashing strip is the same length.

1) Cut the sashing strips the same length as the unfinished blocks. The setting square at each corner will be the same measurement as the cut width measurement of the sashes. Cut the squares. Sew the sashing strips to the blocks of each row, including the top of the first block and the bottom of the last block. Press seams toward sashing.

2) Next, construct the sashing row. Sew a setting square to one end of a sash and make as many as there are blocks in a row. Be sure that a setting square is at both ends of the row. Press the seams toward the sashing.

3) Once this is finished, sew a sashing row onto the right side of every block row, carefully butting the seams that intersect at the sashing and setting squares.

4) Press carefully toward sashing. Now you're ready to join the rows together. Pin the second block row onto the edge of the sashing of row one, carefully butting the seams as before. Check for a perfect fit and adjust if necessary. Once the rows are joined, add the last sashing strip to the left side of row one. Press toward sashing.

Sashing strips can be pieced together using different numbers and widths of strips for different effects. Play and see what you can come up with. You might want to try three strips sewn together for the sashing, then a 9-patch for the setting square.

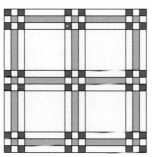

Three strips sewn together: 9-patch

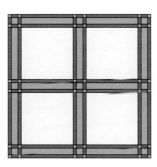

Three strips sewn together: 9-patch variation

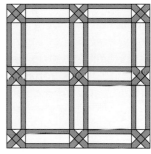

Latticework sashing

One wider sashing strip with a narrower one sewn onto each side is very pleasing, making the setting square a variation of the 9-patch.

You can also create a Latticework (also known as Garden Maze) setting with the triple lattice by changing the cornerstone to an "X". You'll see this sashing used very effectively with many appliquéd or embroidered blocks. Proportion is very important for this sashing. If the latticework is heavy (wide), it may overwhelm a simple pattern, but if it's too dainty (narrow), it can be overwhelmed by a bold design.

Sew sashing to row of blocks

Add last sashing strip

For this example, the lattice will be made from two 1" outer strips and one 2" inner strip, giving a 4" finished sashing strip.

To create templates for a setting square, draw a 4" square on a piece of graph paper. From each corner, mark the width of the outside sashing strip in both directions. Our measurement is 1". Next, connect these marks diagonally in both directions.

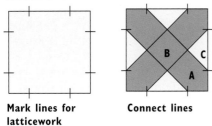

Mark lines for latticework

Connect lines

This will give you the template pieces needed to construct the square. Remember that C is the inner strip fabric and A & B match the outside strips of the sashing. Seam allowances need to be added to each shape

This can also be achieved by piecing three pieces together, then appliquéing a strip finished to the size of the diagonal unit on top of the square. Trim corners.

Identify template shapes

Sew three pieces together

Appliqué strip

If this seems like a lot of work, refer to Sawtooth Star Sashing, to find another way of achieving the latticework look.

Sawtooth Star Sashing

A very easy and effective design is the Sawtooth Star sashing. This incorporates the sashing and setting square into a Sawtooth Star pattern that appears each time four quilt blocks intersect. Look at the *Album Quilt*, page 200 and *Aunt Sukey's Delight*, page 201, and the illustration at right for examples of this sashing.

You'll need two fabrics for the sashing and only two measurements—the length of one side of a quilt block and the width of the sashing that you choose to use.

One way to create this sash is to use templates. Draw a rectangle on graph paper equal to the finished sashing strip. From each corner of the sashing, mark a distance equal to one-half the width of the finished sash.

Connect these points to make right triangles at all four corners of the sash. This drawing can be used to create the templates for both the triangles and the long hexagon (remember to add $\frac{1}{4}$" seam allowances to all sides).

Another very popular method is the sew and flip technique. You need to cut squares equal to half the width of the sashing plus $\frac{1}{2}$". Once the squares are cut, fold them in half diagonally and press. Position the new "triangle" in the corner of the rectangular sashing strip and open, then sew on the fold line.

Repeat with the opposite corner, then the other end. The back part of the square can be cut away, but you can leave the rectangle intact for stability.

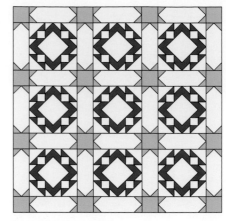

Sawtooth Star sashing

Create templates

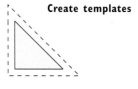

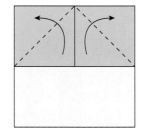

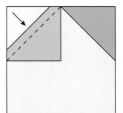

Note See Chapter 6, page 62, under Corner Cutters for a variation on the template method for an easy way to cut the long hexagon shape.

The setting squares will be cut from the same fabric as the star points. Cut them to the width of the sashing plus seam allowances. Once the strips have the points attached, connect them in the same manner as sashing with setting squares. Once all the sashing is joined to the blocks, Sawtooth Stars will appear at every intersection.

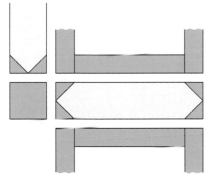

Connect sashing to blocks

You can adapt this method to resemble Latticework sashing without piecing the setting square. Start by adding a framing strip around all four sides of all blocks. Keep the size of these strips proportional to the block. Continue with the Sawtooth Star sashing technique. Because the corners connect with the framing strips, you get latticework instead of stars.

Breakout piecing of Sawtooth Star/ Latticework variation

Sawtooth Star/Latticework variation. A common sashing treatment for appliqué blocks.

Pieced Sashing

One very simple pieced sashing has already been addressed when we talked about the Sawtooth Star set. Another very simple pieced sash creates a Friendship Star block at all the sashed intersections.

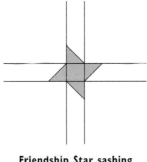

Friendship Star sashing

Your sashing can be divided into much more complicated structures, then colored to create even more variations. How do you begin this process? The answer is graph paper. Start with a piece of graph paper and draw a rectangle equal to the width and length of the finished sash. If you have 9" blocks and you're planning a 3" sash (which, by the way, is a pleasing scale when pieced), then start with a 3" x 9" rectangle. Nine inches divides equally by 1", 1½", 3", and 4½". Using those numbers see what designs you can come up with.

Pieced sashing examples

Once you've determined the design, play with coloration. If you photocopy your design and work strictly in value (light, medium, and dark), you can get a feel for what might happen to the design simply by reversing the position of light and dark.

Window Framing (Coping Strips)

Window framing is the technique of sewing a strip of fabric to each side of the block. These strips can be the same fabric as the background design, or they can be a contrasting fabric. When the strips match the background they will make the block appear to float. When contrasting fabric is used, it will emphasize the blocks.

Window framing is sometimes used to standardize the size of the blocks, a reason you might hear them called "coping" strips. Suppose that you were ready to set your blocks and you discovered that they are not all the same size. If you sew extra wide framing strips to each side of the block, then square up the block, you'd have blocks all the same size, ready to be set in any of the ways mentioned earlier. You might assume that, if you were going to be using the coping strips to standardize the blocks, the strips should match the background fabric so that they wouldn't be seen and the original block sizes would be disguised. However, that isn't necessary. You will see several examples in this book where coping strips have been used to standardize block sizes prior to setting. One such example is *Stars and Cubes*, on page 181 in Chapter 15. If you look closely, you'll notice that the navy prints that surround each of the blocks are not consistent in width. The blocks did not measure the same—some were as far off as $1/2$". Once the quilt was finished, it was hardly noticeable that the strips are different.

Look at the *Ohio Stars* quilt on page 163. High-contrast framing strips were added to each block prior to sashing and corner stones.

Block Framing

Framing can be as simple as strips surrounding the block or as complicated pieced units that create another element to the overall effect. Attic Windows, Square in a Square, and the use of setting squares are a few examples.

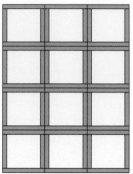

Framing blocks in straight set

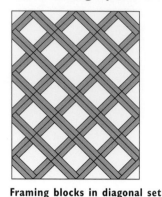

Framing blocks in diagonal set

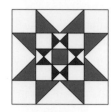

Ohio Star in Sawtooth Star

Attic Window

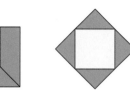

Square in a Square

Setting Squares

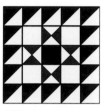

Ohio Star in Lady of the Lake

Another simple way to create a pieced frame for your block is to imagine what your Ohio Star (or any other block) set inside a Sawtooth Star might look like. Or, how about inside a Lady of the Lake?

Any block that has a blank area in the middle can serve as a great frame for other blocks. For that matter, you can simply remove piecing structure from a block and substitute something else for what was there originally.

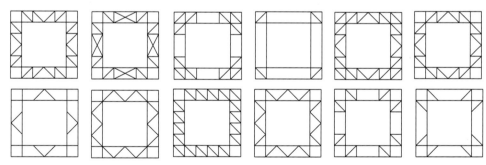

You can't create these more involved sets without understanding the basic components. They aren't hard, but if you don't know how to break down the block, you're going to find it difficult to create intricate sets. So, if you skipped Chapter 5 on drafting (page 51), take time now to go back and review the information.

Ohio Star in coping strips in Sawtooth Star

If you want to put a 6" Ohio Star block inside a 10" Sawtooth Star, how can you make that happen? Coping strips! A 10" Sawtooth Star has an 8" square in the middle. If you sew strips to the Ohio Star block and square it up to $8^1/2$" (remember, that includes the seam allowance) then you can do it. If you don't want framing strips, then you would have a finished 9" Sawtooth Star for the frame of our 6" Ohio Star block.

Zigzag Sets

The zigzag set is a very old set for quilts. It looks more difficult than it is, but a sketch on paper might be a helpful guide.

One way to create this set is to construct triangle units, then join them to plain triangles to form rows. These rows are then sewn together.

Another way to use this set is to work with blocks and join them in a zigzag. Each vertical row of diagonal design blocks has triangles inserted on each side to create straight sides for the rows. These triangles are sewn to the blocks, and the blocks are sewn into rows. Generally, all the setting triangles in this set are the same color, but this is not a rule. You might discover a unique look by experimenting with different fabrics and/or colors.

When joining the rows, the exact center of the long side of each triangle needs to be marked with a crease or light pencil mark. This mark then matches the corner of the diagonal block in the adjacent vertical row when the rows are set together.

Figure 7.1 shows how the rows may need a half block at the top or bottom, which can be either a design or plain block. Design blocks that have a division at this break work especially well for this set. (Don't forget that a 1/4" seam allowance is needed on the diagonal side.) If you don't care for this, consider the following idea. The rows are constructed in the same way, but the outside triangles are made into rows and applied as a border, then finished with the addition of the four corner triangles.

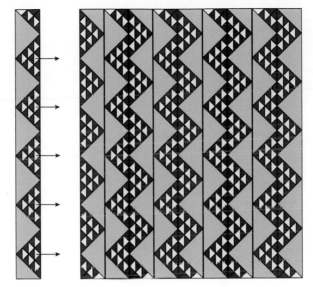

Zigzag set design

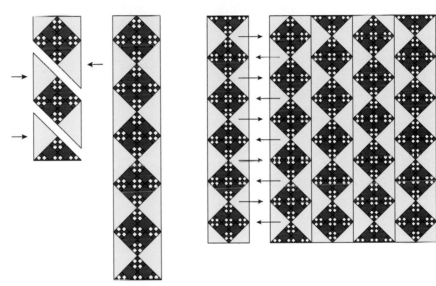

Fig. 7.1 **Constructing rows**

Antique Double Nine Patch, early 1900s, 62" x 73".
Collection of Harriet Hargrave.

Underground Railroad, 1998, 54" x 69".
Pieced and quilted by Deborah Long Mauter.

Bar Sets

Bar sets are simply vertical rows of blocks alternated with rows of strips or combinations of strips. The design blocks are all the same size, and can be straight set or on point. If using a straight set, the blocks are sewn block to block with no separating pieces between the blocks in the vertical row. If on point, you need to add setting triangles to make a straight row. Following are several illustrations of various bar sets.

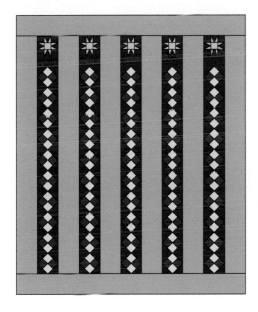

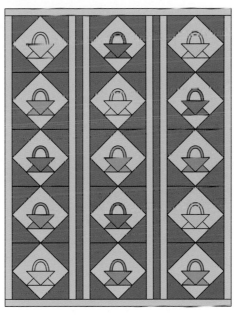

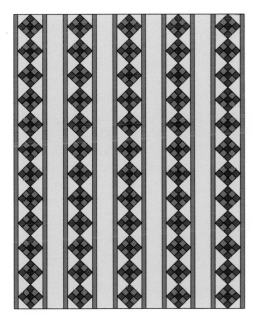

Combination Sets

There is no rule stating that your blocks have to be set all one way. You can set some of your blocks side by side and alternate other blocks with solid squares in the same quilt. You can set some side by side and add sashing to others. Sketching on graph paper will show you how easy these things are to do.

Sharyn's Delectable Mountain variation, which she calls *Sisterhood* (Chapter 13, page 154), is one example of a combination set where some of the blocks are set side by side while others alternate with solid squares. Using the combination this way makes the quilt less predictable and adds a touch of interest.

The basic setting techniques covered in this chapter are just the beginning of a world of design possibilities that you'll discover. What is important now is that you get the basic information. As you go to quilt shows and look through books and magazines, we recommend that you analyze what setting was used with the blocks. It is a good idea to spend a few minutes thumbing through this book looking at the quilts pictured. When you find quilts that you really like, why not put little paper flags to save that page? Can you identify the setting by studying the quilt? If so, you're becoming an independent quiltmaker.

Planning Your Quilt

Harriet and Sharyn have totally different approaches to making quilts. Neither style is right or wrong, just different. Harriet's style is to find a picture of an antique quilt and work to reproduce that quilt as closely as possible in size, color, feel, texture, and so forth. For her, many of the decisions are already determined, based on the quilt as she sees it in the photo. However, her challenge is to find fabrics in today's market that can translate to a quilt made a hundred years ago. Many times it isn't color or pattern that governs her decision to make the quilt, but rather, the extensive quilting she sees on the antique quilt that makes it so appealing.

Sharyn, on the other hand, may find a picture of an antique quilt to work from, but her goal is to use that quilt as a catalyst for color, pattern, or design. She has no intention of reproducing the original quilt. Her finished quilt may bear a family resemblance to the picture, or it may look nothing like the original except for one small aspect. Perhaps Sharyn uses the color formula from the original. Sometimes she uses the same block or maybe the border from the catalyst quilt. She doesn't know how big her finished quilt is going to end up when she starts, nor does she care. For her, quilts just sort of evolve. The quilt may jump-start everything, but size isn't critical. It makes no difference how big the original quilt or its blocks are in real life. If the block is

one she wants to work with, then she picks a size for the block that feels good. The fabric palette can often make the size determination. If large-scale prints are what she wants to work with, then larger scale blocks might be in order. The number of pieces in the block can also be a factor for the finished size. The more pieces, the larger the block. Sharyn cuts until she can't stand cutting any more. Next she pieces blocks until she can't stand sewing. Then she goes to the flannel wall and starts to play. That can take days, weeks, and even months. When in "design-mode," the blocks will just have to mull a while before decisions can be made. Does this sound like too many decisions to make and you're afraid of working this way? For some of you, this is not only too time consuming, but also not enough instant gratification. Each of you will develop a method of working. But before that can happen, you have to make many quilts and experiment with different approaches.

Some people may think that the way Harriet approaches making a quilt is "safe" or without risk. After all, she knows what the quilt is going to look like when it's done. Or, does she? It would be one thing if she could have those exact fabrics to work with. However, those fabrics no longer exist. With today's fabric manufacturers doing a number of reproduction lines, her task has become somewhat easier, but the color of the reproductions is often not authentic, throwing

the right print into the wrong era. The challenge is to find fabrics that have the texture, pattern, and color of the original, and create the illusion of age using new fabric.

Many times the inspiration photo has the actual size of the quilt listed. When that is the case, Harriet uses that measurement as her jumping off place, and works backward to determine block and grid size, as well as sashing and border widths. If the measurements don't feel right to her, she does not hesitate to alter them. For example, she might make the blocks larger or smaller, if that suits her purpose better. Let's say she's looking for a quilt to make for her queen-size bed and falls in love with an antique quilt. If the size of the original is too small, she has to figure out what size block and grid can retain the look and feel of the original, but in a larger format. But it's not just a matter of making more blocks. Scale and balance need to be taken into consideration with the quilting as well as the piecing. While block size can be easily altered, quilting patterns often lose their beauty and balance when enlarged or reduced. If a block gets too large, the desired quilting pattern may not be appropriate any longer. After all, the quilting is one of the most important things to Harriet. Many years of making quilts has led her to that conclusion.

Change is inevitable. Our taste and needs change constantly. Most of us started making quilts because we had a specific need for a quilt. As teachers, Harriet and Sharyn have lost count of the number of new students who came to their first class because they were expecting their first grandchild and wanted to make a quilt for the baby. Maybe a daughter was getting married and they wanted to commemorate that occasion with a quilt or they just wanted a quilt for their own bed. These are valid reasons to make your first quilt, but they won't necessarily inspire you 15 years later.

We have both witnessed a change in each other's quilts and working habits over the years. Harriet began by mass-producing baby quilts for craft shows. This became a full-time business and continued until she opened her store. Once the store was in full swing, she found herself using wild patterned fabrics, rich jewel tones, jazzy patterns and making lots of small projects. She changed block sizes, settings, coloration, and even designed original quilts so that she could always offer new and exciting classes. She discovered over the years that these quilts were not really making her happy. Her students and customers thought they were great and the store benefited greatly, but they weren't making her heart sing. She began to realize that she was making quilts for reasons other than passion. Too often they were made to impress others or promote the fabrics that were in her store.

Her life changed dramatically when she purchased an old farmhouse and started to decorate it. She soon realized her deep love for antiques of the nineteenth century. She started to genuinely study and evaluate the quilts of the 1800s through the 1930s and found that this was where her heart was. Reproducing quilts became the driving force for her quilting style, color, and pattern preferences, as well as for decorating and

her lifestyle. Her goal took the direction of producing timeless heirlooms.

Sharyn's reasons for making quilts have also been influenced by what is going on in her life. In the beginning, it was strictly a desire to put a quilt on her daughter's bed, so it needed to match the wallpaper or work with the furniture.

In 1980 she began teaching quilting in adult education classes. The need to make class samples provided lots of reasons to make quilts. Sharyn made her class samples to give her students choices. To start the students on their way she would make lots of different example quilts. She found herself motivated by the catch phrase "What if?" What if I put the blocks on point? What if I set them straight? What if I used a different kind of sashing? What if I changed the borders? There was always the desire and need to see what the quilt would look like if changes were made.

For many quiltmakers, the most difficult part of making a quilt is picking the "right" fabrics. The decision of which fabrics and colors to use can be paralyzing. Sharyn and Harriet have similar approaches to starting this part of making a quilt. Each decides on a color palette they think they want to work in. That palette often comes directly from the inspiration photo. The next step is to start pulling fabric from the stash. One fabric often leads to the next, and the next, and the next. Many times during this process they stand back and look at the collection to see what might be missing. When building a scrap quilt, which we both love to do, it's important that there be a variety of print types and scales. It's fun to build a color wheel at this time by letting the fabrics fan out from one color to the next. The floor is a great place to work when doing this. Stand back. Look at the collection of fabrics.

Listen to them. Look at the inspiration photo again. Is anything missing that is necessary to complete the look or feel you are going for? Once the quilt has been started, new fabrics can be added or some selected in the beginning can be left out. Just because you selected one fabric to go with the others does not mean it has to end up in the quilt.

Sometimes Sharyn finds a photo from nature to jump-start the color formula for a new quilt. Nature does such an awesome job, why not use something we know works? If you study nature, you see that colors exist in different proportions. It isn't likely that you'll see a situation with exactly 50% red and 50% green. Learn from those things.

Think about your skill level while reading this book. If you need given measurements to make an exact quilt there are patterns in this book that will fill those needs. On the other hand, if you have done this and now feel a need to work more freely, then read through the information in each chapter and experiment with some "What Ifs" of your own. The information you need to be able to branch out is in the pages of this book.

Planning the Size of Your Quilt

How does a new quilter start to unravel the complexities of planning a quilt? It is safe to say that a lot of quilts are made that will never see a bed. They hang on walls, cover the dining room table, and keep the baby warm in the car seat. Many others are made just because we wanted to work in red and black, and we weren't too concerned about the size of the finished product. But what about the times when we want to make a quilt for a particular bed or need the quilt to finish a particular size?

We've shared with you how we approach planning a quilt. Harriet works with a picture or quilt that is already in existence and makes decisions based on a visual aid. Sharyn, when working on design challenges, lets the blocks evolve into what they will, allowing the quilt to be finished when it feels right. It is probably safe to say that most new quilters have a specific quilt in mind that they would like to make—a visual image or picture. Now the task is to assign a finished size to that image, plan the set, and figure out block dimensions.

As we wrote this book, we realized why everyone wants a pattern for every quilt they make. No wonder quilters love the quilt recipe books—all the work and decisions have already been made! But when you rely on patterns, you're not developing the skills that will enable you to take a picture or conceive an idea and work through making it a reality. Can you look at a quilt and assign a desired size to it, figure out what size block is needed to accommodate that size, then proceed? Do you feel that the easiest way to make a quilt larger is to add more borders, regardless of their proportions and suitability? Our goal is to make sure that you never need to buy a pattern again and that you have the knowledge to make these decisions and get the correct answers.

If you want to have a structure to work with, you first need to have an idea of what the finished quilt will be before you start piecing blocks.
■ Is the quilt for a bed? What size bed?
■ How far do you want it to hang over the edges? To the mattress, a few inches over the dust ruffle, or to the floor?
■ Do you need a pillow tuck, or will shams be on top of the quilt?
■ Is the quilt for a wall? If so, what dimensions are needed to fill the space adequately?

Once you've answered these questions, you need to have a quilt layout in mind. Is the quilt layout a simple straight set with borders, straight set with sashing, diagonal set with no sashing, or a diagonal set with sashing and no borders? If you have a photo of the finished quilt and are trying to reproduce it, these questions are already answered. But if you're starting with an idea or concept, you need to start at the beginning and design the quilt first. Start by exploring Chapter 7 on settings (page 64) and getting an idea of what you like. Once you've chosen a set, then block size can be determined.

Design and setting affect the size of the block you'll need for the desired finished size of the quilt. By varying the block size, you can achieve dimensions that are very close to your theoretical finished quilt. On the other hand, the block size can stay the same, and you can design the setting around that size to get the desired quilt size. Does this sound complicated? It really isn't, but it does take planning before fabric is purchased and pieces are cut.

The number and size of the blocks used, as well as the layout of the blocks, can all change the size of the quilt. The number and size of sashing strips can also affect size.

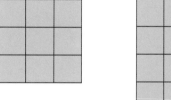

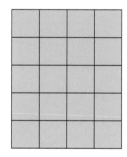

Change the number of blocks

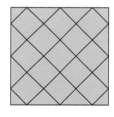
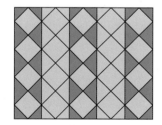

Change the way blocks are set together

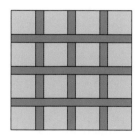

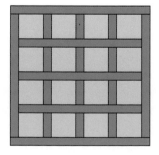

Change the number of sashing strips

Determining the Size of Your Quilt

If possible, start by measuring the bed for which the quilt is intended. Measure with the blankets, sheets, and pillows that will be used with the quilt. If the bed you're making the quilt for is not available, use the chart below for the common surface measurements of mattresses.

Once you have the mattress surface measurements, decide how you want it to look when finished. If the quilt will be used as a blanket and tucked in on three sides, you need to know the thickness of the mattress. If you want the quilt to fall to the top of a dust ruffle, measure the distance from the top of the mattress to the dust ruffle. If the quilt will cover the side rail but not reach the floor, measure from the top of the mattress to this point. If you want a bedspread, you need to measure from the mattress top to the floor. Finally, if you plan to tuck the quilt under the pillows, add 10"-16" to the length for tuck allowance.

There are several decisions that you have to make concerning your personal style, as well as the style and size of the bed. The differences between a water bed, a sleigh bed, a four-poster, and a platform bed will make a difference in the size of the quilt. It is not all mattress size. Does the quilt need to come to just the footboard, as for a sleigh bed, or have a drop at the bottom, like a four poster bed? A waterbed has still different needs.

Commercial bedcoverings can be a guide to needed size. Comforters are generally designed to be used as blankets. They cover the mattress but not necessarily the box springs and generally do not have a pillow tuck. The following sizes can be used as a guideline for a quilt that will be used with a dust ruffle and that does not go over the pillows (based on a 13" drop).

Twin:	65"	x	88"
Full	80"	x	88"
Queen:	86"	x	93"
King:	104"	x	93"

Bedspreads cover the bed, fall almost to the floor, and tuck under the pillows. Below are measurements that represent the maximum dimensions for a bedspread (based on a 21" drop and an 11" pillow tuck).

Twin:	81"	x	107"
Full	96"	x	107"
Queen:	102"	x	112"
King:	120"	x	112"

Besides these given measurements, contraction must also be taken into consideration. Contraction is the slight gathering or pulling in of the layers as they are quilted. An average of 3% to 5% of the finished size of the top can be lost to this. Shrinkage of the batting when washed can also play a part in the finished size of the quilt. We'll call this the contraction rate, CR.

Study Chapter 20 (page 218) for information about batting. Contraction and shrinkage only pose a problem when the quilt must be a particular finished size. The time to accommodate this situation is in the planning stages. If you know that the quilt needs to be 90" x 113" finished, after quilting and washing, but you also know that you'll lose 5% while quilting or possibly washing, add in the 5% to the quilt top dimensions, making it 95" x 119".

Mattress Surface Dimensions	
Bassinet	13" x 28"
Crib	23" x 46"
Playpen	40" x 40"
Youth	32" x 66"
Studio	30" x 75"
Bunk	38" x 75"
Twin	39" x 75"
Long Twin	39" x 80"
Double	54" x 75"
Queen	60" x 80"
King	78" x 80"
California King	72" x 84"

Note The mattress thickness must be measured, as the pillow top mattresses can be up to 17" thick, whereas a standard mattress is 7"-10" thick. If your quilt is going to the floor, be sure to measure the distance from the top of the mattress to the floor. There are no standards for these two measurements.

To simplify things, we have created formulas that you can use to evaluate your measurements. Refer to the diagram of a bed as shown below.

To use these formulas, plug your measurements into the formula up to the CR. Add the measurements together, then multiply the total by your CR percentage (5%). Add this amount to the first total. These numbers give you the general size of the quilt. Let's work through an example:

You need to make a queen size coverlet, tucked under the pillows and hanging to the dust ruffle. The formula would look like this:

Width- $W + 2(A) + CR$
$60" + 2(15) = 90" : 90" + CR(90 \times 0.05 = 4.5") = 94\frac{1}{2}"$
Length- $L + 1(A) + PT + CR$
$80" + 15" + 18" = 113" : 113" + CR(113 \times 0.05 = 5.65") = 118\frac{2}{3}"$

You can round fractions up or down to your choosing. Using this formula, your quilt top needs to be approximately 95" x 119" in order to fit your bed as desired.

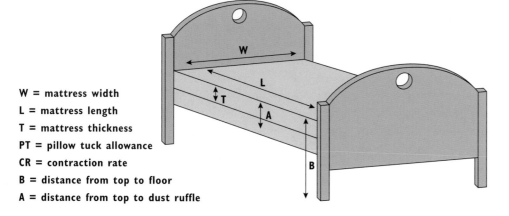

W = mattress width
L = mattress length
T = mattress thickness
PT = pillow tuck allowance
CR = contraction rate
B = distance from top to floor
A = distance from top to dust ruffle

Quilt Styles and Formulas		
Quilt Type	**Width**	**Length**
Blanket (4" tuck allowance)	W + 2T + 8" + CR	L + 1T + 4" + CR
Coverlet - to dust ruffle	W + 2A + CR	L + 1A + CR
Coverlet - tucked under pillow	W + 2A + CR	L + 1A + PT + CR
Bedspread - tucked under	W + 2B + CR	L + 1B + PT + CR
pillow to floor		

Inches Added by Sashing to Straight-Set Quilts									
	Number of Blocks Across or Down Row								
Strip Width	**4**	**5**	**6**	**7**	**8**	**9**	**10**	**11**	**12**	**13**
1/2"		2½	3	3½	4	4½	5	5½	6	6½	7
1"		5	6	7	8	9	10	11	12	13	14
1½"		7½	9	10½	12	13½	15	16½	18	19½	21
2"		10	12	14	16	18	20	22	24	26	28
2½"		12½	15	17½	20	22½	25	27½	30	32½	35
3"		15	18	21	24	27	30	33	36	39	42
3½"		17½	21	24½	28	31½	35	38½	42	45½	48
4"		20	24	28	32	36	40	44	48	52	56
4½"		22½	27	31½	36	40½	45	49½	54	58½	63
5"		25	30	35	40	45	50	55	60	65	70

Determining the Number of Blocks

STRAIGHT BLOCK SETTINGS

If you're not using sashing in the design of the quilt, the next step would be to divide the width of the quilt by the width of the quilt block to determine the number of blocks in a horizontal row. Next, divide the quilt length by the length of the quilt block to determine the number of blocks in a vertical row.

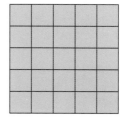

You will find that these rarely come out even. This is when you need to decide whether you want to enlarge the overall quilt size in order to use the quilt block in the given size, add borders so that the quilt block can be used, or re-size the quilt block itself. If you add sashing to the blocks, the figuring becomes more complex.

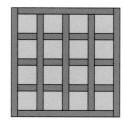

Try more than one approach. If we want to keep the block size a given, say 12", and the top needs to be 95", we will have 7 blocks across the width of the quilt with 11" left over. There will need to be 8 sashing strips across to accommodate the 7 blocks. This would make each strip less than 1½". Probably not a good design idea. So now what? What if we used 6 blocks across, which would equal 72", leaving 23" left for sashing, each being 3" wide. Now you think 3" is too wide, maybe 2"

would look better. That would use 14" of space. Now re-figure. 72" for the blocks, 14" for the sashing, and 9" left for borders, 4½" on each side. This might work.

But how about the length? We need 119". 119 ÷ 12 is 9 blocks, but no room for sashing. Try 8 blocks long—96" plus sashing needs of 18" if it's to be 2" wide. 96" + 18" = 114". That leaves 5" for the bottom border. It will work out great.

To simplify, use the chart on page 90 to determine how the sashing adds to the size of the quilt. For example, if you've chosen the size for the sashing in the design process, refer to the chart to see how it affects the size of the quilt. If you're trying to make a quilt a certain size but don't know what size sashing works with the blocks, refer to the chart from that approach.

Diagonal Block Settings

When using a diagonal setting, the blocks are set on point and the measurements change. The quilt size is determined by the diagonal of the block. Refer to the chart at right for common block sizes and their diagonal measurement.

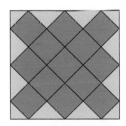

Using these measurements, repeat the process used for the straight set block. Notice that a diagonal set requires the use of half-blocks and quarter-blocks along the outside edges. (Refer to diagram). This is covered in detail in Chapter 7 on page 67.

If you're using sashing in the diagonal set, add the desired width of the sashing to the side of the block. Using the combined dimension, find the length of the diagonal.

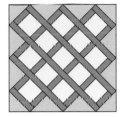

Diagonal set with sashing

Below is another time-saving chart for figuring the size added to the overall size of the quilt when adding sashing to a diagonal set.

Once you've designed your quilt and chosen the size of the blocks and sashing, you're ready to calculate the yardage needed. This is covered in the next chapter.

It always helps to draw diagrams as you go so that you keep the sashing placement and numbers needed straight. This becomes easier as you actually do it. We suggest that you go through the book, pick a couple of quilts, and change their finished size, then figure the blocks needed, options for settings, and so forth. It is good practice, and you might design a new quilt that you just have to make!

As you progress through this book and arrive at the chapters that give the patterns and instructions for the quilts, you'll find that we give you only the yardages and block sizes for the actual sample quilt. What if you love the quilt but need it larger or smaller than the one shown? As we've said, you, the quilter, need to know how to figure out the size you want and what changes you need to make to accommodate your size specifications.

Diagonal Measurements for Blocks			
Square	Diagonal	Square	Diagonal
1.5"	2.12"	11	15.6
2	2.83	12	17
3	4.24	13	18.38
4	5.65	14	19.8
5	7.07	15	21.21
6	8.48	16	22.62
7	9.9	17	24
8	11.31	18	25.45
9	12.73	19	26.87
10	14.14	20	28.28

NOTE: These measurements can be rounded off in either direction.

Inches Added by Sashing to Diagonal-Set Quilts										
	Number of Blocks Across or Down Row									
Strip Width	2	3	4	5	6	7	8	9	10	11
½"	1⅜	2⅛	2⅞	3½	4¼	5	5⅝	6⅜	7⅛	7¾
1"	2⅞	4¼	5⅝	7⅛	8½	9⅞	11⅜	12¾	14⅛	15½
1½"	4¼	6⅜	8½	10⅝	12¾	14⅞	17	19⅛	21¼	23⅜
2"	5⅝	8½	11⅜	14⅛	17	19¾	22⅝	25½	28¼	31⅛
2½"	7⅛	10⅝	14⅛	17⅝	21¼	24¾	28¼	31⅞	35⅜	38⅞
3"	8½	12¾	17	21¼	25½	29¾	34	38⅛	42⅜	46⅝
3½"	9⅞	14⅞	19¾	24¾	29¾	34⅝	39⅝	44½		
4"	11⅜	17	22⅝	28¼	34	39⅝	45¼			

Calculating Yardage

The fabric we purchase today is manufactured to a 44"-45" standard. We seldom see anything narrower than 42" on any of our quilt-making cottons. The selvage, however, has to be taken into consideration when finding the usable width of the cloth, as well as any possible shrinkage if prewashing. It is fairly standard to say that we get 42" of usable width from almost all of our fabrics.

Determine if you'll be cutting strips for the project and assess how you'll be cutting them. Will they be cut across the width or along the selvage edge (the length of the cloth)? If cut crosswise, your measurement will always be 42". If you choose to cut strips lengthwise, the measurement can vary with the yardage available, so you need to assign a measurement to your desired length needed.

Once you begin to think in terms of strips, squares, and triangles, figuring yardage is greatly simplified. When figuring yardage for a quilt with strips, as in the *Fence Post* in Chapter 10 (page 97), everything is being cut from strips. Once you know how long the strips are going to be, think of how many units you can get from each strip, and thus, how many strips are needed to give you the number of units for your quilt. When quilts contain blocks with several different shapes, you need to identify every different shape, size, and color planned for the quilt and how they can be cut from strips to make figuring yardage simplified.

Terminology can sometimes get in the way, so here are brief definitions for the terms used when figuring yardage:

> ***Like Units:*** Pieces that are the same color, shape, size, and position in the block.
>
> ***Running Inches:*** The length of each unit that you cut from a strip or set of strips.
>
> ***Strip Sets:*** The combination of strips sewn together to accommodate the pattern of each row.
>
> ***Like Blocks:*** All blocks that are the same in shape, size, color, and construction.

There are a few givens when figuring yardage. When figuring the sequence of the strips to be sewn together, we read across the top of the block. Running inches of each unit are read up and down the edge of the block. For the following examples, the running length of each strip will be figured on 42".

Sewing sequence of strips

Running inches

Fig. 9.1

Let's look at how this formula works. Try it on the block shown in Figure 9.1.
- Count the total number of like units in a block.
- Multiply that number by their cut length (do this for each different color, shape, and units' position in that block).
- Multiply this number by the total number of like blocks.
- Divide this number by 42". This will give you the number of strips needed of that color, for the unit of that block. (Round this number up if it's a fraction.) This number is the number of strips you need to cut.
- Multiply this number by the cut width of the strip. This measurement is found by reading across the top of the block or row.

The answer given here will be the total number of inches needed for that unit in all of the like blocks. Repeat this formula for each unit and each different block.

Note It is wise to add 1/4 yard to the final amount calculated to allow for mistakes and mis-cutting.

The following formula can be done totally on a calculator.

Like units x cut length x total number of like blocks ÷ 42" (round up to next whole number here) x cut width = total number of inches needed for that unit. Following is a chart that converts yardage into calculator calculations for your convenience.

Yardage to Decimals and Inches		
Fractions	Decimals	Inches
1/8	.125	4 1/2
1/4	.25	9
1/3	.333	12
3/8	.375	13 1/2
1/2	.50	18
5/8	.625	22 1/2
2/3	.666	24
3/4	.75	27
7/8	.875	32 1/2
1	1.00	36

Let's work through an example using the following blocks from Double Irish Chain.

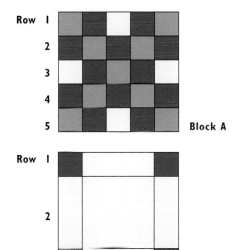

Row 1
2
3
4
5
Block A

Row 1
2
3
Block B

Each of these blocks uses a 2" finished grid. Cut size is 2 1/2". Remember to always use cut sizes when figuring yardage. It is a 5-patch block, so the blocks will finish out to 10". There will be 10 of each block in the quilt (a hypothetical number to keep the math simple). Block A uses three different fabrics. There are 9 pieces from Fabric ▣, 12 from Fabric ■, and 4 from Fabric □. Looking down the left edge of the block, you see that all the squares in each of the rows are

the same size. Looking across the block, the squares are also all the same size. All the squares are 2" finished, 2 1/2" cut. The illustrations below show how the strips for Block A are sewn together.

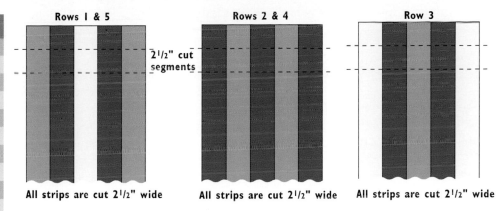

Rows 1 & 5

2 1/2" cut segments

Rows 2 & 4

Row 3

All strips are cut 2 1/2" wide   All strips are cut 2 1/2" wide   All strips are cut 2 1/2" wide

NOW FOR THE FORMULA
Fabric ▣
9 units x 2.5" x 10 blocks ÷ 42" (5.36 rounded up to 6 strips needed) x 2.5" = 15" (cut six 2 1/2" strips).
Fabric ■
12 units x 2.5" x 10 blocks ÷ 42" (7.14 rounded up to 8 strips needed) x 2.5" = 20" (cut eight 2 1/2" strips).
Fabric □
4 units x 2.5" x 10 blocks ÷ 42" (2.38 rounded up to 3 strips) x 2.5" = 7.50" (cut three 2 1/2" strips).

Block B presents some different shapes. Row 1 has two 2" finished squares of Fabric ■, but the center unit is not square. It is taking the space of three grids, or 6". The length of the row is 2" (finished). Row 2 has the same measurements across the top, but now the length is different, and all three units are cut from Fabric □. Row 3 is identical to Row 1.

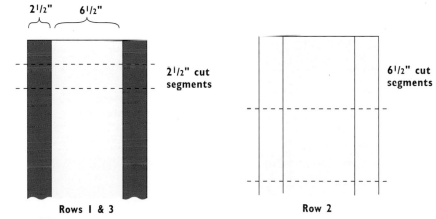

2 1/2"   6 1/2"

2 1/2" cut segments

6 1/2" cut segments

Rows 1 & 3   Row 2

Fabric ■
4 units x 2.5" x 10 blocks ÷ 42" (2.38 rounded up to 3 strips) x 2.5" = 7.50. (Cut three 2 1/2" strips.)

Fabric □ rows 1 and 3:
2 units x 2.5" x 10 blocks ÷ 42" (1.19 rounded up to 2 strips) x 6.5" = 13". (Notice here that the strips have to be cut 6 1/2" wide, and you need a little more than one strip, so you need 13" from the bolt. Cut two strips, each 6 1/2" wide.)

Fabric ☐, row 2:
2 units x 6.5" x 10 blocks ÷ 42"
(3.10 rounded up to 4 strips) x 2.5" =
10" (cut four strips, each 2½" wide).

1 unit x 6.5" x 10 blocks ÷ 42"(1.55
rounded up to 2 strips) x 6.5" = 13"
(cut two strips, each 6½" wide).

If you add all the separate findings
together by fabric, you'll find that
you need the following yardages:

Fabric ■ - 15", rounded up to
½ yard
Fabric ■ - 27.50", rounded up to
⅞ yard
Fabric ☐ - 43.50", rounded up to
1¼ yards

When making strip sets, it's possible
that one or two extra strips may need
to be cut. Add to these measurements any extra that you feel comfortable with. This formula is excellent and easy to use when working

with blocks that contain different
shapes and placements, like Block B.

If you only need to figure yardage
for squares and triangles, the
tables below are very helpful. Both
tables are calculated on cut size, not
on finished size. For ease in use,
look up the finished size on the left
side to get the number of "cut sized"
pieces you can expect from that
yardage. If you prefer a formula, use
the following instructions.

Number of Squares from 42" Strips

Finished Size	¼ yd. (9")	½ yd. (18")	¾ yd. (27")	1 yd. (36")
1"	168	336	504	672
1½"	84	189	273	378
2"	48	112	160	224
2½"	42	84	126	168
3"	24	60	84	120
3½"	20	40	60	90
4"	18	36	54	72
4½"	8	24	40	56
5"	7	21	28	42
5½"	7	21	28	42
6"	6	12	24	30

Number of Half-Square Triangles from 42" Strips

Finished Size	¼ yd. (9")	½ yd. (18")	¾ yd. (27")	1 yd. (36")
1"	168	378	546	756
1½"	96	224	320	448
2"	84	168	252	336
2½"	48	120	168	240
3"	40	80	120	180
3½"	36	72	108	144
4"	16	48	80	112
4½"	14	42	56	84
5"	14	42	56	84

Squares

■ 42" ÷ cut size of square = # of squares per strip (round down).
■ Number of squares needed ÷ # of squares per strip = # of
strips needed (round up).
■ Number of strips needed x cut size of square = amount of
fabric needed.
■ Amount of fabric needed ÷ 36 = # of yards needed, round up
to the next higher ⅛ yard (refer to the chart on page 93).

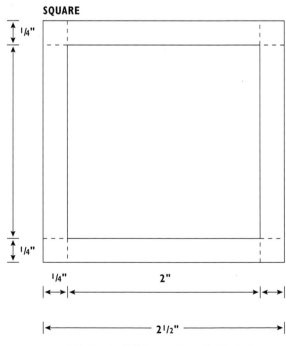

SQUARE

¼"
¼"
¼"
2"
2½"

Cut size is ½" larger than finished size

Half-square Triangles

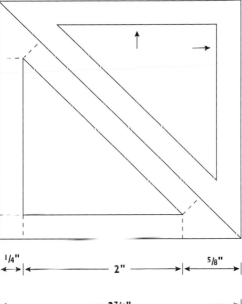

HALF-SQUARE TRIANGLE

- 42" ÷ cut size of triangle (finished measurement of short side + 7/8" for seam allowance) = # of cuts per strip. Round down if necessary.
- Take the # of cuts x 2 (triangles per square) = # of triangles per strip.
- Next, take the # of triangles needed ÷ # per strip = # of strips needed (round up)
- Number of strips needed x cut size of triangle = amount of fabric needed.
- Amount of fabric needed ÷ 36 = # of yards needed (refer to the chart on page 93).

Cut size is 7/8" larger than finished size; triangles are measured on the short sides because they're made in pairs.

1/4" | 2" | 5/8"

2 7/8"

Quarter-square Triangles

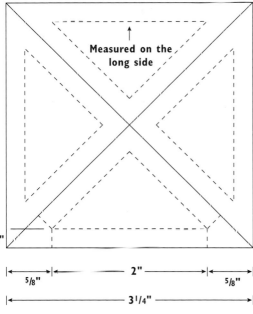

QUARTER-SQUARE TRIANGLE

Measured on the long side

- 42" ÷ (cut size of long side of triangle + 1 1/4" for seam allowance) = # of cuts per strip. Round down if necessary.
- Take the # of cuts x 4 (triangles per square) = # of quarter-square triangles per strip.
- Next, take the # of quarter-square triangles needed ÷ # per strip = # of strips needed (round up).
- Number of strips needed x cut size of triangle = amount of fabric needed.
- Amount of fabric needed ÷ 36" = # of yards needed (refer to the chart on page 93).

1/4"

5/8" | 2" | 5/8"

3 1/4"

Cut size is 1 1/4" larger than finished size because they are made four at a time

Sashing

Figuring yardage for sashing is simply a matter of adding up running inches. Add 1/2" to the finished sash width to accommodate for 1/4" seam allowances. Calculate the number of block-width sashing pieces, as well as the length between the rows.

Borders

Many quilters prefer to cut their border pieces from the length of the fabric, using a continuous piece for each side. Others cut crosswise and piece the strips to the length needed. If cutting cross grain, add all the side measurements together. You will also need to add the width of the border x 4 to this total to allow for the extra length added by the width of the top and bottom border. Remember to add 1/2" to the strip width to allow for 1/4" seam allowances.

BORDERS WITH BUTTED CORNERS

One border length = finished border length + ¹/₂". (Remember to add the width of the border x 2 for the top and bottom to accommodate for the width of the side borders once they are attached).

Second border length = finished border length + (finished border width x 2) + ¹/₂".

BORDERS WITH MITERED CORNERS

One border length = finished border length + (finished border width x 2) + 4"

Backing

There are several configurations into which backings can be sewn that utilize the fabric width most efficiently. Vertical seams utilize the width of the fabric through the width of the quilt, using the yardage length to accommodate the length of the quilt. If your quilt is within the range of one, two, or three widths of fabric sewn together, vertical seams are required. An example is a baby quilt that is 41" wide. Since the 45" fabric yields 42" of usable width, one width would accommodate the 41" of quilt top. A full that is 80" wide can also use vertical seams—42" + 42" = 84". Two panels sewn together would be sufficient. A king that is 92" x 120" is a bit different. 92" ÷ 42 = 2.19. This would be three panels of 45"-wide fabric, each 3¹/₃ yards long, for a total of 10 yards of fabric. If the seams run horizontally, the width of the fabric is better utilized. 120" ÷ 42 = 2.86 (3 panels). 92" ÷ 36 = 2.56 x 3 = 7.68 or 7³/₄ yards, a big savings in yardage and money. Work through your quilt sizes and determine which configuration utilizes your fabric best.

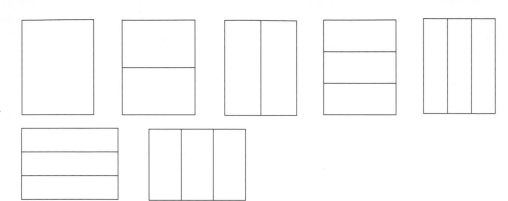

Possible backing configurations

Muslin, both bleached and unbleached, and a limited number of prints and colors are available in 90"- and 108"-wide widths. These wider fabrics eliminate the need for piecing.

Binding

Below are two charts that estimate the yardage needed for both straight grain and bias binding, ¹/₂"-wide finished.

Estimated Yardage for ¹/₂" Wide Straight Grain Binding			
Quilt Size	**# of 2¹/₂" Wide Strips**	**Inches of Fabric**	**Yards of Fabric**
Wallhanging (36" x 36")	5	12¹/₂	³/₈
Twin (54" x 90")	8	20	⁵/₈
Double (72" x 90")	8	20	⁵/₈
Queen (90" x 108")	10	25	³/₄
King (120" x 120")	12	30	⁷/₈

Estimated Yardage for ¹/₂" Bias Binding		
Quilt Size	**Bias Needed**	**Fabric Needed**
Wallhanging (36" x 36")	4¹/₂ yards	22" square
Twin (54" x 90")	8¹/₂ yards	28" square
Double (72" x 90")	9¹/₂ yards	30" square
Queen (90" x 108")	11¹/₂ yards	33" square
King (120" x 120")	14¹/₂ yards	38" square

FORMULAS:
Straight grain binding: perimeter of quilt + 15" ÷ 42" = number of strips (rounded up) x strip width = yardage needed.

Bias binding: perimeter of quilt + 15" = binding strip length
■ Fabric area = binding strip length x binding strip width
■ Sides of square for cutting bias binding = fabric area
■ Yardage = fabric area ÷ 1512 square inches (usable square inches in one yard of fabric).

Basic Strip Piecing

There is an old Chinese proverb that describes our goals in this book:

I hear and I forget
I see and I remember
I do and I understand

How does this apply to you? Well, you can hear about a technique, but it's soon forgotten. You see a technique done and you remember it, but if you miss a step, you get lost. But if you do the technique, you understand it.

This chapter is where you'll actually begin to sew. We have given you a firm foundation. If you've read and studied the first nine chapters of this book and have done the exercises, you're well-equipped to venture into piecing.

Project

We are starting you out with a classic beginner's quilt. We chose a Rail Fence variation because it's very easy to understand how the pattern works, and the sewing is basic. This project establishes the groundwork for the rest of the projects in this book, and probably for the rest of your quiltmaking career.

Fence Post (a Rail Fence Variation)
41^1/$_4$" x 63^3/$_4$" without borders.

This quilt is a simple, three-fabric quilt made entirely from strips. Let's start by looking at the following photo. Look at the layout and answer these questions for yourself:

Fence Post, 1998, 46" x 66". Designed, pieced, and quilted by Harriet Hargrave.

- Is there more than one block in the quilt? If so, what is it?
- How many fabrics are used in the quilt?
- Are different fabrics used in different combinations in the blocks?
- Are all the blocks the same size?
- How many of each block are there in the quilt?

Now check your answers against these:
There is only one block in the quilt. It looks like this:

There are three fabrics used: a blue plaid, a brown plaid, and a tan plaid. The border is a different fabric, but we aren't concerned with this yet. This particular quilt uses border strips that are 5" wide, but this width is a personal decision made after the top is constructed. Borders will be discussed in detail in Chapter 18, page 205.

There are two different fabric combinations, making two different blocks. All the blocks are the same size. There are 17 rows, each containing 11 blocks, making a total of 187 blocks. There are 94 blocks of combination A, and 93 blocks of combination B.

Block A   Block B

Determining Yardage Needed

From this information, you now know the fabrics you need, the sewing combinations of these fabrics, and the total number of each block that needs to be made. Let's work through determining the number of strips needed, at the same time figuring out the yardage needed. The finished block size is $3^3/4$" square (unfinished $4^1/4$"), making each strip $1^1/4$" finished, $1^3/4$" cut. If the strips are an average of 42" long, we can get 9 blocks from each set of strips. (42 ÷ 4.25 = 9). If we need 94 blocks, we will need to construct 11 sets of

strips of each color combination. (94 ÷ 9 = 10.44, rounded up to 11)

Block A is made of two blue strips with a tan strip in the middle. If you need 11 strip sets, you need to cut 22 blue strips and 11 tan strips. Block B is made of two brown strips with a tan strip in the middle. You need 22 brown strips and 11 tan strips.

Total strips needed—all cut $1^3/4$" wide:
    22—blue
    22—brown
    22—tan

Yardage needed is $38^1/2$" of each of the three fabrics used. You will need to purchase $1^1/8$ yard, plus a little extra for safety in cutting. (We suggest $1^1/4$ yards each.) See Chapter 6 for the best way to cut the strips.

Once the strips are cut, lay them out in the order that they appear in the blocks.

Sewing the Strips Together

If you studied the information in Chapter 4 on page 41, you've already determined the best way for you to achieve as accurate a $1/4$" seam allowance as possible. With your machine set up for that seam allowance width, a new size 80/12 needle in the machine, and 50 weight, 3 ply cotton thread in the needle and bobbin, you're ready to sew.

Starting with Block A, the strips should be laid in order, side by side, next to your machine. Pick up one strip from the first pile and put one strip from the second pile on top of it, aligning the right cut edges exactly. Stitch the entire length of the strip. Now pick up another strip from the first pile and one strip from the second pile. Put the second on top of the first, align the edges, and allow the feed dogs to pull this set of strips under the foot.

First set of strips to sew

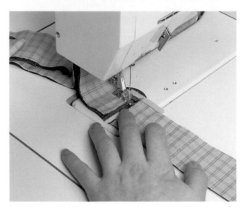

Feed second set of strips

Add third strip to set

This is the basis of string piecing or chain sewing. You will not need to backstitch, as the ends will be trimmed before the blocks are cut from the strips. Continue on until all of piles one and two are sewn together.

Next, pull all the connected strips back through the machine, and, starting with the first set of strips, open it up so that the top strip is on the right. (This is much like opening the pages of a book. You always add to the right.)

Now, place one strip from pile three on top of it, right sides together, then align the right-hand edges and stitch the entire length. Continue chain sewing all of the strips of pile three onto the strips that are chained together. Once the strips are all joined, cut the threads that hinge them together, and you're ready to press the seam allowances. Repeat this process for the strips that make up Block B.

Using the guidelines in Chapter 4 on page 45, press the seam allowances toward the darker strips.

Press seams toward outside strips

Calculating the Accuracy of the Strips

The next step is to cut the strips into segments or, in this case, the actual blocks of the quilt. Measure across several sets of pressed strips. You are looking for the finished width, which should ideally be 4¼" wide. If that is what you've sewn, great! Your accuracy is right on. If it isn't, you need to measure to find your own personal width. We will hope that the strips are consistent with each other. If not, it might be advisable to reassess the method you chose to sew ¼" seams. If the strips are various widths, you'll constantly be making adjustments as you join the blocks. You may end up with a very lumpy finished top due to uneven seams.

■ Check your pressing as well as the sewing.

■ Have you pressed any folds in the seams that would then cause the strip sets to be uneven?

■ Were the strips cut exactly?

■ Are all the seams sewn consistently?

Remember, the actual size is not as important as the consistency. It may be necessary to take out a few seams at this point and correct the problem once you've identified it. If all the seams are the same size and all the strip sets are the same width, you can cut all the blocks square. However, if the strip sets are various widths, how can all the blocks be square? Once you determine the overall width of your strip sets, use that number as the measurement to cut from each set of strips.

The cutting of the blocks, or segments, is very important. You must be very careful to keep the seams perpendicular to the edge you're cutting. Lay the ruler on top of a set of strips. Align the cross lines of the ruler evenly with the sewn seams. Trim the end off of the strip set, wasting as little fabric as possible.

Turn the strip 180°, so the length of the strip is on the same side as the hand you cut with. Next, align the measurement needed (determined by the width of the strip set) with the cut edge, at the same time aligning the ruler lines

parallel to the seams. This will enable you to make a perpendicular cut that results in a perfect square block. Continue until all strip sets are cut into 94 "A" units and 93 "B" units.

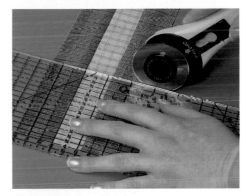

Align ruler to cut segments

Note Many quilters choose to layer cut at this point. This is determined by your accuracy and skill.

Harriet prefers to cut one strip at a time, so that the ruler lays flat on the fabric with no rocking. She doesn't like to take the chance of one seam being slightly out of line, causing a miscut that could cause more work in the end. Sharyn will layer two to three strip rows at a time when cutting segments. You can try both methods, but experiment slowly and deliberately, being as careful as you can with the cutting. Accurate cutting is critical.

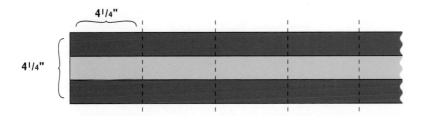

4¼"

4¼"

Sewing the Blocks Together

Now you're ready to lay out the blocks to form the pattern of the quilt. This can be done either on the floor or on a design wall, if you have one. Arrange the blocks, using the photo on page 97 as a guide. Make 17 rows of 11 blocks each. For this particular quilt top, notice that all the Block A's are horizontal and all the Block B's are vertical. Once they are all laid out, stand back and check for any misplaced blocks. Once it all checks out, you're ready to develop a system for chain sewing.

Most beginner quilters assume that you would sew all 11 blocks of Row 1 together, then all 11 of Row 2, and so forth. This is one way, but it's much slower and easier to get mixed up. There are two different ways of approaching this step. We will begin with Harriet's favorite, then give you another option.

With Harriet's system, you develop the rows into stacks, then sew off the stacks, joining all blocks into rows at the same time.

Start by picking up the first block of Row 1, then pick up the next block, putting it under the first one, the third under the second, etc. Once the whole row is in a stack, pin the stack together at the top edge so that you know what is the top and bottom of the stack. Proceed with all the rows

until you have 17 stacks, all pinned at their top edge. Keep them in order, stacking Row 1 on top of Row 2 on top of Row 3, and so forth.

Now take these stacks to your sewing machine. Harriet likes this method because it eliminates jumping up and down to get blocks. You can just sit and continuously sew without stopping. You can use a table to your side, if necessary, and lay out the blocks in order. In this case, you can make three rows of four stacks each and one row of five stacks each.

Once all the stacks are in place, remove the pins. It is really important that you develop a system that makes sense to you—are you working to the right in rows or up and down in rows? Stay consistent to what is most logical to you. Now, start by picking up block one from stack one, and putting block two from stack one on top of it. (Remember the book idea?) Sew the two blocks together along the right edge. Don't cut the thread, as we will chain (or flag) sew all the rows together as we go. Now pick up block one from stack two, put block two from stack two on top, and sew the right side. Continue this until the first two blocks from each stack are stitched together.

Next, pull the chain back through the machine and, starting with row one again, add the top block (this will be block three) onto the right side of the opened pair. You can't sew the block onto the wrong side because you can't turn the chain. Stitch, then pick up the top block from stack two, stitch, and so forth. Continue in this manner until all 11 blocks and 17 rows are stitched together. There will be about a ¼" hinge between each row. These can now be pressed and the rows stitched together or can be cut to separate the rows if you find it easier to press one row at a time. Stack the rows in order, and you're ready to press. Press all the seams to the vertical strips so that no seam allowance is folded back on top of itself. Then sew the rows together.

Another method is to work in pairs. This time, work down the length of the quilt instead of across the width. Start by placing each block in the second vertical row on top of its neighbor in the first row, right sides together. Starting at the top, pick up the pairs and stack them, having pair number one on top. Be careful that you do not turn them on the way to the machine. The edge that will be stitched must stay on the right.

Next, start stitching the first pair, and when you're at the end, feed the second pair under the foot—chain style. Continue on until all the pairs are joined. Don't cut them apart; the chaining keeps them in order. Now repeat this with Rows 3 & 4, 5 & 6, 7 & 8, etc. In this case, you'll have five paired rows with one row left over.

Stacks of rows

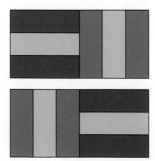

Sew pairs of blocks together

Sew pairs to pairs

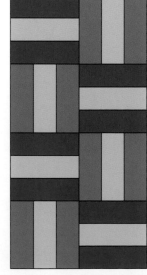

Sew four-block units together

Press the pairs, again pressing the seam allowances toward the vertical strips. They will alternate left and right down the row. This develops the basis of butted seams. Once they're pressed, you're ready to join pairs to pairs. Lay the first pair on top of the second pair. Because the seams are facing opposite directions, you'll find that there is an automatic fitting of the seam allowances, one to the other. This is butting the seams. You can pin this or use your fingers to hold the seams together until they go under the presser foot. What a lot of people like about this method is that there is only one seam to match at any one time, instead of a long row of them as in the first method.

Once this is done down the row, you'll have eight sets of four blocks sewn together, with one pair left over. Next, sew the 4-block units to one another. You will now have 8-unit blocks. Add the last one left over to the last set of units. Continue until all the pairs are totally joined and Rows 1 & 2 are now one long row. Time to press again. If you plan ahead, you'll see that if you press all of the joining seams of Rows 1 & 2 down, and all the same seams of Rows 3 & 4 up, 5 & 6 down, 7 & 8 up, and so on, the seams will be ready to butt together when you sew the newly formed rows together.

Whichever method you find easiest, you should finish with a flat, neat quilt top. Did you? Or did you have trouble with any portion of the project? **You should stop now and evaluate your quilt for any problem areas.**
- Are your strips all cut the same width?
- Was your seam allowance consistent?
- Were your strip rows each the same sewn width?
- Were your blocks all exactly square and the same size?
- Check your pressing of the strip rows.
- Did your blocks line up as you assembled the quilt top? Seams butt perfectly?
Bottom line: You must cut, sew, and press accurately if there is to be any hope of finishing with quality quilts.

Now that you have a basic understanding of how to make the Fence Post quilt, what else can you do with these construction techniques? We're providing a few additional quilts for visual stimulation. Look at each of the quilts and determine what has occurred to change the look, design, and feel of the quilt.
- Is there more than one block in the quilt? If so, what is it?
- What is the fabric recipe? How many fabrics are used in the quilt?
- Are different fabrics used in different combinations in the blocks?
- Are all the blocks the same size?
- How many of each block is there in the quilt?
- Does the block layout create a specific pattern?
- Do you like the blocks set straight or on point?
- What size finished quilt would you like to make?
- What size do you need the blocks to be to make the quilt this size?
- What size would you need to cut the strips to obtain that size of finished block?
- How do you want to border the quilt?

Note When making a very large quilt using these methods, you might find it handier to create 1/4 of the quilt at a time then join the four individual quarters together. If the quilt is quite large, the hinged units (the hinge is the thread connecting the blocks together) can have a tendency to get twisted if you aren't extremely careful.

Scrap Fence Post, 1998, 41" x 56". Pieced and quilted by Harriet Hargrave.

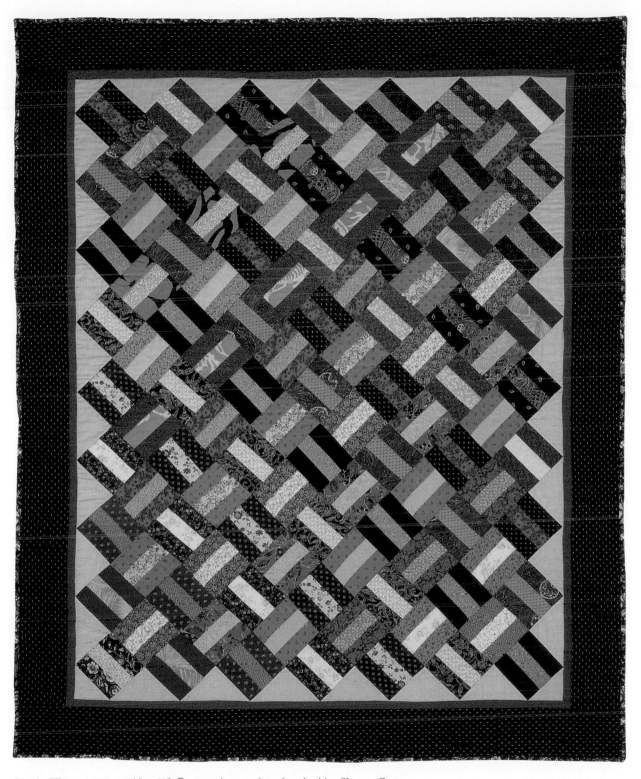

LatticeWeave, 1987, 53½" x 66". Designed, pieced, and quilted by Sharyn Craig.

Barn Fence, 1998, 57¹/₂" x 66¹/₂". Designed and pieced by Sharyn Craig. Quilted by Joanie Keith

Plaid Fence, 1987, 31" x 34". Designed, pieced, and hand quilted by Sharyn Craig.

Strips & Squares

Now that you've completed a very basic block and turned it into a quilt top, you're ready to go on and explore some of the more complex blocks which give you greater design impact.

This quilt is a simple 4-patch, made entirely from strips. Begin by looking at the photo of the quilt and answering the following questions:

■ Is there more than one type of block in the quilt?

■ What components make up these quilt blocks?

■ How can you most effectively go about piecing the shapes together?

■ Are there any units that need to be broken into subunits to make the piecing easier?

■ How many fabrics are used?

■ How many basic shapes are there?

■ Are the blocks all the same size?

■ How many of each block are there in the quilt?

■ What techniques do you know to help you make the shapes quickly and accurately?

Project

This quilt is made from 4" finished blocks. It is made from six different blue prints, a cream solid, and a stripe border. You'll notice that we give you the yardage recommendations for this quilt instead of working through the process as we did for *Fence Post*. If you decide to

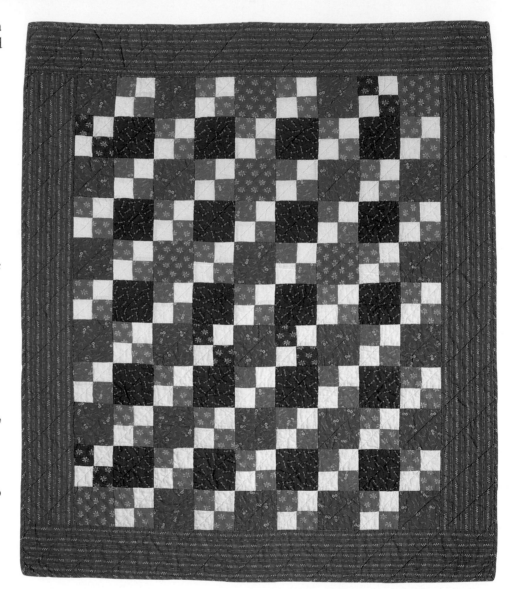

1860s 4-Patch, 1997, 43" x 50" with borders. Pieced and quilted by Harriet Hargrave

change the number of fabrics or the size of the quilt, you can recalculate based on the information in Chapter 9 on figuring yardage (page 92).

This quilt has forty-nine 4" finished 4-patches and fifty 4" finished solid squares.

You will need:
$\frac{1}{4}$ yard medium blue #1
$\frac{1}{2}$ yard medium blue #2
$\frac{1}{2}$ yard dark navy #1
$\frac{1}{8}$ yard dark navy #2
$\frac{1}{3}$ yard light blue #1
$\frac{1}{4}$ yard light blue #2
$\frac{1}{2}$ yard cream solid or shirting print
$1\frac{5}{8}$ yards medium blue stripe for border

Cut:
Six $2\frac{1}{2}$" strips of cream or shirting print
One $2\frac{1}{2}$" strip dark navy #2
Four $2\frac{1}{2}$" strips light blue #1
Two $2\frac{1}{2}$" strips light blue #2
Sew each blue strip together with a cream strip using a $\frac{1}{4}$" seam allowance. Once sewn, press the seam allowance toward the blue strip. Using your ruler, cut each strip into $2\frac{1}{2}$" segments. Remember to check that the ruler lines are parallel with the seam before cutting the segments. Position two units right sides together so that the seam allowances butt and alternate. Make sure that the darker fabric goes into the sewing machine first as you sew the right-hand edge. The natural action of the sewing machine will help push the seam lines together when the seam allowance is pointing toward the foot of the machine as you are stitching.

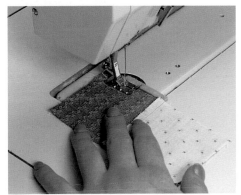

Feed units through with seam allowance pointing toward the foot

Repeat with all the units, chaining one after another. Clip units apart. Press seam allowance.

(a)

(b)

(c) **Creating a fanned intersection**

Tip If you're looking for a really slick way to finger-press this center seam allowance that reduces bulk in the middle of the 4-patch, you might want to try this little trick. With the 4-patch wrong side up, position the fleshy pads of your thumbs on the darker portion of the seam allowance, one on either side of it. Gently push the seam allowance toward the lighter squares of the 4-patches. This will cause approximately two stitches to release and fan around as shown in the photo.

This tip definitely reduces bulk, and the block lies very flat at the center. This same method of fanning the seam allowances can work on other blocks, such as 9-patches and Pinwheels. Any time you have straight across matches that alternate, you can use this technique. Would you always use it? Not necessarily. But once you know how to do it you can determine for yourself when the reduction of bulk is a big plus. At this point you may iron the units if desired.

Once sewn, you should have the following quantities of 4-patches:
Five dark navy #2 and cream
Thirty light blue #1 and cream
Fourteen light blue #2 and cream

Each 4-patch should measure $4\frac{1}{2}$". If not, use your actual measurement and cut the following strips:
Cut:
Three $4\frac{1}{2}$" strips medium blue #2
One $4\frac{1}{2}$" strip medium blue #1
Three $4\frac{1}{2}$" strip dark navy #1

From these strips cut:
Twenty-four $4\frac{1}{2}$" squares medium blue #2
Six $4\frac{1}{2}$" squares medium blue #1
Twenty $4\frac{1}{2}$" squares dark navy #1

Lay out the quilt top:
Starting with Row 1, make every other position a medium blue square, and randomly place the 4-patch blocks between. The medium blue squares are used in Rows 1,3,5,7, and 9. The navy squares are used in Rows 2,4,6, and 8. Keep the 4-patch blocks scattered.

Assemble the Quilt Top
Using your favorite chain sewing procedure (Chapter 10, page 98), sew all the rows together. Once the top is joined, press thoroughly and check for evenness and flatness.

ADD BORDERS

The borders are cut 5½" wide. Refer to Chapter 18 (page 205) for specific instructions on adding borders to a quilt top.

You should finish with a flat, neat quilt top. Is it? Or did you have trouble with any portion of the project? **You should stop now and evaluate your quilt for any problem areas.**

- Are your strips all cut the same width?
- Was your seam allowance consistent?
- Were your strip rows each the same sewn width?
- Do your 4-patch intersecting seams butt?
- Were your 4-patch units all exactly square and the same size?
- Did your rows line up as you assembled the quilt top? Seams butt perfectly?

The 1860s 4-patch is made from a controlled number of fabrics and colors. This pattern is also stunning when made scrappy, as shown in Sharyn's two flannel quilts at right. Because there is a larger variety of fabrics and they are placed more randomly, the techniques to construct them are slightly different than using just strips.

4-Patch Quilts: From Individual Squares

It is possible to cut and piece the entire 4-patch quilt from individual squares. If making very scrappy 4-patches, it's often easier to cut and piece separate squares, rather than using the strip method. The individual squares can be cut either with your ruler or with a template. If you would like to try cutting the individual squares with a template, we are providing a 2" square pattern piece for your template guide. Use one of the template-creating processes discussed in Chapter 5 (page 58) to make this pattern guide into a sturdy, usable template for rotary cutting.

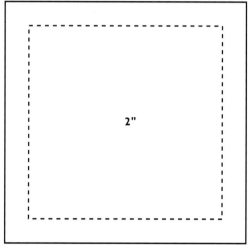

2" square pattern piece

Cut 2½" strips of assorted light- and dark-value fabrics. Leave the strips folded in fourths. Begin cutting at the end of the folded strips where the selvages are. Cut off the selvages to square the end. Continue cutting the strip into squares. If cutting with the ruler, cut every 2½", taking care to line up the ruler lines with the edges of the strip. If cutting with the template, simply position the template on the strip and cut.

Randomly pair a dark and a light square right sides together and sew. Repeat with the remaining dark and light squares. Press the seam allowance toward the darker fabric. At this point you would continue making the 4-patches using methods described in the project quilt.

Seam allowance toward darker fabric

4-Patch Quilts: Combining Templates and Strip Piecing

Cut assorted 2½" strips of light-and dark-value fabrics. You can work with full-width strips or shorter strips if you desire a more random, scrappy quilt. Pair up one dark and one light strip, right sides facing, and sew them together the entire length.

Leaving the sewn strip in the closed position, place the square template on the sewn strip and cut 2½" squares. (If you're careful you can stack 2 to 3 sewn strips one on top of another and cut the squares.)

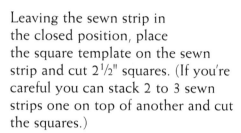

Template

Once the unit is cut, press the seam allowance toward the darker fabric. Continue pairing the units as previously described. Finger-press seam allowances to create the fanned central intersection.

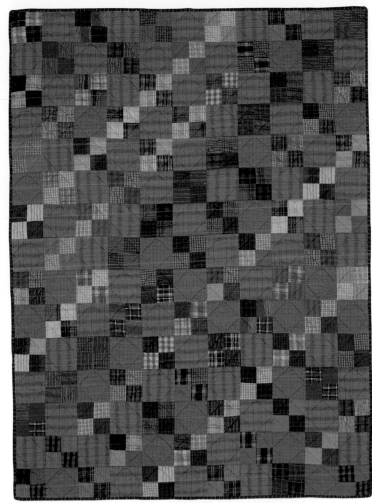

Old Flannel 4-Patch,
1998, 40¹/₂" x 55¹/₂". Designed,
pieced, and quilted by Sharyn Craig.

New Flannel 4-Patch,
1998, 42" x 57".
Designed, pieced, and
quilted by Sharyn Craig.

Keep Going!!

Apply the techniques that you've learned to the following blocks for practice. This is a good time to choose a quilt size, design the quilt around a block, and work through figuring the yardage requirements. Keep your designs simple and straightforward at first. Then, as you get more comfortable with the process, make the quilt designs more complex.

Let's start with a simple 9-patch.

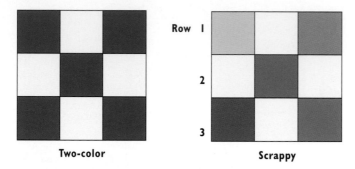

Two-color   Scrappy

All the units are the same—squares. But how many fabrics are used? One is a two-fabric block, the other is a scrap block. Starting with the two fabric block, ask yourself, "How can I efficiently piece it?" Rows 1 & 3 are the same, so you can sew together strips in this combination, then cut the segments to obtain both Rows 1 & 3 from one set of strips. Row 2 is a different setup, so it will be a different set of strips.

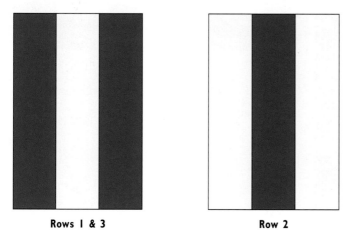

Rows 1 & 3   Row 2

If all the blocks in the quilt are the same, this block would be most effectively pieced using two different strip sets. The scrap block, on the other hand, needs to be approached from another angle. Because all the colored fabrics are different, it can either be constructed using individual squares cut and sewn together one by one (which would produce the most random fabric placement for a scrap quilt), or various combinations of fabrics can be sewn into short strip sets, then segmented into the rows. This will give more repeats of the same combinations of fabrics, but the final effect is much the same in a scrap quilt.

Obviously, the two fabric block is the fastest and easiest when you consider only the sewing time, but the scrap quilt gives more variety in exchange for a bit more time and effort.

Single Irish Chain, 1986, 53" x 66".
Pieced by Sharyn Craig. Quilted by Judy Tyrell. An example of a 9-patch quilt.

Project

Double Irish Chain

A classic favorite is the Double Irish Chain. Again, this quilt is made from only two blocks. Traditionally it was made with two or three fabrics.

Identify the two blocks.

Next, decide what size you want the finished block to be or what size you want each separate square to be. A 1½" finished grid is very pleasing for this pattern and is what we will use for the project.

Block A has 5 rows of 5 units each. Rows 1 & 5 are the same, Row 2 is the same as Row 4, Row 3 is different from any of the rest, so you need to make three different strip sets for Block A. This project is 5 blocks x 5 blocks, so you need thirteen A blocks and twelve B blocks.

Block A

You will need to sew:
Two strip sets for Rows 1 & 5
Two strip sets for Rows 2 & 4
One strip set for Row 3

To do this, cut:
Four 2" strips of background (white)
Nine 2" strips of color #1 (green)
Twelve 2" strips of color #2 (red)
Refer to the illustrations, above right, for color placement and sew the strip sets in the order shown.

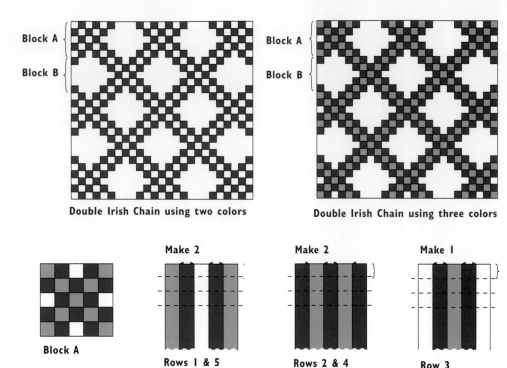

Double Irish Chain using two colors

Double Irish Chain using three colors

Block A

Make 2
Rows 1 & 5

Make 2
Rows 2 & 4

Make 1
Row 3

Press all seams toward the color #2 (red) strips. This will cause the seams to automatically butt when you join the segments into the blocks.

Cut all of the strip sets into 2" segments. Place a stack of thirteen Row 1 segments by your machine. Next to that, place thirteen Row 2 segments, and continue on until you have thirteen segments for each row in the proper sewing order. Now all you have to do is pick up one of the Row 1 segments, place a Row 2 segment on top, right sides together, and stitch them together, being very careful to butt the seams as accurately as possible. Repeat until all thirteen are joined.

Pull the joined segments back toward you and add Row 3 onto the second row of all thirteen blocks. Continue until all 5 rows are stitched together. This completes all of Block A. Press.

Block B

Block B can be a bit confusing, so let's walk through it carefully. There are only two strip sets needed for this block. The measurement for the wide strip comes from Block A. Turn an A block over and measure from the outside raw edge of the seam allowance of the second strip to the outside raw edge of the fourth strip. The combined three center strips plus seam allowance is the cutting width of the center strip needed for Block B.

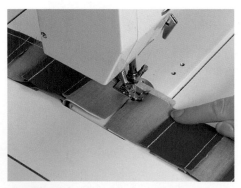

Double Irish Chain block assembly

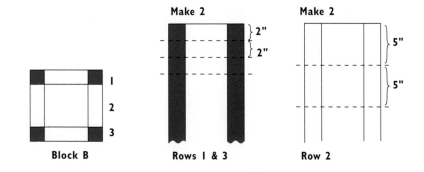

Block B

Make 2
Rows 1 & 3

2"
2"

Make 2
Row 2

5"
5"

1
2
3

You will need:

One set of strips plus 6" more (use short strips) for Rows 1 & 3, and two sets of strips for Row 2.

Cut:

Four 2" strips of color #2 (red)

Four 5" (or your actual measurement) strips of background (white)

Four 2" strips of background (white)

Lay out strips according to the diagram and sew them together. Press the seams toward the background on the strip set for Row 1. Press them toward the narrow strips for Row 2. Now you're ready to cut the strips into segments.

The Row 1 set is cut into 2" segments. The Row 2 set, however, is cut the same length as the center strip was cut wide: 5" (or your actual measurement).

Note Since row two is all the same fabric, some quilters like to keep it seamless. If you'd prefer this, cut the strip as wide as the block to eliminate any seams. Some prefer this for seamless quilting, others like the balance that the seams provide.

Lay out the segments and chain sew the rows together. Now you can lay out the blocks into the overall pattern. Remember that a Block A is always in the corner. Using the stacking or pairs system explained in Chapter 10 (page 100), pick up the blocks and proceed to sew the top together.

Look at the *Triple Irish Chain* variation to the right. How is it different? What are the blocks? How would you piece this variation? What strip combinations would you use?

Christmas Double Irish Chain, 1998, 47" x 47". Designed, pieced, and quilted by Harriet Hargrave.

Triple Irish Chain, 1998, 68" x 90". Pieced and quilted by Harriet Hargrave.

Mountain Homespun

Now it's time to look at blocks that use a combination of sub-units. We call this next quilt Mountain Homespun.

The block is made up of three different units. One is a square, one is a 9-patch, and one is a Rail Fence block. It is always wise to start with the most complex unit. Because there are more seams in more complex units, there is a greater chance of size change when sewing seam allowances. Which is the most complex unit in this block?

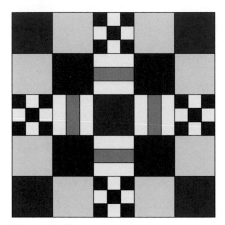

Mountain Homespun

You're right, the 9-patch has the most seams and is therefore most complex. What size is the finished block going to be? Let's say that we want it to be 15" finished. That makes the grid 3" (the size of each patch in the 5-patch block: 15" ÷ 5 = 3"). So the 9-patch is made up of three 1" finished units (3" ÷ 3 = 1"). The strips for the 9-patch would be cut 1½" wide. Once these strips are sewn together, you'll have the measurement that the segments need to be cut. The Rail Fence block is just three 1½" strips sewn together and cut as long as they are wide, which should be the same as the finished 9-patch unit.

Mountain Homespun, 1998, 70" x 85". Designed and pieced by Harriet Hargrave. Quilted by Cathy Franks.

Dots and Dashes

This is a fun little variation that is very similar to the Mountain Homespun quilt on a much simpler scale. To make the quilt, you also need 9-patch blocks, Fence Post (Rail Fence) blocks, and solid squares. Because the blocks are set diagonally, you also need setting triangles for along the edges. Sharyn actually made this quilt from lots of leftover blocks from other 9-patch quilts and Fence Post type quilts. In fact, if you look closely at the quilt, *Lattice Weave*, in Chapter 10 (page 103), you'll probably recognize some of the very same fence block units. Keep this quilt in mind as you're learning to make the blocks from this chapter. Who knows what wonderful things could happen just because you ended up with extra blocks!

Dots and Dashes, 1990, 58 1/2" x 47". Designed, pieced, and quilted by Sharyn Craig.

The "H" Quilt

Let's look at an even more complex block. Harriet bought this antique quilt because of all the H's she saw in it. It seemed appropriate because of the double H's in her name. The quilt is 5 x 6 blocks. Can you identify the blocks as you look at the whole quilt?

Once Harriet started to really look at the quilt, she found that it's simply an adaptation of the well known Burgoyne Surrounded block. Look at the two blocks on page 116 and see if you can identify the changes made.

Burgoyne Surrounded uses a combination of 9-patch and 4-patch blocks together, solid squares in the center of the block, and a sashing. The "H" Quilt uses 4-patches, with the blocks sewn next to one another. Both quilts are made of all strips and squares, but the piecing is more complex than we have seen up to now. Let's look closely at how the *"H" Quilt* is made.

"H" Quilt, 62" x 75". Burgoyne Surrounded variation. From the collection of Harriet Hargrave

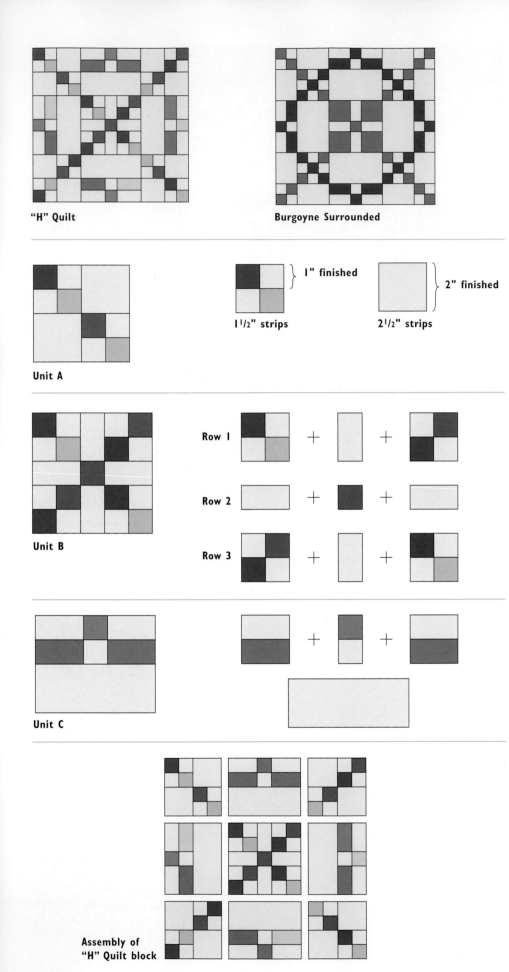

"H" Quilt

Burgoyne Surrounded

Unit A

1" finished

1 1/2" strips

2" finished

2 1/2" strips

Unit B

Row 1   +   +

Row 2   +   +

Row 3   +   +

Unit C

+   +

Assembly of "H" Quilt block

The block is made up of three subunits and is 13" finished, using a 1" grid.

Starting with Unit A, we see that it contains two 4-patch units and two solid squares.

Therefore, each unit of the 4-patch is a 1" square. If each 4-patch finishes to 2", the solid squares will also be 2" finished, 2 1/2" cut.

The color placement of the 4-patch blocks is the beginning of the chain that runs through the entire quilt, so be careful to place them carefully before sewing these four units together. All four corners of the block are identical.

Next look at Unit B. It is constructed from 4-patches and a segment from a strip set (or templates can be used if desired). The unit in between the 4-patches in Rows 1 & 3 is cut 1 1/2" wide by the length of a completed 4-patch. Row 2 is made from two strips cut the width of a finished 4-patch, and another strip cut 1 1/2" wide.

When the Row 2 strips are sewn together, press the seams toward the wider strips and cut into segments 1 1/2" wide. To construct the whole unit, sew a 4-patch unit on either side of the 1 1/2"-wide piece. Do this for both Rows 1 & 3. Join these two sections onto either side of the strip segment. Press.

Unit C gets its measurements from Unit B. It utilizes the size of a 4-patch and the measurement of the finished unit. The solid strip is cut the width of the 4-patch and the length of the unit. The pieced side uses measurements from the 4-patch again. Once all the units are constructed, lay them out into the configuration of the block, next to your machine.

THE ART OF CLASSIC QUILTMAKING

All the blocks can be constructed at once by stacking the units on top of one another. Using the process you're most comfortable with, start to pick up the units in pairs and sew them together, proceeding until all 3 rows of all the blocks are joined. Continue by joining the rows into the finished blocks.

Can you assign another grid measurement to this block and figure out where to start? Can you look at the Burgoyne Surrounded block and see the difference? If so, do you now know where to start and how to proceed?

When Sharyn looked at this quilt, she immediately thought "What if I substituted S's or C's for the H's? Or, what if I made an alphabet quilt, with a different letter or number in each of the 'H' spaces?" She settled for *The Craig Quilt* you see here.

We're providing you with block lettering for all 26 letters and 10 numbers. You might have to make a few adjustments for some of the letters in order to make them fit properly, but we know you can do it. Feel free to innovate and create to your heart's content. After all, isn't that what we've been encouraging you to do all the way through this book?

The object of walking through so many different blocks is so that these questions become second nature to you when you look at a block or a quilt. If you can start to dissect the quilts into blocks, the blocks into units, assign a grid, and know where to start cutting and sewing, you're well on your way to pattern-free quiltmaking.

The Craig Quilt, 1998, 37" x 37". Designed, pieced, and quilted by Sharyn Craig.

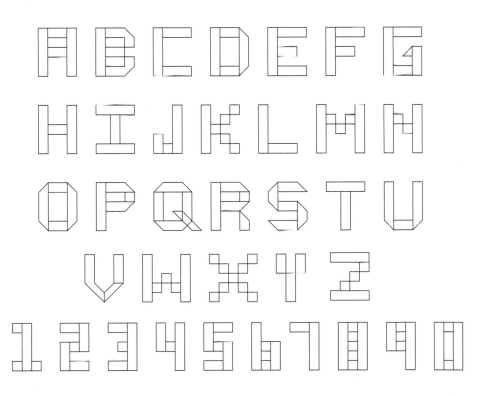

CHAPTER 12

Log Cabins & Pineapples

The Log Cabin pattern is probably one the most popular patterns in quilting. It's an age-old pattern, going back centuries to a look-alike item found in King Tut's tomb. Today's versions resemble the quilts of the middle 1800s, when the Log Cabin pattern was popularized during Abraham Lincoln's era. It is one of the few traditional designs that did not lose popularity during the Victorian era.

There seems to be an infinite number of variations to the Log Cabin pattern. That is perhaps what makes it so appealing. Let's start by looking at a basic, common Log Cabin block.

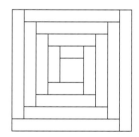

Basic Log Cabin block

When examining the block, you'll see that the block is built from a center square and is surrounded by strips. These strips are nearly always divided by color so that one diagonal half of the block is light, the other dark. This color layout lends itself to endless design possibilities. When constructing the block, the strips are added to the center square, working around the square equally. Tradition has it that the

center square was red to depict the chimney of the Log Cabin, and it's very commonly found this way in a wide variety of antique Log Cabin quilts. The center is frequently two or three times as wide as the strips, but this is not a rule. You will sometimes see the center as narrow as the strip itself or as wide as four strips. The number of strips used on each side can vary.

A study of old quilts shows that there was an amazing variety of construction techniques for the basic unit. Generally, four to six strips of both light and dark are used. The width of the strips can vary from $1/4$" to $1\frac{1}{2}$" wide. Today's most popular widths tends to fall within the 1" to $1\frac{1}{2}$" range.

There is no "right way" to make a Log Cabin block. When studying old quilts, you start to identify interesting discrepancies. Strips can be added to the center to form V-shaped sides or L-shaped sides. First the light strips are attached to two sides of the center square, then dark strips are added to the other two sides of the center square, resulting in a "V" formation. An "L" formation is made by adding one light strip to one side of the square first, then placing two dark strips on the next two sides of the center, and finally ending the first round with a light strip. Examine Figure 12-1 to see the difference this color placement makes.

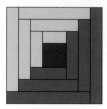 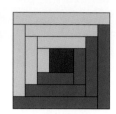

Fig. 12-1 **"V" formation**   **"L" formation**

You will most often see the blocks constructed starting with the light strips, but you can certainly start with the dark if you prefer. Below is a breakout of the pattern.

Piecing order for Log Cabin blocks

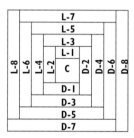

Four "rounds"

Log Cabin blocks are unique in their piecing order—working in "rounds." The basic block is constructed by joining the first light strip (L-1) to the center square (C). Rotate the center and add L-2. Then add D-1 and D-2. These are the first and second dark strips and the end of the first round. Continue on, adding L-3 and L-4, then D-3 and D-4, completing the second round. This process keeps repeating until all the desired rounds are added and the block is square.

You have a variety of sewing techniques to choose from. The traditional method was to work on a base cloth— the original quilt-as-you-go idea. You will sometimes hear this technique called pressed piecing or foundation piecing. This is a great method when working with difficult fabrics such as silks, sheers, velvets, and mismatched textures, which is quite possibly how this technique got started. Many old Log Cabin quilts were made from these fabrics, often sewing fine silks next to suiting wools.

The Log Cabin block can also be constructed without the base square. Individual logs can be cut to size then pieced, or long strips can be added to a unit, sewn to the desired length, then cut off. Assembly-line piecing— made popular by Eleanor Burns in the early 1980s with her Quilt-In-A-Day® ideas—is a very fast technique when a limited number of fabrics are used. We would suggest that you try each method to see the benefits and drawbacks of all of them. Also, learn which method gives you the most accuracy in the finished block.

Study the variety of Log Cabin quilts you see pictured here, or anywhere else for that matter. When you're ready to start making a Log Cabin, begin by deciding whether you want to work with scrappy or controlled fabric and colors. Choose a strip width to work with and think about what size finished blocks you'll want to make. Strip width and finished block size will determine how many rounds you sew. By now, if you've been working through the book, you'll be ready to make some of these decisions for yourself. If you're still a bit intimidated by calculating yardage, remember that you can never run out of fabric if you work scrappy!

It can be useful to create a notebook of the various methods prior to starting a quilt. If you make one

block using each method, you will be able to confidently choose one that you'll enjoy making enough of for an entire quilt.

TECHNIQUE ONE:
Base Block (Pressed-Piecing or Foundation) Method

1) First, cut a square of fabric slightly larger than the finished size of the block. This is the base. Fold the base square in half diagonally in both directions and crease lightly. **2)** Position the center square for the block in the center of the base, right side up. **3)** Placing right sides together, lay a light strip on top of the center square, aligning the raw edges carefully. Cut the light strip to size and stitch through all three layers. Turn the strip over to its right side and press along the seam allowance, pressing flat against the base square. **4)** Now rotate the base clockwise and repeat with the second light strip. Position it on the second side of the center square, cut to size, and stitch in place.

5) The next clockwise rotation will begin the addition of the dark strips. This process is continued in a light-light/dark-dark color sequence until each side has the desired number of strips. This completes the block.

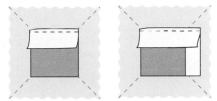

Quilt-as-you-go technique

Using Basic Fabric as Backing

Many antique quilts did not add a separate backing and batting at this stage. You can use a fabric for the base block you desire as a backing, then finish the blocks in the same manner as the antique quilts. Once you check the blocks for squareness, pin the strips of two blocks together along one edge, right sides together. Sew a 1/4" seam to join the strips. Be careful not to catch the backing in the seam. Open the two blocks, then place them face side down. Press the seam. Where the two backing pieces come together, smooth one backing piece under the other. Turn under the edge of the top piece of backing 1/4" and blind stitch in place through the other piece of backing. Continue to add blocks to make rows in this manner, then join the rows.

You may choose to use a trim piece instead. In this method, sew two blocks together through all layers with a 1/4" seam. On the back, baste the seams down to one side. Cut 1"-wide strips of the backing fabric, or a contrasting fabric if you desire, and turn the edges in 1/4". The finished strips are about 1/2" wide. Center the strip over the seam and blind stitch in place on both sides. This technique gives a lattice appearance to the back.

Join blocks for quilt-as-you-go

Finish seam with strip

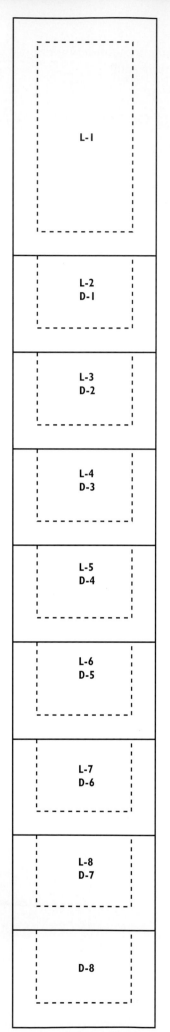

If you would like to add a batting and backing, the layers can be joined together by tying or ditch quilting. A more modern method of quilt-as-you-go, introduced by Marti Michell, is to place batting between the base fabric (actually the backing fabric in this case) and the strips as they are joined together. As the strips are stitched into their position, the seams are quilted at the same time. Each block is quilted as it is pieced.

TECHNIQUE TWO:

Individual Pre-Cut Logs

When a great deal of variety is needed in the block for a very scrappy look, it's often easiest to precut the log pieces and randomly stack them so that no two fabrics are in the same placement in the blocks. We have provided you with a set of templates that give you the cut sizes of each log for each color. Cut the needed number and proceed with the piecing as described on page 118.

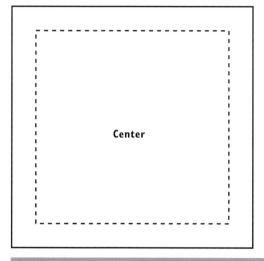

Use the following chart to determine the template size you need for logs in various sized blocks.

Log Sizes Used in Various Sized Blocks			
(Example uses a 2" center square)			
Unit	Length Formula	Finished Size	Cut Size
center	c	2"	2$\frac{1}{2}$"
L-1	c	2"	2$\frac{1}{2}$"
L-2	c+w (width)	3"	3$\frac{1}{2}$"
D-1	c+w	3"	3$\frac{1}{2}$"
D-2	c+2w	4"	4$\frac{1}{2}$"
L-3	c+2w	4"	4$\frac{1}{2}$"
L-4	c+3w	5"	5$\frac{1}{2}$"
D-3	c+3w	5"	5$\frac{1}{2}$"
D-4	c+4w	6"	6$\frac{1}{2}$"
L-5	c+4w	6"	6$\frac{1}{2}$"
L-6	c+5w	7"	7$\frac{1}{2}$"
D-5	c+5w	7"	7$\frac{1}{2}$"
D-6	c+6w	8"	8$\frac{1}{2}$"
L-7	c+6w	8"	8$\frac{1}{2}$"
L-8	c+7w	9"	9$\frac{1}{2}$"
D-7	c+7w	9"	9$\frac{1}{2}$"
D-8	c+8w	10"	10$\frac{1}{2}$"

TECHNIQUE THREE:
Stitch and Cut Piecing Method

This technique lends itself to scrap or more controlled blocks. If you want a lot of different fabrics, trim each strip after each addition, changing strips for each log on each block. For less variety, sew several block units onto each strip before cutting it off. This will result in that fabric appearing in that position in several blocks.

Begin by cutting all the strips to the desired width. After cutting a strip of the fabric chosen for the center square, cut it into individual squares. Place a center square and a light strip right sides together. Stitch with a ¼" seam allowance. Cut this strip off even with the center square. Open and press the seam allowance toward the log.

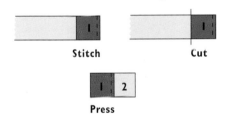

Lay the squares on top of another light strip. Be sure that the light square is at the top so that the block is rotating counterclockwise. Stitch on the right side of the unit. Trim the strip even with the center square. Open and press the seam allowance toward the log.

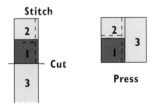

Rotate the unit so that the log that you just pressed is at the top and position it on top of a dark strip. Align the edges and stitch. Cut off strip, open, and press.

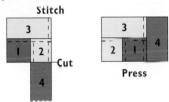

Next, position the unit over another dark strip, being sure that the last log is at the top. Align, stitch, cut, open, and press. You are now back to a square—or should be.

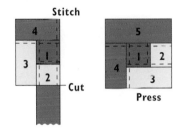

Continue adding and cutting until you have a total of four logs on each side of the center square.

TECHNIQUE FOUR:
Assembly-line Piecing Method

This is the ultimate piecing technique for speed, but achieves the least variety of fabrics. This process will give you many blocks—possibly all of them—that will have the same fabrics in the same position.

Begin by placing a strip of the center square fabric on top of a light strip. Align the edges on the right side and stitch the length needed. Using a rotary cutter and ruler, measure the size needed for the center square and cut the length of the strips into squares. Be careful to align the ruler with the stitch line. Press toward the light log.

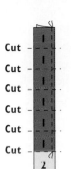

Position the unit on top of another light strip, making sure that the log is at the top. Stitch the first one in place, position another, and continue stitching.

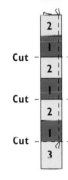

Continue this process until the second strip is added to all the first units. At the cutting mat, again cut the units apart, keeping them square and straight. Press seam allowances toward log.

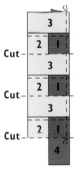

Place the three piece units over a dark strip in the same manner as above. Cut apart and press.

Continue stitching the units to strips, cutting them apart and pressing, until you have four complete rows of logs.

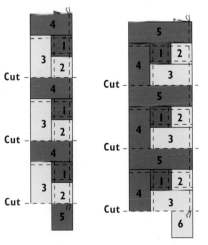

Using the antique quilt pictured on the next page for inspiration, try your hand at creating a scrap Log Cabin quilt using any of the previously discussed techniques.

For your first attempt at a Log Cabin you might want to work with this formula. Make the center twice the width of the strips (2") and add the strips counterclockwise, beginning with the light fabrics. The strips are 1" wide finished. You might want to go only four rounds, making the completed block a 10" square.

Endless Design Possibilities

Once you know the construction techniques of the basic Log Cabin block, you're ready to discover a whole world of design using different configurations of the logs around different centers. The traditional diagonal effect of the Log Cabin block can be jazzed up in several ways. Consider the following possibilities.

Change the center. Use a half-square triangle, a 4-patch, a different color, or a pieced star. Refer to Figures 12-2 through 12-5.

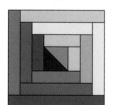
Fig. 12-2

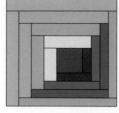
Fig. 12-3

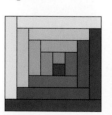
Fig. 12-4

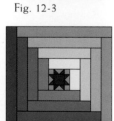
Fig. 12-5

Different center squares

Change the size of the strips, making either the dark or light narrower than the other.

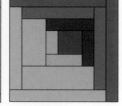
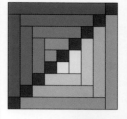

Different size strips

Change the position of the value sequence. Use the same fabric for a full round around the center, the second fabric is the second round, and so forth.

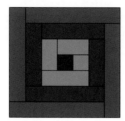

Repeat fabric in ring

Use only two fabrics and alternate them in such a way as to form a spiral.

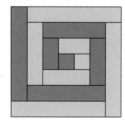

Fabric placement creates a spiral

Add squares or half-square triangles to the ends of each log to create the Chimneys & Cornerstones effect.

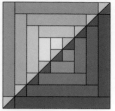
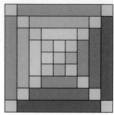

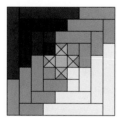

Blocks with cornerstones

Combine values within each log to give a surprising effect. Refer to the quilt shown on page 127 for an example.

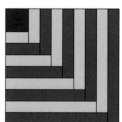

Block with different type of logs

Keep the center square in a corner and build a chevron by adding logs to only two sides of the center square.

Chevron Log Cabin

And more.

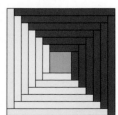
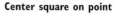

Center square on point   Control the number and placement of fabrics

Barnraising Log Cabin, 1880s, 57" x 57". Antique blocks set together and quilted by Harriet Hargrave.

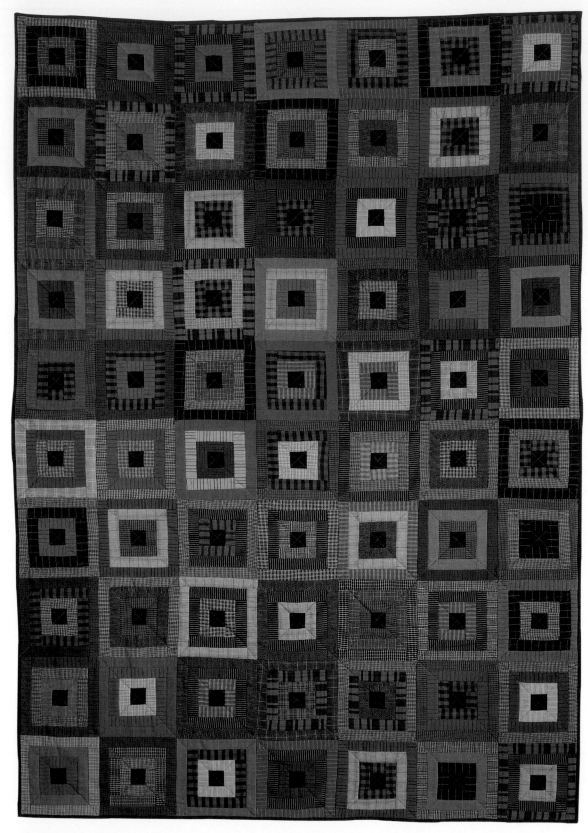

Primitive Log Cabin, 1997, 50" x 71". Designed, pieced, and quilted by Mary Radke.

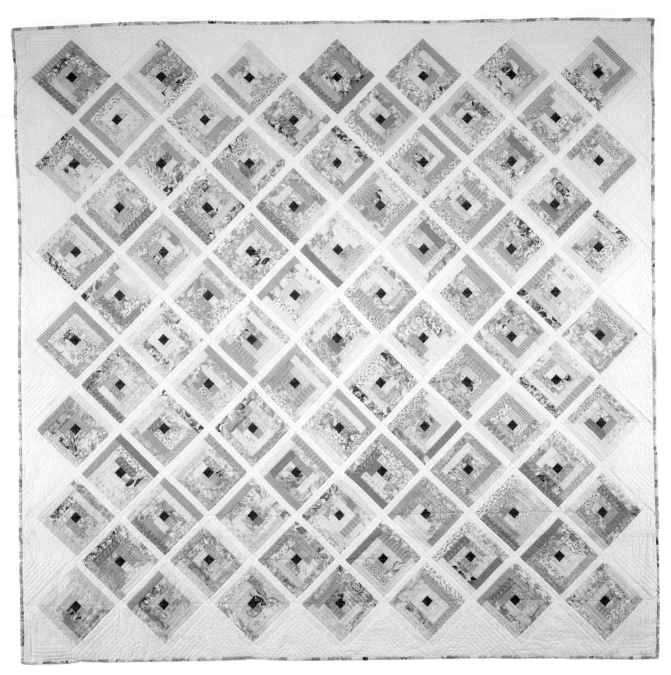

Cabin in the Cotton, 1993, 80" x 80". Pieced and quilted by Georgia Mueller and Pam Gable.
Based on a pattern by Mountain Mist/The Stearns Technical Textile Company. Owned by Gail Mullinax

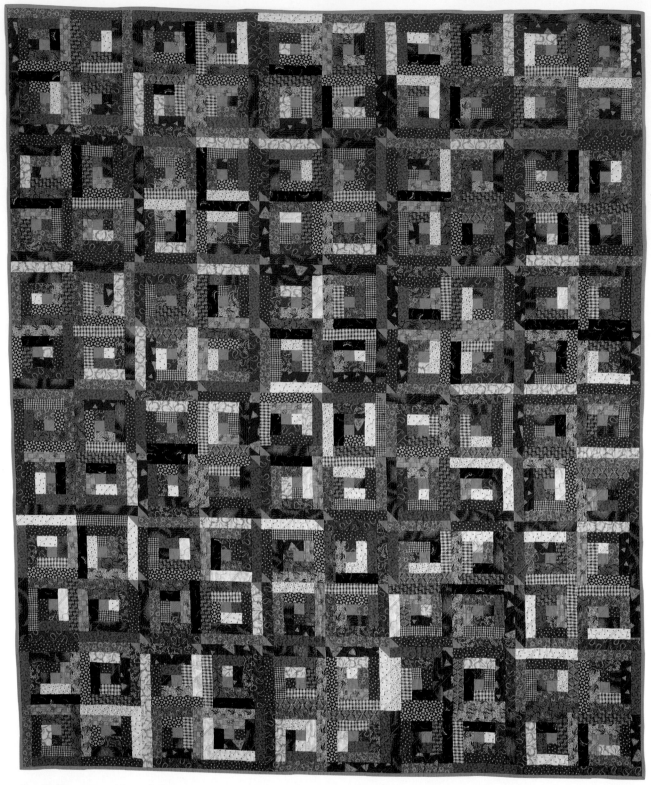

Log Cabin , 1995, 57" x 68". Designed, pieced, and quilted by Christine Husak.

Ozark Log Cabin, 1998, 74" x 74". Pieced by Harriet Hargrave and Sharyn Craig.
Quilted by Cathy Franks. Block designed by Judy Martin, first published in her
book *Scraps, Blocks and Quilts*, 1991.

There are endless layout possibilities for the blocks once they are constructed. Below are a few of the more traditional layouts. You can spend hours manipulating the blocks into a myriad of designs. Have fun!!

Log Cabin Layout Designs

THE ART OF CLASSIC QUILTMAKING

Courthouse Steps: A Variation of the Basic Log Cabin Block

Courthouse Steps is the division of the light and dark values into quadrants instead of halves. Traditionally, the center is black to represent the judge's flowing robes, but old quilts show that there are many interpretations of this idea that use other colors in the centers.

Instead of adding the strips around the center square, either clockwise or counterclockwise, they are added in an alternating manner from side to side. Two light (or dark) strips are added to opposite sides of the center square, then the opposite value is added to the remaining two sides.

Any of the techniques used to piece a traditional Log Cabin block can be used in the piecing process for Courthouse Steps. Just change the order in which the strips are sewn.

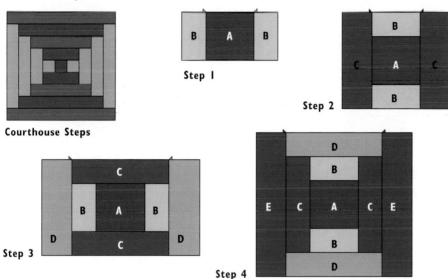

Courthouse Steps

Step 1

Step 2

Step 3

Step 4

1) Begin by sewing light logs on opposite sides of the center square.
2) If working from strips, trim, then press both seam allowances toward the logs. Next, add dark strips to the two opposite sides of the center square. Trim and press.
3) Light strips are then added to the same side of the center as before. Trim and press.
4) Now dark strips are added. Trim and press.
Keep going, adding as many rounds as you need. This block has superb design potential. Review the design ideas given for the traditional block and apply them to the Courthouse Steps block.

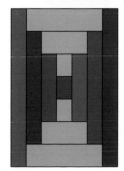
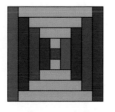
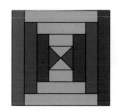
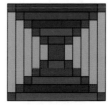

Courthouse Steps variations

Log Cabin can be as traditional or as contemporary as you want to make it. When you start looking for Log Cabin ideas, you'll be amazed at the possibilities this block offers. Following are some more brain teasers.

■ To get a really scrappy look, put all the light strips and dark strips into separate paper bags and make yourself sew whatever comes out. This will prevent you from trying to have all the fabrics look "good" next to one another.

■ Use any block that is made up of half-square triangles as a layout design. The Log Cabin block is truly only a half-square triangle—a big one! Instead of looking at the block as if it were just a center with logs surrounding it, look at it as if it were just two triangles sewn together—light and dark. Look at blocks in books and, wherever there is a triangle unit, ask yourself if a Log Cabin block could be substituted. What would the final effect be? What if all the triangle units became Log Cabin blocks?

■ Use triangles to create a "mock" Log Cabin look. Refer to *Pilgrim's Progress* and *Terrific Triangles* in the Chapter 13 photo gallery (pages 154-157).

■ Look at different blocks that have two different values on either side of a diagonal. Wouldn't they work great in a Log Cabin traditional set? Consider Drunkard's Path, Split 9-Patch, and others.

■ Start a file of Log Cabin ideas. You'll be fascinated at how versatile this block truly is!

To precut the logs from the strips, start by stacking between 4 and 8 different dark strips one on top of another, all right side up. (Don't stack more strips than you can comfortably cut through at one time.)

Stack eight different dark strips one on top of another

Eliminate the selvage on the end of the stack of strips. Next, segment the stack into the number of pieces at the assigned lengths that you need according to the chart on page 133.

FOR 6" FINISHED BLOCK

Let's use 2"-wide strips as an example. Segment at 2", 3½", 5", and 6½".

Segment dark strips

Scramble the strips. You need to mix up the order of the fabrics so that you won't make any block with the same fabric in it twice. To accomplish this in a very easy manner, we recommend the following system. Leave the smallest size segments alone. Place the top fabric from Pile 2 on the bottom of the stack. Place the top two fabrics from Pile 3 on the bottom of the stack. Place the top three fabrics from Pile 4 on the bottom of the stack.

To Scramble Dark Strips

Leave alone

Pile 2 Move 1 strip from top to bottom

Pile 3 Move 2 strips from top to bottom

Pile 4 Move 3 strips from top to bottom

Repeat segmenting and scrambling with the remainder of the dark strips.

Next, repeat the process with the light strips. Stack up to eight strips, all right sides up. Remove selvages and segment into the required number of pieces. Scramble the light logs in the same way you scrambled the dark logs.

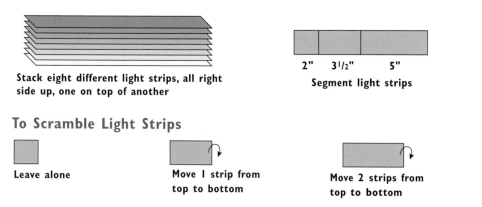

Stack eight different light strips, all right side up, one on top of another

Segment light strips
2"   3½"   5"

To Scramble Light Strips

Leave alone

Move 1 strip from top to bottom

Move 2 strips from top to bottom

Lay out the precut logs to form the block as shown in Figure 12-7. Remember, all the odd numbers are dark strips and all the even numbers are light strips.

Watch the direction of the pieces carefully! When laying the pieces out, it's recommended that you lay them out to the left of the sewing machine. Stack all the logs one on top of another for the total number of blocks you'll be making.

> **Note** If you prefer, you can stack logs for eight blocks at a time, rather than ALL of them.
> Once logs are cut and blocks are laid out, you can usually sew about 8 blocks together in 30 minutes. It is often easier to come up with a 30-minute block of time than it is 6-hour blocks of time. If you like being able to finish something in your small bites of time, working on no more than 8 blocks at once might be a good solution.

Sew the logs together in the numbered order. Sew all the number one seams first. Next sew all the number two seams, and so on.

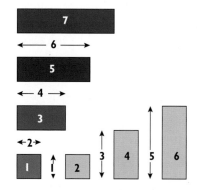

Fig. 12-7 **Lay out block as shown. Sew in numbered order.**

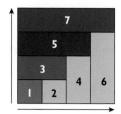

Seam allowances are all directionally guided away from #1 square

Half Log Cabin, 1998, 56" x 56". Blocks set on point into a Barn Raising format. Designed and pieced by Sharyn Craig. Quilted by Joanie Keith.

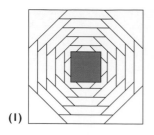

(1)

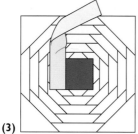

(2)

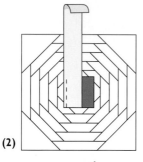

(3)

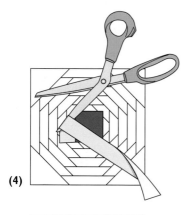

(4)

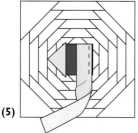

(5)

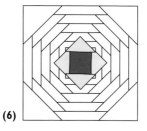

(6)

THE PIECING PROCESS

(1) Cut a square of fabric for the center and pin in place, right side up.

(2) Using a ¼" seam allowance, sew the first strip along one side of the square, with right sides together.

(3) Open the fabric to the right side and press the strip. If the seam has been sewn accurately, the fabric will reach the next parallel line. If it does not, or if it extends beyond the line, correct the seam allowance, then press.

(4) Cut the strip on the diagonal. The diagonal cut will be on the fabric placement line for the next row.

(5) Repeat this process with the same fabric on the opposite side of the square. The notch formed by the first cut on the strip can be used to position the fabric as a starting point for the second placement.

(6) Repeat this process again with the same fabric on the two remaining sides of the square.

(7) The contrasting fabric for the other four sides is next. Position a strip right side down along the edge of two of the first-row pieces. It is helpful to pin the pieces that were just sewn to the foundation to prevent them from slipping. Do not pin the strip you are now attaching. Repeat the sewing process, first sewing opposite sides, starting and stopping at the diagonal lines. Check to be sure that the seams are exactly at the corners of the center square. Press open and cut. Repeat with the same fabric on the remaining sides to complete the second row.

Return to the first fabric and add four pieces to form row three. Continue alternating the values around the center until the corners are reached. Use a strip wide enough to fill the corners and attach.
Turn the block to the back side and trim to the edge of the foundation, leaving ¼" seam allowance. Once all the blocks are sewn together, the paper can be removed.

METHOD TWO
This method uses no foundation, and therefore accuracy in sewing and cutting is a must. Its benefit is that there is no foundation to remove at the end. This technique utilizes 1½" cut strips. You can either cut the strips to length using the templates at the end of the chapter (see pages 142 through 143) or cut the ends after stitching. With either method, it's necessary to keep the seam widths absolutely consistent and the stitching lines perfectly straight. The order of piecing is the same as in the foundation method. Following Figures 12-9 through 12-17 will guide you through the construction process.

Once the blocks are finished, be very careful in handling them when joining one to another. Remember that all the ends of the strips were cut on the bias. All the edges have the potential to stretch because of this. Heavy starching during construction will help this problem considerably.

Fig. 12-9

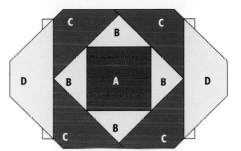

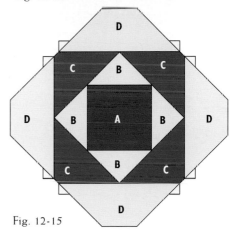

Fig. 12-14

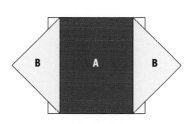

Fig. 12-10

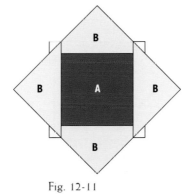

Fig. 12-11

Fig. 12-15

Using strips instead of template units

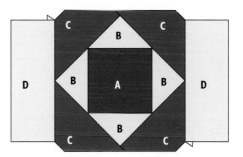

Fig. 12-16

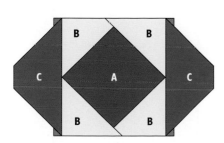

Fig. 12-12

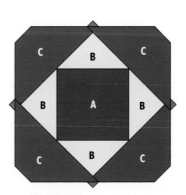

Fig. 12-13

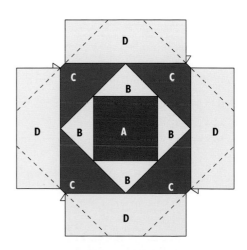

Fig. 12-17 **Strips attached then trimmed**

Pineapple Design Patterns

Note: All patterns include ¹/₄" seam allowance.

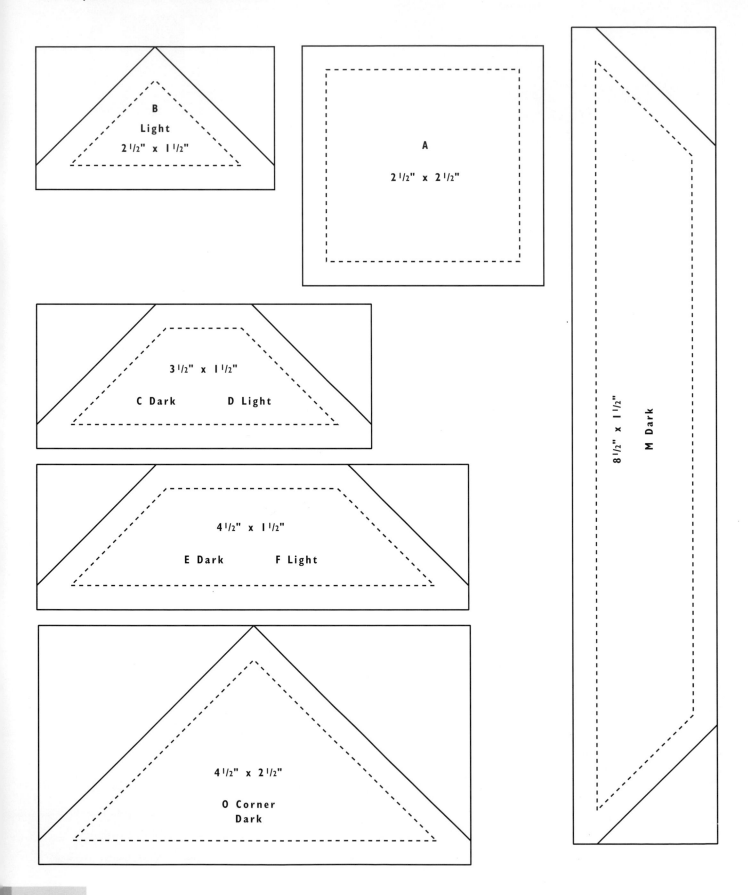

B
Light
2¹/₂" x 1¹/₂"

A
2¹/₂" x 2¹/₂"

3¹/₂" x 1¹/₂"

C Dark   D Light

4¹/₂" x 1¹/₂"

E Dark   F Light

4¹/₂" x 2¹/₂"

O Corner
Dark

8¹/₂" x 1¹/₂"

M Dark

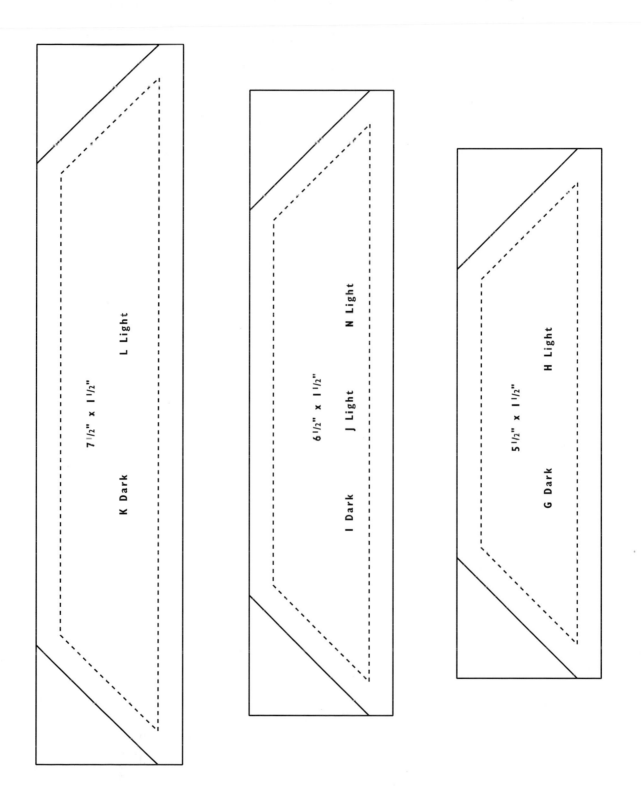

7 1/2" x 1 1/2"   L Light

K Dark

6 1/2" x 1 1/2"   N Light

J Light

I Dark

5 1/2" x 1 1/2"   H Light

G Dark

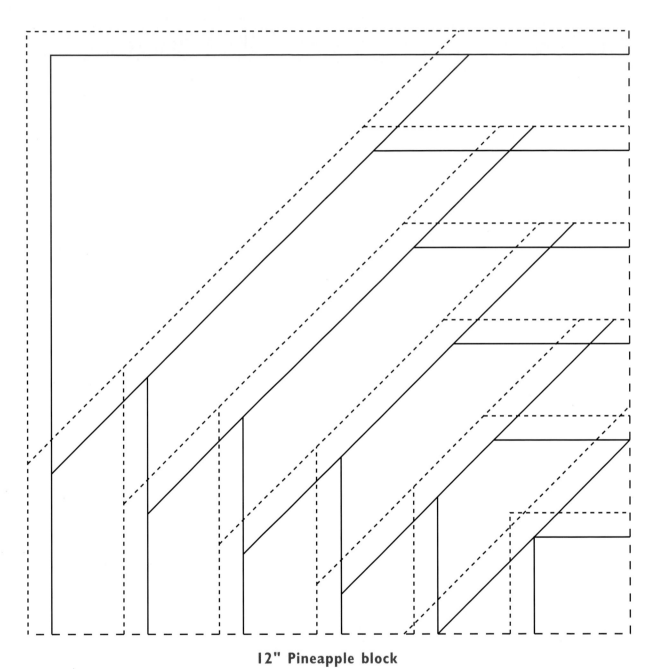

12" Pineapple block

Foundation pattern for one quarter of block

Triangles

In this chapter we explore two different kinds of triangles: half- and quarter-square triangles. A half-square triangle is just what it sounds like: half of a square. If you take a square and divide it in half diagonally, you'll have two half-square triangles. A quarter-square triangle is one-quarter of a square. Take a square, divide it diagonally twice, and you'll have four quarter-square triangles.

 Half and quarter square triangles

We will begin with the half-square triangle and explore different techniques for creating them for use in patchwork blocks. We will give you several different techniques for both cutting and constructing the triangle-square units. Some of the methods cut and piece individual triangles, while other methods sew first, then cut, yielding finished sewn units. All methods use a rotary cutter for the cutting. Some patchwork blocks need both single triangles and triangle-square units, so it's important that you know how to create both. It is our hope that you'll try each of the different techniques. We have both used all of the methods at one time or another. Sometimes we find one method serves our purpose better than another. If you try the various methods, you'll be better able to determine which of the methods might work more satisfactorily for you at different times. You're much less likely to forget a method if you've tried it.

Double 9-Patch Pinwheel, 1998, 60" x 60". Designed, pieced, and quilted by Harriet Hargrave.

Project

We've selected a Double 9 Pinwheel quilt for you to explore the half-square triangle techniques. If you make enough Pinwheel units (5) for one full Double 9 Pinwheel block with each of the techniques given, then by the time you've done all the techniques, you'll be ready to choose the one you prefer to complete this quilt. As you're experimenting with the techniques and making pinwheels, you can either leave them as single pinwheels until they are all made, or you can assemble the Double 9 Pinwheel blocks as you go along.

Double 9 Pinwheel

The project quilt (page 145) is constructed using only three fabrics. The background remains the same throughout, the same brown is used for all the pinwheels, and the border is made from a third fabric and the background fabric. The quilt is 60" square finished.

You will need:

3 yards background
$7/8$ yard brown for pinwheel
$1/3$ yard brown for border triangles

Project Quilt Option

Sharyn's rendition (at right) of this quilt is scrappy, making yardage requirements less exact. If you study the photo, you'll see that the background for all the pinwheels is the same.

You will need:

$1^1/2$ yards light background for triangles
Numerous scraps for colored half of triangles
12 different 18" long x $4^1/2$" wide strips of print for squares within Double 9-patch Pinwheel block
$1^1/4$ yards for sashing

Pinwheel Possibilities, 1998, 50" x 65". Designed, pieced, and quilted by Sharyn Craig.

Note Be prepared. Every technique might not yield units of exactly the same size. This is why you're trying every technique. One or two methods always work better for an individual while the rest seem to go awry. Just remember that this is not only a project, but also a learning process. If any of the triangles turn out too small to use, set them aside for use in a future project. If they turn out too large, they can always be trimmed to the size needed. At least you'll know what techniques to stay away from next time!

Half-Square Triangle Techniques

TECHNIQUE ONE:
Cutting and Sewing Individual Triangles

We will discuss three different methods for cutting and sewing individual triangles. The first method is to cut the fabric using a template. This template can be one you make or one you've purchased, such as Pandora's Box™, Marti Michell's templates, or any other brand of your choosing. Method Two will cut the fabric using a specialty triangle called Easy Angle™. Method Three allows you to cut the triangles from fabric by using a regular rotary ruler and the numbers that were discussed in Chapter 6 (page 61).

Position template to cut

METHOD ONE: TEMPLATES

In this quilt we are using 4" finished Pinwheel blocks that need a finished 2" half-square triangle. A pattern guide for the 2" half-square triangle is provided below. Feel free to trace this guide, following the methods from Chapter 5, and turn the paper pattern piece into a sturdy template for rotary cutting. Or perhaps you've purchased one of the commercial sets of templates and it has a 2" plexi-template that can be used. However you've accomplished this, you now have the 2" template and are ready to cut fabric.

The first decision to make is where you want the straight of grain to be on the finished triangle. This is determined by the position of the triangle in the block or quilt. The goal is to have straight grain along the outside edge of the block or quilt wherever possible. For our Double 9 Pinwheels, the straight grain is going to be on the two short sides of the triangle.

Once you've determined straight grain position, begin by measuring your template, edge to edge. That measurement is the size to cut a strip of fabric.

Measure template

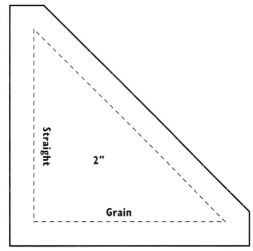

Straight

2"

Grain

To cut a strip to accommodate the 2" half-square triangle template, you need a strip 2½" wide. This strip size assumes that the template you're using has blunted tips like our provided pattern piece. If using a commercial template, you must measure it to determine the strip width you need.

Cut your strip. Leaving the strip folded in fourths, place the folded strip of fabric on the cutting mat as illustrated.

Selvages

Fold

Right-hand strip position

Left-hand strip position

Eliminate the selvage/fold edge of the strip. Position the triangle template on the strip and, with your rotary cutter, carefully cut along the edge of the template. Flip the template to the opposite edge of the strip and cut again.

Your template should fit the strip exactly. You should only have one edge, and if your template is "blunted," one blunt, per triangle to cut. Because our fabric strip is four layers deep, each time we cut, we actually have four single triangles. One Double 9 Pinwheel block needs five finished Pinwheel block units. Each Pinwheel block unit needs four dark and four light triangles, for a total of 20 dark and 20 light finished, 2" half-square triangles per Double 9 Pinwheel. Cutting around the template five times per light and per dark strip will give you enough pieces for one Double 9 Pinwheel block. One strip of light and one strip of dark will give you enough triangles to make six Pinwheel units.

To sew the individual triangles together, position one light and one dark triangle right sides together, carefully matching up the three edges. (If the fabric triangles don't match, you might want to re-check the fabric with your template.) Carefully sew the diagonal edge of the triangles. You can chain stitch the triangle pieces one after another. Clip the units apart and press the seam allowance toward the darker of the two triangles. You now have the triangle-square units and are ready to begin sewing the Pinwheel blocks together.

Chain stitch and clip apart

Press seam allowance toward dark

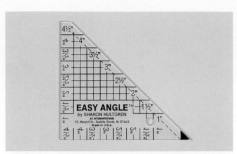

The Easy Angle ruler

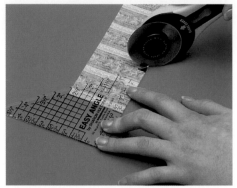

Position the Easy Angle for first cut

Flip over for second cut

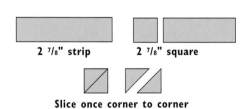

2 ⁷/₈" strip   2 ⁷/₈" square

Slice once corner to corner

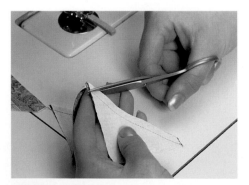

Clipping and blunting

METHOD TWO: EASY ANGLE™

Sharon Hultgren developed an extremely clever ruler for cutting accurate triangles from strips, called the Easy Angle.

To use this tool, cut strips of each fabric used in the triangle-square unit ¹/₂" wider than the finished square desired. For example, if you're making 2" triangle-square units, cut the strips 2¹/₂" wide.

Place one of each of the different fabric strips right sides together, being very careful to keep the long edges even. Lay them on your cutting mat. Position the Easy Angle to the left of the strip until the number that corresponds with the width of the fabric appears in the left corner. In this example, the fabric strips are being cut 2¹/₂", so the Easy Angle number will be 2¹/₂.

Once the ruler is aligned properly, cut the angle with a rotary cutter.

For the next cut, flip the Easy Angle as shown in the third photo to the left, lining up the tip. Line up the top edge of fabric with the corresponding number on the Easy Angle, which is 2¹/₂.

Continue down the length of the strip in this manner. You will need one strip of each color to cut enough triangles for one Double 9 Pinwheel block. Chain stitch the triangle sets together, being careful not to stretch the bias edge as you sew. Cut triangle units apart and press. Lay out and construct the Pinwheel blocks.

METHOD THREE:
CUTTING WITHOUT TEMPLATES

This next method allows you to cut individual triangles without using any kind of template or guide. Cutting without a guide means you must always use the math numbers for those pieces. To cut a half-square triangle and get straight grain on the two short sides of the triangle, take the size of the finished triangle, in this case 2", and to that number add ⁷/₈". (2 + ⁷/₈ = 2⁷/₈"). Cut a strip of light and a strip of dark at 2⁷/₈". One strip at a time, eliminate the selvage/fold edge from the folded strip of fabric. Next, measure over 2⁷/₈" and cut a 2⁷/₈" square. Turn the ruler corner to corner and slice once, creating two half-square triangles. One strip of light fabric and one of dark fabric, when cut this way, will give you enough triangles for 6 individual Pinwheel units.

To sew these pieces together, position a dark and light triangle right sides together, carefully matching all three edges. If the triangle pieces don't match, it's a bit more difficult to find where you're off, but you need to carefully check the sizes you've cut the fabric. If your triangle pieces are off now, then your triangle-square units will be off later. Sewing and assembly of these units follows the same procedure as previous individual triangle methods.

Remember: To cut individual half-square triangles without a template you take the size of the finished triangle and add ⁷/₈". Cut a strip, then a square, and slice once corner to corner. Two of these triangles, when sewn together, yield a square, with straight grain on the outside edges of the unit.

Tip   **Optional cutting method:** Place one light and one dark strip right sides together. Measure over 2⁷/₈" and slice. Carefully turn your ruler corner to corner on the resulting square and slice once. The resulting triangle pairs, when sewn together, will give you a finished 2" unit.

HINT: When cutting without a template, the fabric triangles have long skinny points. These are unlike the blunted points that we have when working with templates. These fabric "ears" need to be cut away to avoid shadowing through or affecting the quilting later. An easy way to cut those "ears" is to clip the chain apart and blunt the triangle in one stroke of the scissors. To determine which direction to blunt the triangle, clip the first unit, press the seam allowance, and clip the "ears" even with the edge of the square. Fold the triangle unit on the stitching once again and study the direction of the blunt in relationship to the sides of the original triangles. With that knowledge, you can clip and blunt in one stroke, eliminating a lot of time spent cutting later. (See photo at bottom left of page 148).

TECHNIQUE TWO:

Cutting Triangle-Square Units

A triangle-square unit is one that is already sewn together prior to cutting. There are several different methods for accomplishing this. Barbara Johannah and Ernest Haight independently developed the first of these methods in the early 1970s. This method is commonly referred to as "sheeting up," and requires that you draw the units on the fabric before sewing. A modern-day interpretation of this technique uses paper foundations with the grids marked on the paper. A third method we will explore is commonly called Bias Strip Piecing. This method starts with bias strips of fabric, but results in square units with straight grain on the outside edge of the finished unit. We will explore two different methods of Bias Strip Piecing, one method using a template, and the other a plexiruler designed for this purpose.

METHOD ONE: SHEETING

This is not a good method for scrap quilts where variety is key, but is wonderful when a great quantity of the same fabric combination is needed. Fat quarters (18" x 22") are typically used for the sheeting process. This is a very manageable piece of fabric to sew. Start by placing one fat quarter of each fabric, right sides together, with the light fabric on top, and press. This helps the fabrics to stick together. Draw a grid directly onto the light fabric. The math stays the same as before—use the finished size of the square plus $7/8$". In this case, draw $2^7/8$" squares. Every square you draw results in two finished units.

(1) Using a long ruler, draw a line parallel to and 1" from the selvage along the entire length of the fabric. Continue to draw parallel lines, each $2^7/8$" apart, across the fabric.

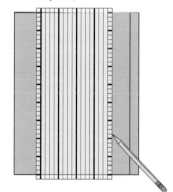

(1) Draw parallel lines for sheeting

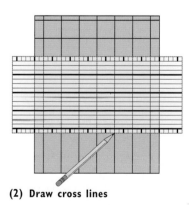

(2) Draw cross lines

(2) Now you're ready to draw the cross lines. Using the horizontal lines on the ruler, line them up exactly with the lines on the fabric.

The first line will be close to one edge. Again, continue drawing lines $2^7/8$" apart, intersecting with the previously drawn lines perfectly, until you're out of fabric.

(3) Next, draw diagonal lines in every other square, starting in one corner.

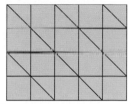

(3) Draw first set of diagonal lines

(4) Now, draw diagonal lines in the opposite direction in the remaining empty squares. Once all the lines are drawn, pin in every blank space.

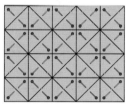

(4) Draw second set of diagonal lines

(5) Choose a foot that allows you to measure $1/4$" from the needle to the edge of the foot. You will begin the stitching as shown below. Align the right side of the presser foot exactly along the left side of the line. Stitch in one continuous line, using the same side of your presser foot all the time. You will be sewing beyond lines on the edge and turning corners. Continue sewing until all the diagonal lines have stitching on both sides.

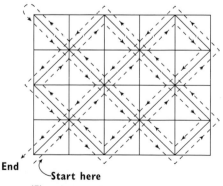

End   **Start here**

(5) Stitch in direction of arrows

(6) Using your rotary cutter and ruler, begin separating the rows by cutting on all the straight lines of one direction.

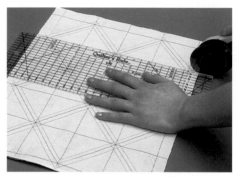

(6) Cut straight lines in one direction

(7) Continue by carefully aligning the ruler with the cut edges and cut on the remaining straight lines to cut the rows into squares.

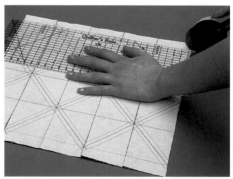

(7) Cut rows into squares

(8) The last cut is the diagonals.

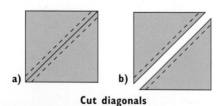

a)   b)

Cut diagonals

(9) Now you're ready to clip the ears and press the square open.

METHOD TWO: PAPER ROLLS AND SHEET TRIANGLES

Sheeting up has been made even easier by the advent of Triangles on a Roll™ and Half-Square Triangle Paper™. Both products come in various sizes and eliminate the need to draw lines on the fabric. The grid and a guide for sewing are printed on a sheet or roll of paper that is pinned to the fabric.

Determine how many units you need. Remember that each square yields two finished triangle-square units. Cut a length off the roll or a section from the sheet to accommodate the number needed. Layer two fabrics right sides together and press. Pin the grid paper on top through the fabrics. Place the pins in the blank areas so you won't sew over them.

Use 15 stitches per inch (about 1.5) so that the paper is perforated when stitched. This makes removing the paper easier in the end. Stitch, following the instructions for sheet triangles on page 149.

We're providing you with a paper guide so you can try the technique (see page 158). Photocopy this guide at 100% for the practice exercise.

If you liked working with the paper, you can find the previously mentioned products in your local quilt shop or mail-order catalog.

METHOD THREE: BIAS STRIP PIECING

Start with a 9" square of both the light and dark fabrics. Position the two pieces of fabric right sides together and press. For our 4" pinwheels, cut bias strips 2½" wide. One 9" square will give you 16 triangle-square units.

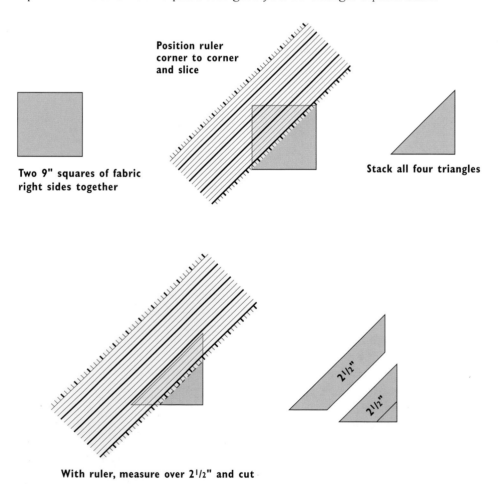

Position ruler corner to corner and slice

Two 9" squares of fabric right sides together

Stack all four triangles

With ruler, measure over 2½" and cut

2½"
2½"

The chart provided will help determine the width of strips needed for other sizes.

Bias Strip Piecing Sizes for Half-Square Triangles		
Finished Half-Square Size	Strip Width of Bias to Cut	Cut Size of Bias Square (Ruler Method)
1"	1³/₄"	1"
1¹/₂"	2¹/₄"	1¹/₂"
2"	2¹/₂"	2"
2¹/₂"	2³/₄"	2¹/₂"
3"	3¹/₄"	3"
3¹/₂"	3¹/₂"	3¹/₂"
4"	4"	4"

Option One: Templates

Seam the strips of bias together down both long edges. Position the triangle template (be sure to use the template provided on page 147) on the sewn edge so that the blunt tips of the triangle intersect the stitching exactly.

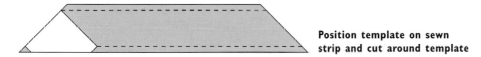

Position template on sewn strip and cut around template

Carefully cut around the template with your rotary cutter. Position the template on the opposite edge and cut. Flip the triangle from edge to edge, cutting the number of triangle-square units needed.

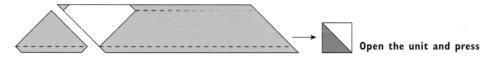

Open the unit and press

Open the unit, popping out the stitching at the point if necessary. Press the seam allowance toward the darker of the two fabrics.

Option Two: Bias Square™ Rulers

Cut the strips of bias the same way as in Method One. This time, seam the strips together down the long edge. Press the seam allowance. For squares that finish 1³/₄" or smaller, it's recommended that you press the seam allowance open. For squares larger than that, press the seams toward the darker fabric.

Using a Bias Square and rotary cutter, begin at the lowest points, as shown, and cut squares that are slightly larger than desired. Turn cut unit around and trim to exact size needed. Continue cutting the number of units you need.

It is possible to seam several sets of bias strips together before cutting units out.

This method of cutting results in triangle pieces left over along the outside edges of the strips. These triangular pieces can be cut into individual triangles with a template or by using one of the triangle ruler guides.

Using a Bias Square Ruler

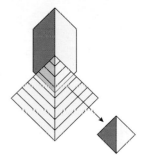

Bias squares cut with Bias Square ruler

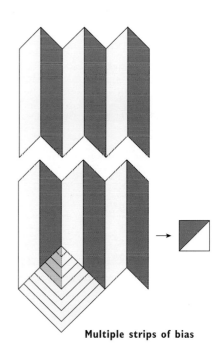

Multiple strips of bias

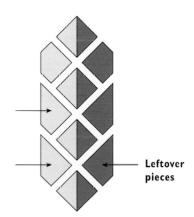

Leftover pieces

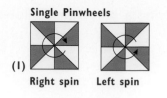

Single Pinwheels

(1)

Right spin   **Left spin**

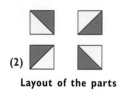

(2)

Layout of the parts

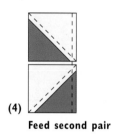

First pair

(3)   ← **Stop short**

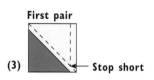

(4)

Feed second pair

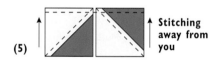

(5)   ↑ **Stitching away from you**

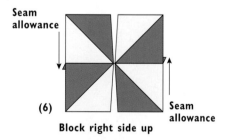

Seam allowance

(6)   **Seam allowance**

Block right side up

Sew
↓

Seam allowance ↑

(7)

Piecing a Pinwheel

(1) Once the four sub-units are made, your next step will be to piece the Pinwheel block. Pinwheel blocks are directional and can spin right or left depending on how you lay out the sub-units.

(2) If it's important to you that the pinwheels all spin in the same direction, be very careful during layout. There is not a right and wrong decision to be made as to the same spin or both spins in the same quilt, but you need to realize that this is a part of the block.

(3) Pick up the top right-hand unit and position it on top of the left-hand unit, carefully matching up the right-hand edge and making sure that the diagonal seams of both butt accurately. Because we directionally pressed the seam allowances toward the dark triangles, you'll now be able to alternate and butt up these seam edges. Sew the right-hand edge, stopping just short of the end of the two pieces. Stopping short on the first pair helps in feeding the second pair snug. You want to avoid extra stitches, which create a gap between units.

(4) Pick up the bottom right-hand unit and position it on top of the bottom left-hand unit, again alternating and butting the seam allowances between the triangles. Feed this second pair of sub-units as close together to the first unit as you can.

(5) When you remove the sewn units from the sewing machine, do not clip the thread that connects the two units. This thread can, for some quilters, actually replace the need to pin when lining up the units. The snugger these two units are with this thread hinge (thread pin), the better chance you'll have to make the points come out perfectly without adding a straight pin. Position the sewn units as shown, with the previously stitched seam pointing away from you:

(6) Unfold the units and directionally guide the seam allowance for the unit on the right away from you, and the seam allowance for the unit on the left toward you.

(7) Next, lay the units on top of one another, with the thread "pin" carefully connecting the two units. The seam allowance of the top unit is now heading toward the sewing machine while you sew. Positioning the seam allowance this way will allow the sewing machine action to "seat" the units together as the alternating seam allowances butt snugly together.

As you stitch the point, also make sure that the diagonal seams, as well as the seam connecting the joined units, butt and align. If you check that these all alternate and butt together, your chances of getting a square finished block with perfectly matched points are much better.

Many quilters have trouble matching triangle points in the middle of the pinwheel. To match the points, it's important to have an approximate ¼" seam allowance beyond the point. If the thread hinge (thread pin) didn't give you nice points in the center, try placing a pin in the point at the cross seam of both units. If possible, have the point on top and sew one thread beyond the point. (This will make a slightly smaller seam allowance.)

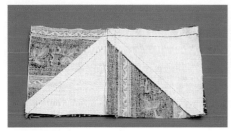

Matching points

Remove the unit from the machine and clip the thread pin that held the units during this last stitching. Clipping the thread will allow you to "fan" the seam allowances, as we did for the 4-patches in Chapter 11 (see page 107). Fanning the seam allowances in the center will reduce the bulk at that central intersection.

HINT: Once you get comfortable with piecing pinwheels, you can start to streamline the piecing process by stacking several blocks, one on top of another, for construction. If you stack the sub-units one on top of another, be consistent in positioning top right on top of top left, followed immediately by bottom right on top of bottom left. Next, go back to the top: top right on top left, bottom right on bottom left, and so forth. When you remove the blocks from the machine, clip the blocks apart, but do not clip the thread pin holding the four units of each block.

Finish Your Quilt

You're now ready to finish your quilt top. Our Double 9 Pinwheel project quilt is a simple straight set with solid cream alternating blocks. The Double 9 Pinwheel blocks take five Pinwheels and four solid squares per block. Follow the guidelines in Chapter 8 (page 86) to finish constructing this quilt top.

By now you may be ready to play with other setting options. Feel free to play and experiment. For example, what if your Double 9 Pinwheels were sashed instead of alternating with large solid squares? That's what Sharyn did with her Pinwheel blocks in *Pinwheel Possibilities*. What other ideas can you come up with?

Before we move into quarter-square triangles, you might enjoy looking at some other quilts that were also made with half-square triangles.

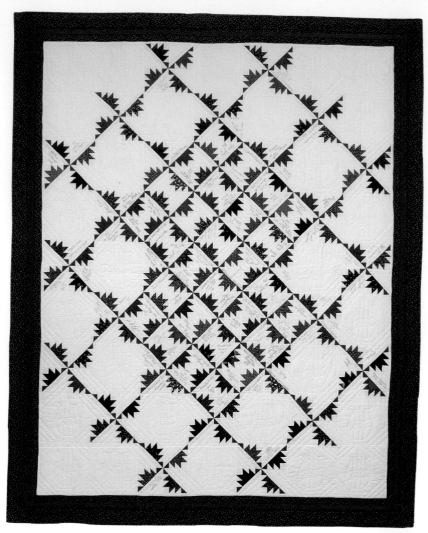

Sisterhood, 1993, 65" x 81".
This quilt is based on the Delectable
Mountains block. Designed, pieced,
and hand quilted by Sharyn Craig
for her daughter, Amy.

Pilgrim's Progress, 1994, 69" x 69". Design based
on combining a pieced triangle unit and a solid
fabric unit to make the half-square block. Designed,
pieced, and quilted by Harriet Hargrave.

Northwind, 1996, 47" x 58¹/₂". The blocks are set into a Pinwheel formation to create the diagonal lines of the quilt. Pieced by Sharyn Craig. Quilted by Joanie Keith.

Fox and Geese, 1996, 65" x 77". Designed, pieced, and quilted by Christine Husak.

London Square, 1992, 70" x 85".
Designed and pieced by Harriet
Hargrave. Quilted by Barbara Trumbo.

Terrific Triangles #1, 1986, 40" x 40".
The blocks were initially set into a Barn
Raising formation, then the corners
were playfully rearranged to create the
overall medallion look. Designed and
pieced by Sharyn Craig. Hand quilted
by Sandy Andersen.

2" finished block

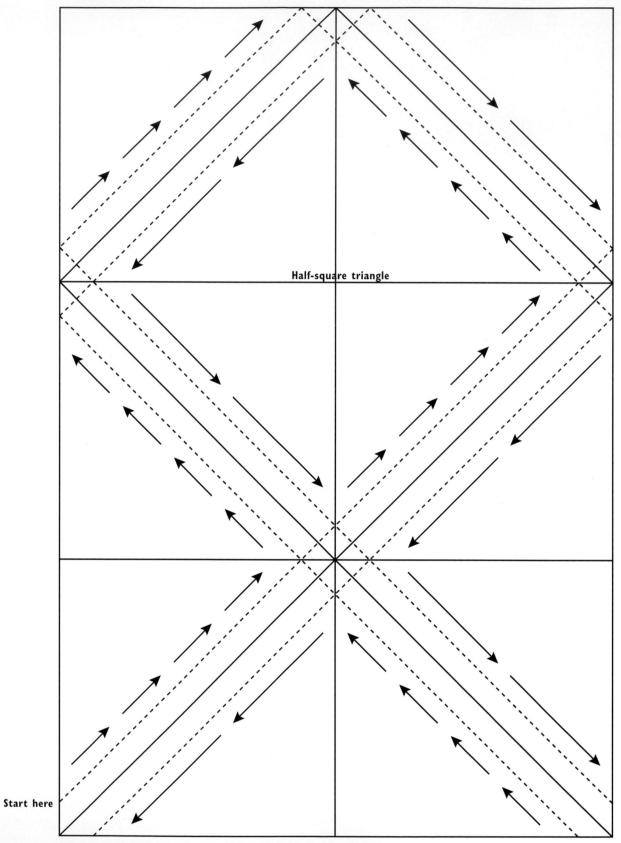

Half-square triangle

Start here

Cut fabric 6" wide by length to obtain desired number of blocks.
Layer two fabrics right sides together, sew following arrows, rotary cut all solid lines, and tear away paper.
Permission to photocopy graciously granted by Anne Dutton, creator of Triangles on a Roll.

Project
Quarter-Square Triangles

Our project quilt for the quarter-square triangle units is the blue-and-white quilt named *Yankee Puzzle*. Harriet's quilt measures 56" x 56".

Yankee Puzzle, 1997, 56" x 56". Designed, pieced, and quilted by Harriet Hargrave.

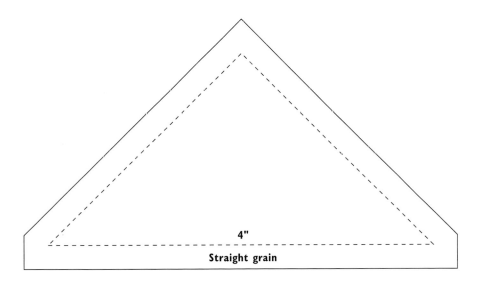

4"

Straight grain

You will need:
A total of 1¼ yards of assorted light, medium, and dark blues
1¼ yards of background for the triangle units
1½ yards of light shirting for the alternate blocks

Below is an illustration of one block. Each block in the quilt is an 8" square finished. One block is made from four quarter-square triangle units. Each 8" block uses eight assorted blue triangles and eight light triangles.

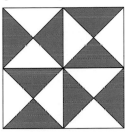

Yankee Puzzle

TECHNIQUE ONE:
Cutting and Sewing Individual Triangles

METHOD ONE: TEMPLATES
Before beginning, ask yourself where the straight of grain needs to be positioned in order to give the best result to your block. Normally, in a quarter-square triangle, the straight grain is on the long edge of the piece. There may be the occasional situation that the straight of grain needs to be on the short sides instead. Once you've made the determination of grain placement, then measure your template, edge to edge. The resulting measurement is the size you need to cut the strip of fabric.

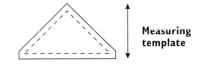

Measuring template

Our finished triangle size is 4". If you measure the 4" template you'll see you need a strip 2⅝". Cut strips 2⅝" wide. Trim off the selvage/fold edge of the fabric.

TRIANGLES   **159**

Position the triangle template on the strip and cut carefully along the edge of the template with your rotary cutter. Flip the triangle template to the opposite edge of the strip and cut. Your template should fit the strip exactly. You'll have only one edge and, if the template is "blunted," two blunts per triangle to cut. If our fabric strip is four layers, every time you cut around the template you'll have four fabric triangle pieces.

Cutting quarter-square triangles with template

Once you've cut the required number of triangles, you'll be ready to sew them together. Quarter-square triangles are directional units, and as such, they can easily be sewn together on the wrong edge. Lay the pieces out to form the unit, then carefully position the triangle on the right on top of the triangle on the left and sew the right-hand edge of the pieces. If you lay the pieces out correctly and always position right on top of left, you'll always get the right position.

For sewing this unit: Since the unit we are making is structured as opposing dark and light triangles, lay the unit out as shown.

Quarter square triangle layout

Sew the first set from "point to square corner," then immediately chain the second unit from "square corner to point." Repeat.

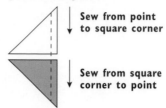

Clip the units apart between the "points," leaving the square corners connected.

Press the seam allowances toward the darker triangles. Fold the two halves together (the thread pin secures the units, eliminating the need for a straight pin). Sew from point to point. Chain remaining units the same way. Clip units apart. Clip the original thread pin.

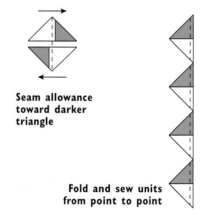

Fan the seam allowances as described in Chapter 11 (page 107). The same technique will work here and will reduce the bulk at that intersection. Press carefully. If you can develop this system of sewing the quarter-square triangles, you won't sew any of them backwards.

METHOD TWO:
CUTTING WITHOUT TEMPLATES
The "magic" number you need to remember when cutting quarter-square triangles is $1\frac{1}{4}$". When you know your finished size of the long edge of the triangle, take that number and add $1\frac{1}{4}$". Cut a strip, then a square, and slice twice corner to corner. Our project quilt uses 4" quarter-square triangles. $4" + 1\frac{1}{4}" = 5\frac{1}{4}"$. Cut a strip at $5\frac{1}{4}"$. Cut a square $5\frac{1}{4}"$. Slice the square twice corner to corner.

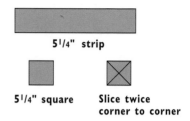

The square, made by sewing together four of these triangles, will be 4" finished. These triangles can be sewn together using the same system as the individual triangles we cut using templates. You will need to blunt the points after sewing. You can clip and blunt in one scissors stroke using the same hint taught under half-square triangles (page 149).

Draw line on half square triangle

Stitch squares together

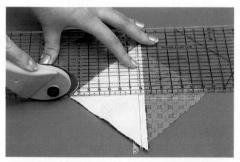
Cut on line

Four different fabrics needed

TECHNIQUE TWO:
Sheeting and Triangle Paper

A triangle-square unit is one that is sewn together prior to cutting. This method for quarter-square units requires two steps.

When marking the grid on the fabric, you need to add $1^1/2$" to the finished size instead of $1^1/4$". This accommodates the additional seam allowance that will be taken from each triangle-square unit. Draw the lines as in the instructions for sheeting (page 149) using the new measurement. Continue with the sewing and cutting.

Once the triangle-square unit seam allowances are pressed to the dark side, turn half of them over to the wrong side and draw a line diagonally across the seam, corner to corner.

Next, place two triangle-square units on top of one another (one marked, one unmarked) with the diagonal line on top. Match the seams—they will interlock very easily here. Pin if necessary and stitch $1/4$" on each side of the marked line. This can be accomplished by chain sewing all the squares on one side at once, then turning them around and stitching the other side.

Cut on the line between the stitching and press the seam. Clip any ears and measure for accuracy.

When you need a four-color quarter-square triangle unit, make triangle-squares from different combinations of fabrics. When putting two squares together, just make sure that all four fabrics are different.

The commercially available triangle rolls and papers make this even easier. The rolls are marked with quarter-square triangles of a certain size. The thinking has been done for you already, as the grid is printed with the formula of finished size plus $1^1/2$". Just make sure you read the label and get the type of triangle unit you want. The following quilts use quarter-square triangles.

Primitive Sawtooth Star, 1997, 57" x 80". The center square is the quarter-square triangle unit.
Designed, pieced, and quilted by Mary Radke.

Ohio Stars, 1998, 59" x 59". Designed and pieced by Sharyn Craig. Quilted by Joanie Keith.

Ohio Stars, 1997, 37" x 37". Designed and pieced by Sharyn Craig. Quilted by Joanie Keith.

Flying Geese

This chapter is devoted to three different techniques of four different methods for making the traditional Flying Geese units. One "goose" is made up of three triangles, which when sewn together, make a rectangle whose width is twice the size of the short height.

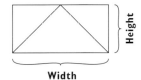

Height

Width

Project Our project quilt, *Migration*, will allow you the opportunity to experiment with each method so you'll have choices for the future.

Migration has four rows of 18 geese each. If you make each row with a different technique, you will be able to decide which method you liked best. Geese are incredibly versatile little units. We're hoping that after you complete the project quilt, you might then be interested in doing one of the variations pictured in this chapter. Or perhaps you'll simply use the methods explored to create some of the geese variation blocks provided at the end of the chapter. Whatever the outcome, it's time to play!

Our project quilt fabric recipe calls for three fabrics: one light, one dark, and one medium value. Our geese units are each made with the light yellow for the large triangle,

Migration, 1998, 33" x 39". Pieced by Sharyn Craig. Quilted by Phyllis Reddish.

dark green for the flanking triangles, and red for the separating strips. You certainly can make your quilt any colors you like. You can also work scrappy if you prefer.

Migration has been done with a 1½" x 3" finished goose. There are a total of 72 geese. The finished size, with borders, is 33" x 39".

You will need:
Light (yellow) ¹/₂ yard
Medium (red) 1¹/₄ yards
Dark (green) 1 yard

 Yardage recommendations are generous (dark yardage based on squares and rectangles technique). The medium yardage allows enough for binding the edge.

If you want a bigger quilt, you can make bigger geese—perhaps a 2" x 4" finished goose. (Remember that the basic single goose has a width that is twice the height.) You can add more rows of geese or more geese to each row of the quilt if you wish. **The multiplying factors for calculating the quilt size is 11 across by 26 down.**
Example:
11 x width of one goose = finished width of quilt
26 x height of one goose = finished length of quilt
If you add additional rows of geese to the desired quilt, increase the "across" multiplier by 2.
Example:
5 row quilt = 13 x width of one goose
Increasing from 18 to 24 geese per row will add 6 to the "down" number.
Example:
24 geese = 32 x height of one goose
Feel free to experiment with other numbers

Project Worksheet:
Migration calls for 4 rows of 18 geese each
3 separation sashing strips
(each strip = width of 1 goose)
Example of Outer Borders
1¹/₂", 3", 1¹/₂" for project quilt.
These are finished sizes.
Border 1—height of one goose
Border 2—width of one goose
Border 3—height of one goose

Migration				
Finished Size	Quilt Size	Yardage Recommended		
		Dark	Medium	Light
1¹/₂" x 3"	33" x 39"	1	1	¹/₂
2" x 4"	44" x 52"	1¹/₂	1¹/₈	⁵/₈
2¹/₂" x 5"	56" x 65"	2¹/₄	1¹/₂	³/₄

TECHNIQUE ONE:
Squares and Rectangles

Cut two 2" strips of your dark value fabric designated for small triangles into 2" squares. To make the 18 geese units for one row, you need a total of 36 2" dark squares, which will become the small triangles. Cut two strips of the light value print at 2". Next, cut eighteen 2" x 3¹/₂" rectangles, which will become the larger triangles.

(1) Position a dark square on one end of the rectangle and sew corner to corner across the square.

(2) Fold the square in half toward the corner and press.

(3) Position a second dark square at the opposite end of the rectangle and sew diagonally as illustrated. Fold the square toward the corner and press.

(1) (2) (3)

(4) Trimming the excess fabric from under the top dark triangle is optional. Some quilters like to remove the bulk, while others feel that it gives stability and increases accuracy.

Sewing Corner to Corner

For some, it's easy to "eyeball" the diagonal of the square while sewing corner to corner. For others, the sewn line has a tendency to curve. You may prefer to take the time to draw a line lightly from corner to corner on the square, then sew on the line. Another way to find the diagonal is to fold the square corner to corner and lightly crease the diagonal line before sewing. Sharyn likes to put a tape guide on the bed of the sewing machine, which allows her to line up the corner of the square during sewing. To create this tape guide, raise the presser foot and lower the needle. Position a ruler up to the edge of the needle as shown in photo.

Place tape along edge of ruler

Drop the presser foot to hold the ruler in place. Take a piece of ¹/₄" masking tape and position it at the edge of the ruler up to, but not interfering with, the feed dog of the machine and coming toward you approximately 3".

Now when you sew corner to corner on the square, you'll line up the corner of the square with the left edge of the tape. Keep the corner of the square along the left edge of the tape and sew. This works because the left edge of the tape is in direct line with the needle.

Line up corner of square with left edge of tape

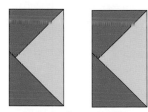

Tip There is a product called The Angler™ available at quilt shops that you can buy and use to assist you in sewing straight seams.

Make your eighteen individual geese units this way. Press carefully. Next you need to join them together. Lay the units out as illustrated, with nine geese in each stack.

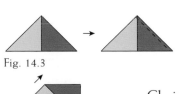

Layout of geese units

Starting from the right, position the goose on the right on top of the goose on the left, right sides together. You will be sewing the right-hand edge. When you position the geese (Figure 14.1) for sewing, you'll be able to see the "x" of stitches on the underneath side of the unit. You are aiming for that "x" when sewing the geese together, but remember to sew just beyond (short of) the actual middle of the "x" in order to not cut off the points.

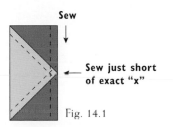

Sew

Sew just short of exact "x"

Fig. 14.1

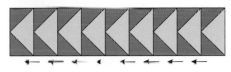

Fig. 14.2   Seam allowance

If you lay the geese out in the opposite direction, you can't see the "x" and run the risk of cutting off the points as you sew.

First, make units of two geese each. Set aside one 2-geese unit. Then join the 2-geese units together to make 4-geese units, then 4's into 8's, 8's into 16. Take the last remaining unit of two and add it to complete your row of 18. Directionally press the seam allowances as shown in Figure 14.2.

TECHNIQUE TWO:
Cutting and Piecing Individual Triangles

The large triangle is a quarter-square triangle. The little triangles are half-square triangles. For our project quilt, the large triangles are 3" quarter-square triangles. The little ones are 1½" half-square triangles. We're giving you two different methods for this technique, one cutting the pieces with templates, one cutting the triangles without templates. It is recommended that you make one row of 18 geese each way.

METHOD ONE:
CUTTING WITHOUT TEMPLATES
Cut 2⅜" strips of your dark fabric. Then cut into 2⅜" squares, and slice once corner to corner. For the eighteen geese units, you need a total of thirty-six 2⅜" triangles, so you'll cut two strips at 2⅜".

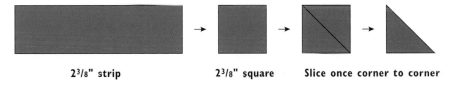

2³/₈" strip   2³/₈" square   Slice once corner to corner

For the light triangles, begin by cutting 4¼" light strips. Cut 4¼" squares. Slice each square twice corner to corner. You need a total of 18 triangles for our 18 geese. (5 squares = 20 triangles).

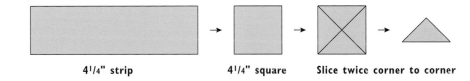

4¹/₄" strip   4¹/₄" square   Slice twice corner to corner

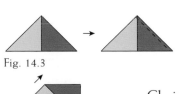

Fig. 14.3

Seam allowance

To sew the triangles together, begin by positioning a small triangle right sides together with a large triangle. Sew as shown in Figure 14.3.

Chain all large triangles with a small triangle in this fashion. Clip apart. Press seam allowance toward the little triangle.

Hint: Remember the clipping and blunting tip presented in Chapter 13 (page 149), this can save you time later.

Add the second small triangle to each unit as illustrated:
Chain all units. Clip apart. Press. Join individual geese together in the same manner as described in Technique One (page 166).

METHOD TWO:
CUTTING WITH TEMPLATES
You will need a 3" quarter-square triangle template and a 1½" half-square triangle template. You can use our pattern pieces to create your own templates, draft your own, or use ones from a commercial set.

Straight grain on the 3" quarter-square triangle will be on the long edge. Straight grain on the 1½" half-square triangle will be on the two short sides. From your dark value fabric, cut a 2" strip. Position the template and cut as described on page 160. From your light value fabrics, cut a 2⅛" strip. Position template and repeat process. You need a total of 36 dark-value, small triangles and 18 light-value, large triangles. Sew the triangles together as described on page 167.

Note We've provided a paper foundation pattern that can be reproduced at 100% to use for this technique. There are commercially printed papers available in various sizes that can also be used.

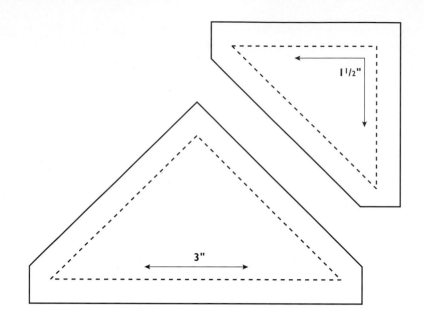

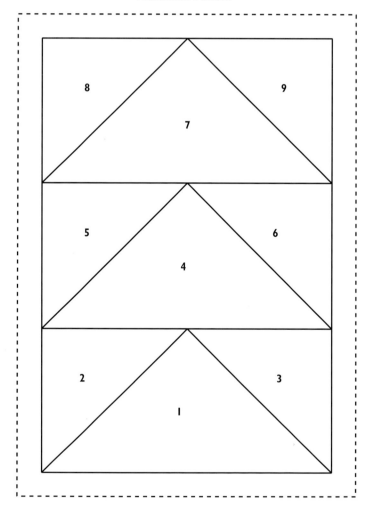

Foundation Pattern

TECHNIQUE THREE:
Paper Foundation

If you liked the foundation methods from Chapter 13 (page 150), you may really like the foundation method for making the Flying Geese units. To make the paper foundation a workable size, we suggest a strip of three geese at a time. The 3 geese unit is the base of several of our other inspiration quilts, so working in 3's definitely has merit.

To create your paper foundation, take a piece of ¼" grid graph paper and draw a rectangle 3" x 4½". Next, divide the rectangle into three equal 1½" sections.

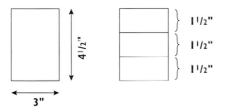

Divide the 1½" sections into triangles as shown. Add a ¼" seam allowance around the outside edge of the original rectangle.

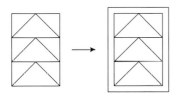

Add ¼" seam allowance

The piecing order will begin from the bottom large triangle and go "center, left, right." Continue to the second goose, "center, left, right," as shown to the right.

Piecing order

It can be quite helpful to precut fabric for the areas instead of guessing what size and shape is necessary. Recommended pieces to cut are 2½" squares of dark fabric sliced once for the small triangles, and 4½" squares

Position fabric to paper foundation

**Position first piece to be stitched.
Stitch and open.**

of light value fabric, sliced twice for the large triangles. You need a total of 36 small dark triangles and 18 large light triangles.

Experiment with different needle sizes as well as different paper types and weights for the combination that tears away most easily after stitching. (There are now several different plain papers packaged expressly for creating your own paper piecing patterns available at quilt shops). Refer to page 39 for needle and thread recommendations.

You'll be placing the fabric on the blank side of the paper and sewing on the lines on the opposite side. A tiny dot of glue stick can help hold fabric #1 in position. Position fabric triangle #2. Holding the paper up to a light can be helpful to make sure the fabric is positioned correctly and that at least ¼" of fabric extends beyond the stitching line on all sides.

Flip the paper foundation over to the printed side with the lines and stitch on the line between #1 and #2. Open the little triangle so that it covers paper triangle #2 and finger-press carefully. Position fabric triangle #3 on the other side of #1, matching raw edges. Sew. Open. Finger-press. Continue in this manner until the foundation is covered. ***See page 170 for a slick trick that our friend Carol Doak has allowed us to share with you.***

Press the entire unit while paper is still in position. Trim around the outside edge of the foundation on the cutting line. Continue making a total of 6 units this way for one row of our project quilt. Join the 3 geese units together to make one row of 18 geese. Press carefully. Remove paper.

> *Tip* If you have access to a photocopy machine that can reproduce at 100%, you can copy the master foundation pattern as many times as you need instead of drawing it each time. Keep the original intact to be used as your copy "master." Even machines that can reproduce at 100% can distort, so check copies against the master.

Assembling Project Quilt

To complete the assembly of our project quilt, lay out the geese rows as shown in the photo on page 165. The separating spacer strips are cut 3½" x 27½" (or the actual length of your sewn rows). Sew the geese rows together with the strips. The framing borders for this quilt were strips cut 2" from a medium (red) and 3½" from a dark (green). Attach borders.

Inspiration Quilts and "What If?" Ideas

Once you learn how much fun it is to make the geese units, you'll certainly want to make many more quilts. Pictured here are a few more quilts to get your creative juices flowing. There are endless possibilities for how you can arrange the geese to give totally different designs. Don't be afraid to play. You may want to browse through books that feature antique quilts for additional ideas. Harriet has made two quilts using geese in different ways. *Homeward Flight* uses geese as the sashings. Notice that the sashing between the blocks is a different size than the sashing between the rows.

Northern Flight, is a multiple-piece goose unit. Because of the size of the pieces, Harriet decided to paper piece this one as well. Foundation patterns for these two quilts can be found on pages 172 and 173.

CARD TRICK

Place an index card on the next sewing line (the line between #1 and #2). Fold the paper back along the edge of the card to expose the excess fabric beyond the seam line. Place the ¼" line of your rotary ruler on the fold and trim the excess fabric ¼" from the fold. This card not only allows you to trim the previous fabric(s) ¼" from the next seam line, but also allows you to align the next piece of fabric ¼" from this seam line. Carol Doak's "card trick" is from her book *Show Me How To Paper Piece*, reprinted with permission of Carol Doak and That Patchwork Place/Martingale & Company.

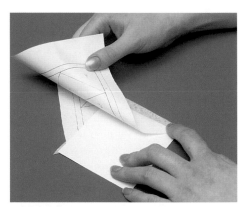

Fold back paper along edge of card

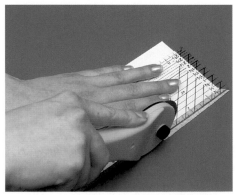

Position ruler and cut ¼" seam allowance

Homeward Flight, 1997, 35" x 40". Inspired by an antique quilt top in Harriet's collection. Pieced and quilted by Harriet Hargrave.

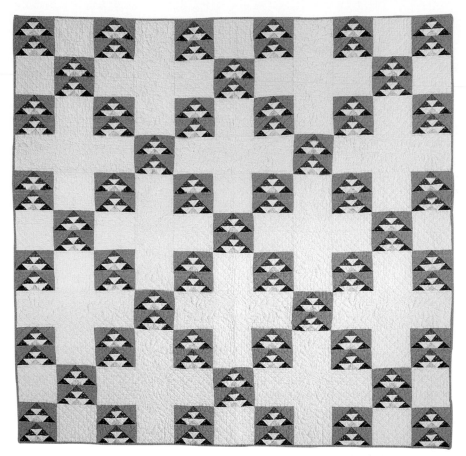

Northern Flight, 1997, 56" x 56".
Designed, pieced, and quilted by
Harriet Hargrave.

Geese Tracks, 1998, 55¹/₂" x 55¹/₂".
Pieced by Sharyn Craig. Quilted
by Joanie Keith.

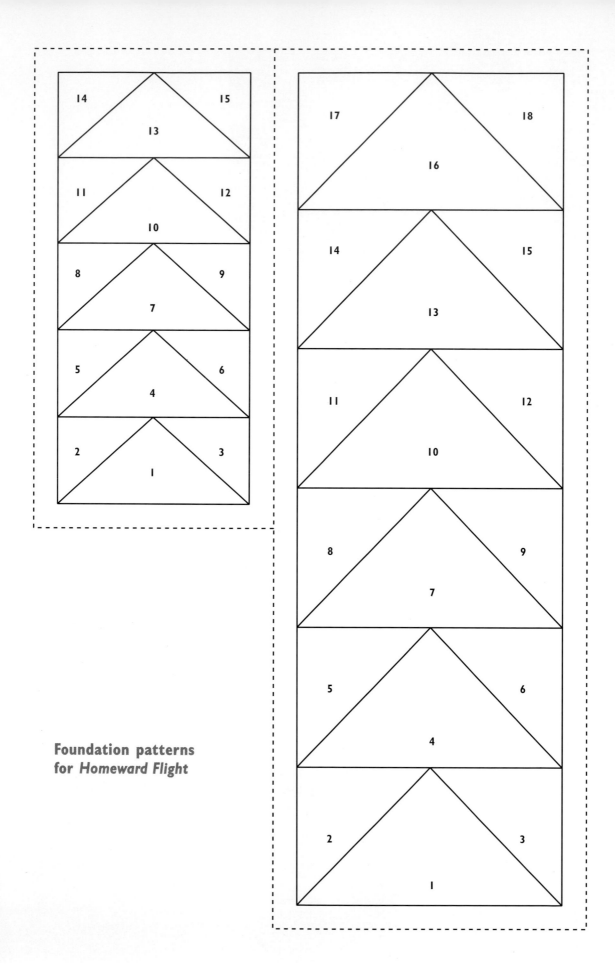

Foundation patterns for *Homeward Flight*

Foundation patterns for *Northern Flight*

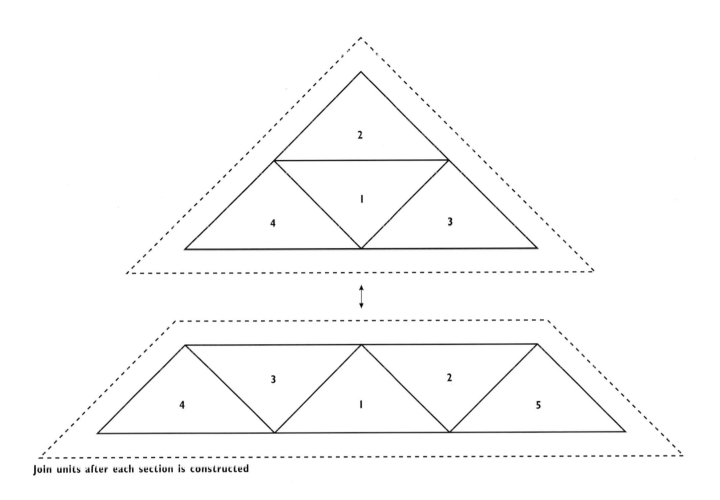

Join units after each section is constructed

A-Maze-ing Geese, 1994, 46" x 57". A block called Ribbon was used to create the pieced border for the quilt. Designed, pieced, and quilted by Sharyn Craig.

Half Log Cabin, 35" x 48". This quilt is set in Fields and Furrows with a Flying Geese border. Designed and pieced by Sharyn Craig. Quilted by Stephanie Cornet.

THESE BLOCKS ARE MADE WITH LOTS OF "GEESE!"

In addition to a number of all-over geese-style quilts, there are an amazing number of traditional pieced blocks that have geese units in them. We are showing some here just to get your attention. Once you've determined the method you like to work with to produce the geese, then when you see a particular block you like that has geese as an integral portion of the block, you can decide how to construct the block accordingly.

The way you determine to color the block can directly impact on your decision as to method. But now you have choices. You don't have to rely on someone else's recipe. You are in control!

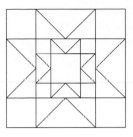

Rising Star

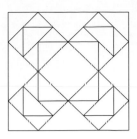

Rambler

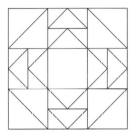

Cut the Corners

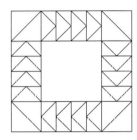

Fox and Geese

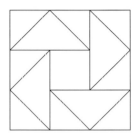

Ribbon

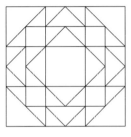

Aunt Sukey's Choice

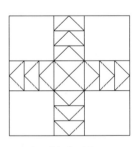

Jacob's Ladder

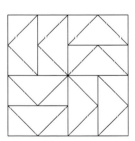

Dutchman's Puzzle

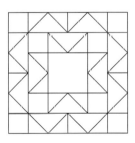

Eddystone Light

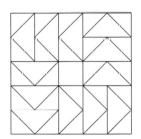

Flying Geese

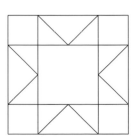

Sawtooth Star

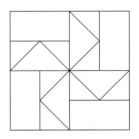

Louisiana

Set-In Piecing

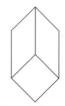

Many quilters avoid set-in piecing (sometimes called Y-seaming) because it appears too hard to do. They think in order to create the 3-seam unit it must be "hand pieced" or, perhaps because no technique they have tried has worked for them, they have been left with puckers, pleats, and pieces that don't lay flat. Set-in piecing is not hard, and it can successfully be done on the sewing machine. If you follow the procedure presented here, then practice it several times, we guarantee you'll be rewarded with flat blocks and nice corners at the Y-seam intersections.

Basic Y-Seam Construction

Your basic Y-seam is made up of three different pieces that come together to create a "Y." Some examples are shown as follows.

Diamonds to half-square triangle

Parallelograms to half-square triangle

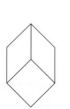

Diamonds to square

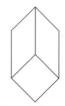

Parallelograms to square

To sew the Y-seam, lay the fabric pieces to the left of your sewing machine so that the "Y" you see is upside down.

Units laid out to left of sewing machine

A helpful hint when doing set-in piecing is to use either a straight stitch foot or an open-toed appliqué foot on your machine. What you want is a foot that has nothing impeding your vision. When there is space between the toes, it's much easier to see the previous stitching line when it is time to "lock" the stitches.

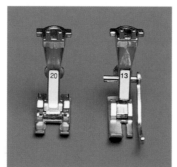

Open-toed foot and straight stitch foot

Sew the seams in the numbered order

You will put the middle piece (this is the one with the 90° angle; you can remember it as the one with a "square corner") on top of the piece to its left, and sew end to end. Finger-press seam allowance as shown.

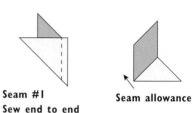

Seam #1 Sew end to end   **Seam allowance**

Position seam #2 pieces together, placing the piece on the right on top of the piece on the left, then flipping the pieces over so that the piece with the 90° angle (square corner) is on top as you sew. You will begin sewing at the outer point and stop sewing at the previous stitching line. You must lock the stitches at this point. Some machines have a locking stitch. On other machines, you must backstitch to lock the stitches. It is important to lock the stitches because we do not cross over the stitching line with Y-seaming. If you do not lock at this point, then the stitching is in danger of pulling out.

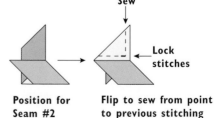

Position for Seam #2   **Flip to sew from point to previous stitching**

LeMoyne Star, 1998, 51" x 51". Pieced and quilted by Sharyn Craig.

Bring the remaining two edges together and sew from point to previous stitching line, locking stitches at both ends of the seam.

Sew from point to previous stitches

Lock stitches

Finger-press the seam allowance from the right side of the unit toward the piece on the right, as you look at the "Y" upside down.

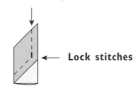

Arrows indicate seam allowance direction

(Unit is right side up)

Project Lots of blocks contain some set-in piecing (see the example blocks at the end of the chapter, page 180), but the LeMoyne Star is all Ys. It is for this reason that we chose the *LeMoyne Star* as our project quilt for this chapter.

Our project quilt has twenty-five 6" LeMoyne Stars and twenty-four solid squares. The blocks are set in an alternating pattern with 7 blocks across and 7 down. Quilt size prior to bordering is 42" square. An additional 6" finished border in the same fabric as the alternating squares adds a nice finishing touch. One benefit of this alternating set is that you reduce the number of star blocks needed.

If you cut and piece four LeMoyne Star blocks, you'll be well on your way to becoming an expert at set-in piecing. We recommend that you select three fabrics to practice with: one for the background and two different fabrics for the diamonds that create the star. From the practice fabric, cut out enough background squares and triangles for four blocks. Do the same with the diamonds. After you cut and piece four blocks, you can decide whether

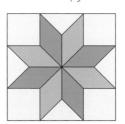

LeMoyne Star

you want to go on with making more of these 6" LeMoyne Star blocks, or if you want to change the fabric recipe.

Cutting the LeMoyne Star pieces out can be done either with or without templates. For our project exercise, we are making 6" finished LeMoyne Stars. The pattern pieces you need are a finished $1^{3}/_{4}$" square, half-square triangle, and diamond. Pattern pieces are provided for these templates, or you can draft your own following the instructions in Chapter 5 (page 51). Note the grainline arrows indicated on each pattern piece. Proper grainline is crucial if the stars are to lay flat. If you prefer to cut your fabric pieces out without templates, you can follow the rotary cutting guide numbers printed on each pattern piece in parentheses. For instructions on cutting the pieces without templates, see Chapter 6 (page 61).

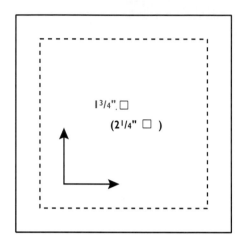

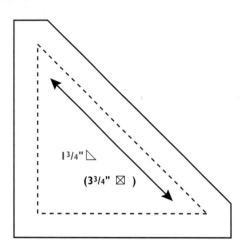

$1^{3}/_{4}$", □
($2^{1}/_{4}$" □)

$1^{3}/_{4}$" ◺
($3^{3}/_{4}$" ⊠)

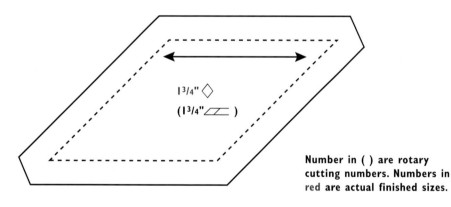

$1^{3}/_{4}$" ◇
($1^{3}/_{4}$" ▱)

Number in ( ) are rotary cutting numbers. Numbers in red are actual finished sizes.

Note These numbers include seam allowances and take proper grainline into consideration.

YARDAGE RECOMMENDATIONS

All the stars in our quilt are scrappy, with many different backgrounds and fabrics in the diamonds that create the stars. You can work in as few as two fabrics for the stars (one for the background and one for the stars) or you too can make your stars scrappy.

For the background on the stars, you need approximately 1 yard. For the diamonds creating the stars, you need a total of 18 strips, each cut at $1^{3}/_{4}$". (Two $1^{3}/_{4}$" strips yields enough diamonds for three stars.) For the alternating solid squares and framing border, you need $1^{3}/_{4}$ yard.

CONSTRUCTING THE LEMOYNE STAR

Looking at the basic LeMoyne Star block you'll see that there are two different sub-units, each with set-in piecing.

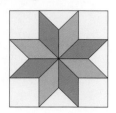

LeMoyne Star

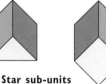

Star sub-units

(1) It is recommended that you begin construction with the triangle and two-diamond "Y" unit. Since the block has four of these identical sub-units, you can lay the sub-units out one on top of another, four deep. You can chain piece seam #1 for each unit, one after another. Remember that seam #1 is always sewn end to end. Refer to Basic Y-seam construction on pages 176-177.

Begin with this unit. Stack four deep in each pile. Chain sew seam #1, end to end.

(1)

(2) Finger-press the seam allowance toward the diamond. Re-stack the units one on top of another. Next sew seam #2 by placing the diamond on top of the triangle. Before sewing, flip the pieces over so that the triangle is on top. You'll be sewing from tip to previous stitching line. Lock the stitches. Finger-press the seam allowance toward the diamond. Re-stack the sub-units.

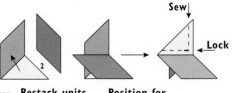

Sew

Lock

(2) **Restack units four deep** **Position for seam #2**

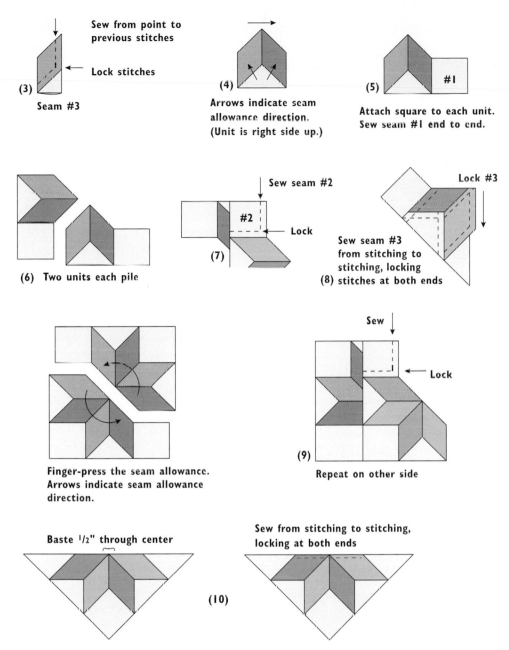

(3) Sew from point to previous stitches — Lock stitches

(3) Seam #3

(4) Arrows indicate seam allowance direction. (Unit is right side up.)

(5) #1 Attach square to each unit. Sew seam #1 end to end.

(6) Two units each pile

Sew seam #2

(7) #2 — Lock

Lock #3 Sew seam #3 from stitching to stitching, locking (8) stitches at both ends

Finger-press the seam allowance. Arrows indicate seam allowance direction.

Sew — Lock

(9) Repeat on other side

Baste 1/2" through center

Sew from stitching to stitching, locking at both ends

(10)

(8) Seam #3 in this phase is a bit different, so pay careful attention. If you follow these steps, you'll give your star a nice flat center intersection where all 8 diamonds come together. Position the two pieces right sides together, matching up the diamonds and the alternating seam allowances. (This is why we always press the seam allowances toward the diamond on the right.) You'll be sewing from *stitching to stitching* this time, being certain to lock the stitches at both the beginning and the end.

(9) Next, begin sewing the two halves together. You've already sewn a seam, which attached the square to the diamond. Now you must sew a second seam, which is a square to diamond, locking at the previous stitching. Do this at each end.

(10) The final seam will close up the center of the star. Technically, you'll sew from end to end, locking at each end. You also want to work toward having all 8 diamonds intersect at the same point. You may want to try this hint. Lengthen your stitch length to a long basting stitch. Match the diamonds (all seam allowances butt and alternate, which helps). Sew only 1/2", right at the star point intersection. Remove the block from your machine and check for the diamond points. If you're happy with the results, shorten your stitch back to regular stitch length and sew the entire seam, remembering to lock the stitches both at the beginning and the end. If you aren't pleased with the way the diamonds intersect, you have only to remove about four basting stitches. Correct the problem until you're satisfied, then do the final stitching. It is an extra step, but if you've ripped that last seam in a block, you know what a pain it can be.

The seam allowances should naturally fan in the center of the star, as in 4-patches or Pinwheels. (This is because of that earlier step you did of sewing only stitching to stitching.)

(3) For seam #3, position the two diamonds right sides together and sew from tip to previous stitching. Use your fingers to gently guide the seam allowances out of the way. Don't stitch through the seam allowances. Lock the stitches. Repeat with the other three sub-units.

(4) Finger-press the seam allowance toward the diamond that is on the right (when the "Y" is upside down and the sewn unit is right side up as shown).

(5) Next attach a square to the right diamond as illustrated. This is seam #1 and, as such, is sewn end to end.

(6) This seam allowance is eventually going to be guided toward the square, but for the time being, simply push it toward the diamond so you can see the stitching line when sewing seam #2. Lay sub-units out two deep as shown.

(7) Position the unit on the right on top of the unit on the left. Flip the pieces over and sew with the square on top, from outer edge to previous stitching. Lock the stitches.

In the final star, the seam allowances between diamonds and triangles go toward the diamonds. Between diamonds and squares, they go toward the corner squares. All seam allowances between diamonds should go around in a complete circle. Final pressing should be done with an iron.

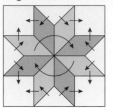

Recommended direction to guide seam allowances

Directionally "fan" seam allowances at center

Once again we cannot stress the importance of practice. Four stars should be your minimum number to cut and sew. Ideally, you should cut and sew all four stars in the same day to become comfortable with the procedure. The more time that elapses between each star, the more you are going to feel like you're starting all over again. The idea is to become proficient at this technique. If you make four stars and each star has 8 "Ys", by the time you've finished four blocks, you'll have made 32 "Y" seams. That's probably going to make you comfortable, wouldn't you agree? If the four practice stars you make turn out really good, then there is no reason that they can't be used in your project quilt. If one or more isn't perfect, then there's not too much that has been wasted.

Troubleshooting

■ If you have problems with the star, be sure to check for accuracy in cutting, sewing, and pressing. If you do not cut accurately, there is no way your pieces are going to fit nicely together.

■ If the corners of your set-in pieces tend to pucker, make sure you haven't stitched too far. Should puckering occur, it's usually just a matter of cutting the culprit stitch. You're better off sewing "short" rather than too far. There is always fabric behind the corners, so there won't be a "hole" if you've sewn "short."

Other Examples of Blocks Containing Set-in Piecing

There are lots of other blocks that have the same Y-seaming as an integral part of the design. We're giving you a few examples to entice you and whet your appetite.

Another place you find the set-in piecing is on the simple Attic Window block.

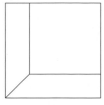

Attic Window

Not only is the Attic Window a fun little block all by itself, but it also can be used as a frame for other blocks. Think about how much fun it might be to set your LeMoyne Star blocks into an Attic Window. It'd be like looking out the window at the stars!

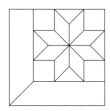

Here are some more quilts that also share the common bond of set-in pieces. If you master the Y-seaming now, you'll never be put off by the more integral blocks again!

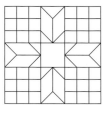

Arrow Star

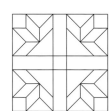

Sage Tracks

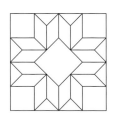

Michigan Beauty

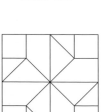

Whirling Pinwheels

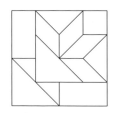

Cactus Basket

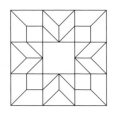

Star Born

Stars and Cubes, 1998, 64¹/₂" x 84". Designed and pieced by Harriet Hargrave.
Blocks pieced by Nancy Barrett. Quilted by Cathy Franks.

LeMoyne on the Double, 1997, 37" x 37". Designed, pieced, and quilted by Sharyn Craig.
LeMoyne Star block set into a Double Irish Chain.

Morning Star, 1997, 52" x 52". Designed and pieced by Sharyn Craig. Quilted by Joanie Keith.

Snow Crystals, 1999, 60" x 94". Blocks from Harriet Hargrave.
Designed and constructed by Sharyn Craig. Quilted by Joanie Keith.

CHAPTER 16

Curved Seam Piecing

Blocks with curved seams have long intrigued quiltmakers. Double Wedding Ring, Drunkard's Path, Orange Peel, Robbing Peter to Pay Paul, Glorified Nine Patch, and Grandmother's Fan are only some of the names that quilters are familiar with. It is not recommended that quilters begin piecing with curved seams, but once you are competently cutting and piecing straight-line patchwork blocks, there is no reason you can't be equally successful piecing curves.

To begin our lesson on curved seams, let's look at the simple Drunkard's Path unit. We'll use this unit to discuss the basic terminology pertaining to the drafting, template making, and piecing for the curve lesson. We are not, however, going to be using the Drunkard's Path for our project quilt. Instead, we have selected a very old but little-seen pattern called Royal Cross.

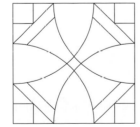

Drunkard's Path

Royal Cross

The reason for this is simple. The Drunkard's Path unit has all the parts we need for the preliminary discussion; however, due to its small

size, it isn't the easiest curve for beginners to piece. Royal Cross is a larger block with more pieces, making the curve much easier to sew. Once you're comfortable piecing the Royal Cross, you can move to Drunkard's Path.

Drafting and Template Making

To draft a block with curved seams you need graph paper, a ruler, a good compass (not the 29-cent variety), and Scotch tape. The success you have drawing the pattern will be directly related to the quality of your compass. You do not have to have an expensive engineering compass, but it does have to be adjustable in width and have the ability to hold its position. For about $5.00 at the better office supply stores, college bookstores, and engineering supply houses, you can find an adjustable compass with a screw to tighten the two legs during the drawing process that works great.

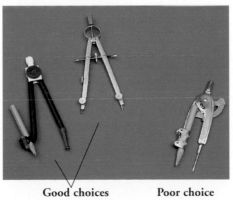

Good choices   **Poor choice**

Looking at the two pieces in the Drunkard's Path unit, you'll see one piece has an inner curve, called the concave curve and the other piece has an outer curve called the convex curve. An easy way to remember the difference is the concave curve "caves in."

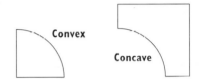

Convex

Concave

We are using the Drunkard's Path unit in a 3" finished size for the initial drafting exercise. Take one sheet of graph paper and securely tape it to your rotary cutter mat. Draw a 3" square on your graph paper. Position the pointed part of the compass on one corner of the square, allowing it to sink into the mat for stability. Extend the pencil 2" (making a 2" radius). Scribe a quarter-circle arc as illustrated.

3" square

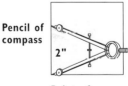

Pencil of compass

2"

Point of compass

Scribe a quarter circle arc

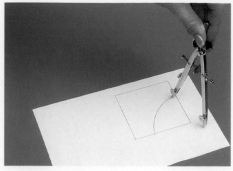
Creating a gentler curve

Trace each piece

Carefully draw around template

Cut out template

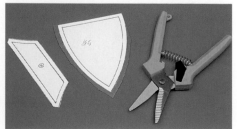
Create pattern pieces

That's it. You now have your finished Drunkard's Path unit. That wasn't so difficult was it? Check to make sure that your pencil intersected both edges of the original square exactly at 2". If it didn't, make sure you're holding the compass properly, from the top, not the legs, and that it's upright, not leaning into the curve as you draw.

You can adjust the distance between the original point and the scribed arc as suits your personal taste. There is nothing concrete about that distance being two-thirds the distance of the total square size, but that does seem to be the amount used most often. To obtain a "flatter," more gentle curve, position the point of the compass outside of the original square and scribe, still at 2" on the original square. You're using a smaller portion of the total circle; some find this easier to piece. Feel free to play with the design.

Making Templates

The next step is to make templates. Tape template plastic on top of your drawing and carefully trace each piece with the seam allowances added. Trace one piece with seam allowances, then move the template plastic and trace the second piece with its seam allowances. Use your ruler on all straight lines and the compass on the curve. When adding the seam allowance to the convex curve (outer curve), adjust the compass $1/4$" larger and scribe. To add the seam allowance to the concave curve, adjust the compass $1/4$" smaller than the original arc.

These templates are not good for use with rotary cutters. To use these templates, you need to carefully draw around the template with a pencil on the wrong side of your fabric, and cut with good fabric cutting scissors. Another option for making all templates, except the concave curve, is to use the John Flynn Cut Your Own Template Kit material. If you want to make your own templates for all but the inside curve (so you can rotary cut these pieces), then instead of taping template plastic on top of the original drawing, tape another sheet of paper on top. Create each pattern piece, with seam allowances, on the paper. Cut out the paper pattern piece. Glue to the template laminate material and cut out the templates with the special cutter provided for this material.

There are commercially available templates for many curved pieced blocks, including Drunkard's Path, Wheel of Mystery, Winding Ways, Double Wedding Ring, Glorified Nine Patch, and Royal Cross. John Flynn has available some templates made out of his laminate material, and there are plexi-templates by a number of manufacturers, including Come Quilt With Me® and Quilter's Rule®.

These commercial templates are used with rotary cutters quite successfully. Many quilters do find it easier to cut the concave curve with the 28mm rotary cutter, particularly if it's a tight inside curve like the one found on a 3" Drunkard's Path. Again, you need to experiment with the various cutting methods to find what works best for you. The bottom line is that you must have accurate templates and cut accurately if you expect to successfully piece your block.

Piecing the Curve

When piecing a curve, many quilters like the security of what are referred to as "registration marks." A registration mark acts like the notches found on patterns in dressmaking. A registration mark on each piece of fabric needs to line up during piecing. On the simple Drunkard's Path, it's easy enough to fold each piece in half and crease at the halfway mark. During piecing of the edge, you'll line these two creases up.

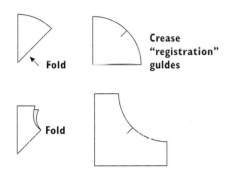

Fold

Crease "registration" guides

Fold

Another way to create registration marks is to draw them on during the drafting phase and actually notch the template. With the template notched, you can either draw with a pencil to indicate that mark or cut $^1/8$" into the seam allowance.

Mark registration guide marks on original drafting, which gets transferred to templates

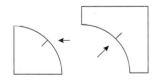

Notch each template

Many quilters prefer to sew a curved seam with the concave piece on top and lots of pins to hold the units together. Others find it easier to piece with the convex curve on top and use pins sparingly, if at all. You are going to have to try both ways to determine which way will work better for you.

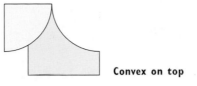

Convex on top

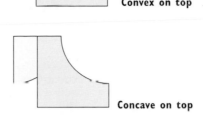

Concave on top

There are some things you can do during sewing to ensure success.

■ Lengthen your stitch slightly. This helps ease the fabric layers together.
■ If available, use the needle-down feature on your sewing machine. This keeps the layers from slipping while your fingers are easing the edges together.
■ Slow down. This is not a race. A slower, more definite pace will allow you to control the fabric.
■ Keep your fabric edges together. While this is always a good idea in piecing, it is particularly important with curves.
■ Sew an accurate $^1/4$" seam allowance. In fact, think of these last three little tips as your mantra while piecing curves. Say them to yourself over and over while sewing, and you'll actually start to relax and enjoy the process. We can't be in a hurry when sewing curves or we will get in trouble every time.

Some books recommend clipping into the seam allowance before piecing. We do not sanction this practice. Our experience is that a clip can not only weaken the seam, but also can create pointy spots along the curve. If you find it necessary to clip the seam after sewing but prior to pressing, then do so, but be very cautious.

Royal Cross

Now it's time to look at our project quilt block in earnest. We used a $10^1/2$" finished block. To draft the block, begin by drawing a $10^1/2$" square on graph paper. You may have to tape several sheets together if you don't have one of the larger sheets of graph paper. Again, tape the paper securely to the rotary mat.

(1) The Royal Cross block is based on a 9-patch grid: 3 equal divisions across the block. $10^1/2$" ÷ 3 = $3^1/2$" per division. Along each edge of the square, make tiny reference marks to divide the edge into three equal parts.

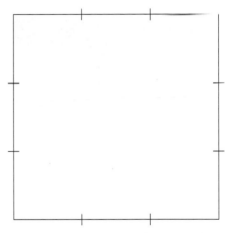

(1) Original square with reference marks

(2) Position the point of the compass on one corner of the block. Extend the pencil two-thirds of the way to the second little reference mark, and scribe a quarter circle.

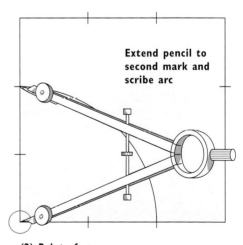

Extend pencil to second mark and scribe arc

(2) Point of compass

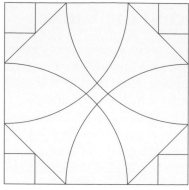

(5) Halfway between the corner of the block and the arc, draw in the corner squares

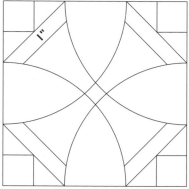

(6) Positioning your ruler on the diagonal line at the corner, measure 1" and draw a line

(This last line is drawn at an arbitrary distance created by what seems visually pleasing to the eye. You may prefer to have your band wider or narrower, depending on your fabric choices.)

(7) Let's talk about piece #3, the small square in the center. It's recommended, for ease of both creating the templates and sewing the block, that you eliminate the slight curve to the edges. Do this by laying a ruler corner to corner and drawing straight lines. We used a red pencil when doing this to remind us which line to follow when making templates.

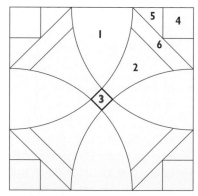

(7) Eliminate slight curve of piece #3

Royal Cross, 1999, 36" x 36". Designed and pieced by Sharyn Craig. Quilted by Joanie Keith.

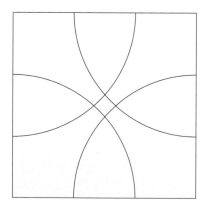

(3) Repeat at each of the other three corners

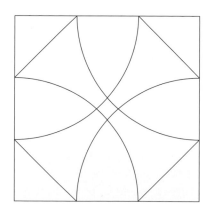

(4) Draw a line across each corner of the block, connecting the ends of the arcs

This affects the bottom of the #2 pieces, as well as the #3 square. It does not affect the eye's perception that the entire line is curved. See for yourself by looking at the quilts pictured here. Can you tell it has been slightly flattened in this area?

Project

ROYAL CROSS TEMPLATES

Using the full-scale drawings on page 190 as your pattern guides, prepare your templates. A premade template set is also available from John Flynn. See Resources page 234.

Note Pieces #4 and #5 are the 1 3/4" square and half-square triangle that were used to make the 6" LeMoyne Star. If you already have those two templates, it isn't necessary to make new ones unless you would prefer to have a second set that you store with the rest of the pieces for this block.

Royal Cross, 1999, 48" x 60". Designed and pieced by Sharyn Craig. Quilted by Joanie Keith.

FABRIC

We don't tell you how much fabric you need or how many different fabrics to use for this project. Instead, we have numbered each piece and provided the yield per strip information needed for you to make your own decisions. After all, you might want to make the entire quilt with three fabrics, or you might want to make it scrappy. You might want some parts controlled and others scrappy. How are you going to set your blocks? The two example quilts shown here are totally different. The quilt on page 188 sets the blocks tangent, creating exciting circular designs for the viewer. Setting the blocks tangent means you have the extra consideration of making the pieces all match between the blocks. Maybe you don't want to have to hassle with that aspect of the design. The quilt shown above sets the blocks with sashing and cornerstones. The red and white 9-patches were created when the corner squares of the block were the same color as the cornerstones of the sashing.

How are you going to color your blocks? Feel free to play with col- ored pencils and the line drawing of the block. You can photocopy the drawing we have provided several times for the coloring process if that sounds like fun to you.

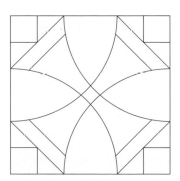

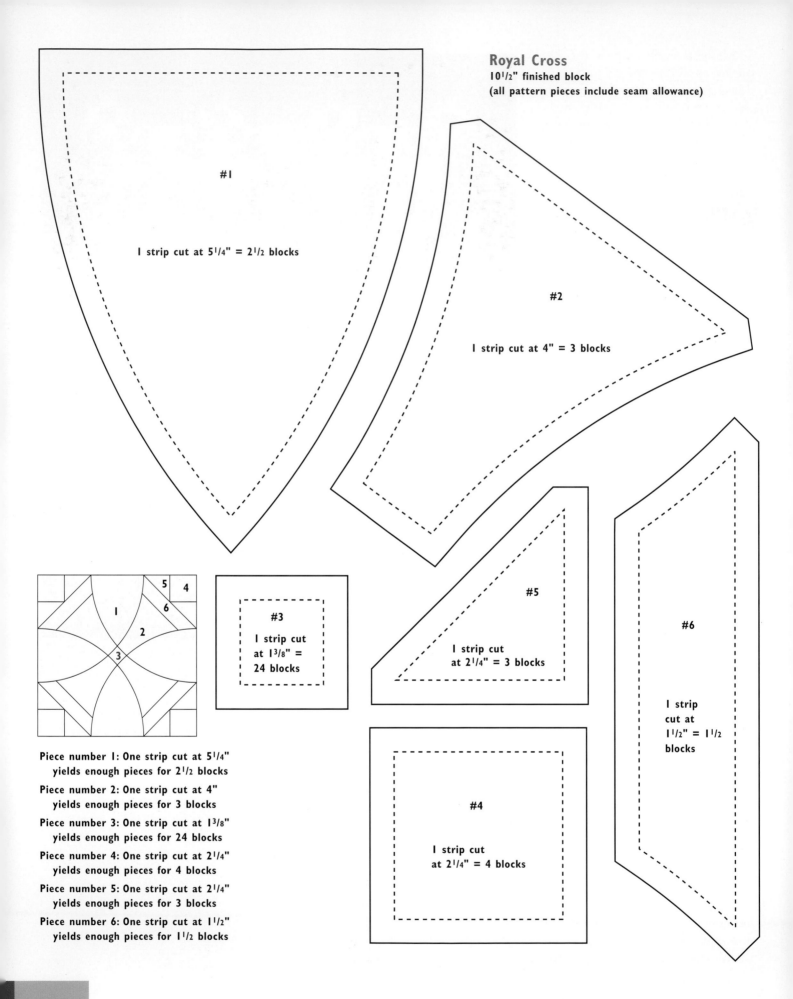

Royal Cross
10¹/₂" finished block
(all pattern pieces include seam allowance)

#1

I strip cut at 5¹/₄" = 2¹/₂ blocks

#2

I strip cut at 4" = 3 blocks

#3
I strip cut
at 1³/₈" =
24 blocks

#5

I strip cut
at 2¹/₄" = 3 blocks

#6

I strip
cut at
1¹/₂" = 1¹/₂
blocks

#4

I strip cut
at 2¹/₄" = 4 blocks

Piece number 1: One strip cut at 5¹/₄"
    yields enough pieces for 2¹/₂ blocks
Piece number 2: One strip cut at 4"
    yields enough pieces for 3 blocks
Piece number 3: One strip cut at 1³/₈"
    yields enough pieces for 24 blocks
Piece number 4: One strip cut at 2¹/₄"
    yields enough pieces for 4 blocks
Piece number 5: One strip cut at 2¹/₄"
    yields enough pieces for 3 blocks
Piece number 6: One strip cut at 1¹/₂"
    yields enough pieces for 1¹/₂ blocks

To calculate total yardage, decide how many blocks you want to make. Once you've determined how many blocks you anticipate making, complete the calculations for how much of each fabric you'll need.

PIECING ORDER FOR ROYAL CROSS

The following diagrams show the order in which to piece the block. The arrows show the suggested direction to push the seam allowances. You will be creating sub-units, which you'll join together to make the block. It is strongly recommended that you cut and piece one block before you cut the pieces for the rest of the quilt. Make sure your templates are correct and that you've cut accurately.

Remember:
- Lengthen your stitch slightly
- Use needle-down function if your machine has it
- Slow down during sewing
- Keep your fabric edges together
- Sew with an accurate 1/4" seam allowance.

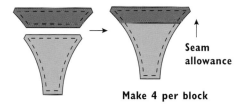

Seam allowance

Make 4 per block

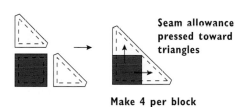

Seam allowance pressed toward triangles

Make 4 per block

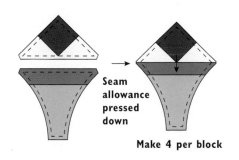

Seam allowance pressed down

Make 4 per block

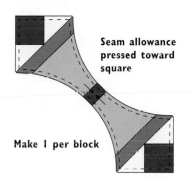

Seam allowance pressed toward square

Make 1 per block

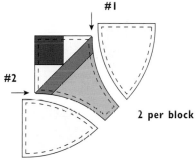

#1

#2

2 per block

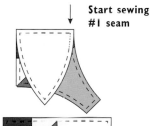

Start sewing #1 seam

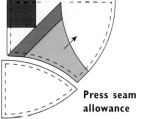

Press seam allowance

Flip and rotate the unit 90°. Start sewing #2 seam at the arrow.

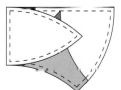

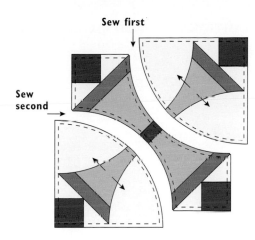

Sew first

Sew second

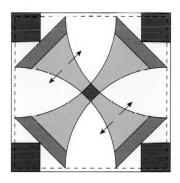

SEWING CURVED PIECES TOGETHER

When piecing the concave and convex curves together to create the halves, it's recommended that you stitch from the outer edge down. Carefully and deliberately start the sewing with the top edges totally even. Using the needle-down button on your machine is a definite advantage, because it helps you keep your position while using your hands to manipulate the fabric. Sew about a half-inch, then slowly ease the top piece around to match the bottom piece. Keep the edges together. Sew slowly. Draw the edges together every 1/2" or so. When you're about halfway down the edge, begin making the bottom edge match up by pushing the remaining edge together gently with your finger tips.

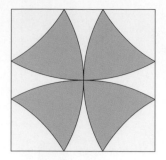

Wheel of Mystery

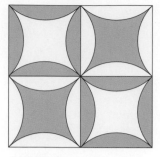

Robbing Peter to Pay Paul

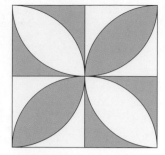

Orange Peel

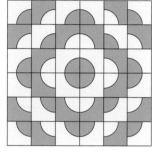

Love Ring

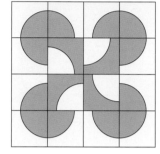

Fool's Puzzle

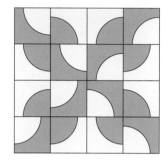

Rocky Road to California

Glorified Nine Patch

Let's talk about another curved block design called the Glorified Nine Patch. The quilt you see on page 193 was made from a set of antique blocks and pieces purchased by Sandy Andersen. It's an all-over pattern connected with the elliptical shapes. Sharyn's quilt on the same page is constructed in square blocks with half-ellipses. If you make the quilt in squares instead of the all-over pattern, your final quilt can have more design flexibility. Sharyn used sashing and cornerstones with her Glorified Nine Patch blocks instead of running the design together. You get a larger quilt without as many blocks to piece, you don't have to worry about those tiny points meeting up, and you don't have long rows of curved sections to maneuver at a time. We are simply giving you some food for thought and permission to play with this or any other design. Just because it appears one way in the original quilt does not mean it has to stay that way.

And, because we want you to be able to play with curved piecing, we are providing pattern pieces for 9" Glorified Nine Patch units. The ellipse is marked for a half-piece or whole to let you decide how you would prefer to piece your quilt.

Here's another thing to think about; look at Laurine Leeke's quilt on page 195. Notice how she used the Drunkard's Path units to frame Ohio Star blocks. How else might you use the Drunkard's Path units? What other blocks might you frame with the unit? Could the unit be used as a border on a quilt?

Throughout this book we have tried to not only teach techniques, but also to build independent quiltmakers. Once you know the "how-to" we hope you're going to want to use the information to develop your own style of quilts. Many of the blocks and designs can be very successfully intermingled to create fun quilts. How you use the information is entirely up to you. Now have fun!

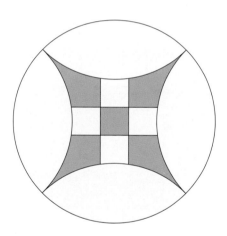

Glorified Nine Patch: Option I

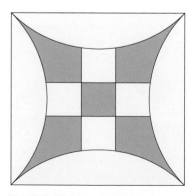

Glorified Nine Patch: Option 2

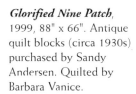

Glorified Nine Patch,
1999, 88" x 66". Antique
quilt blocks (circa 1930s)
purchased by Sandy
Andersen. Quilted by
Barbara Vanice.

Glorified Nine Patch,
1999, 40" x 52".
Designed, pieced, and
quilted by Sharyn Craig.

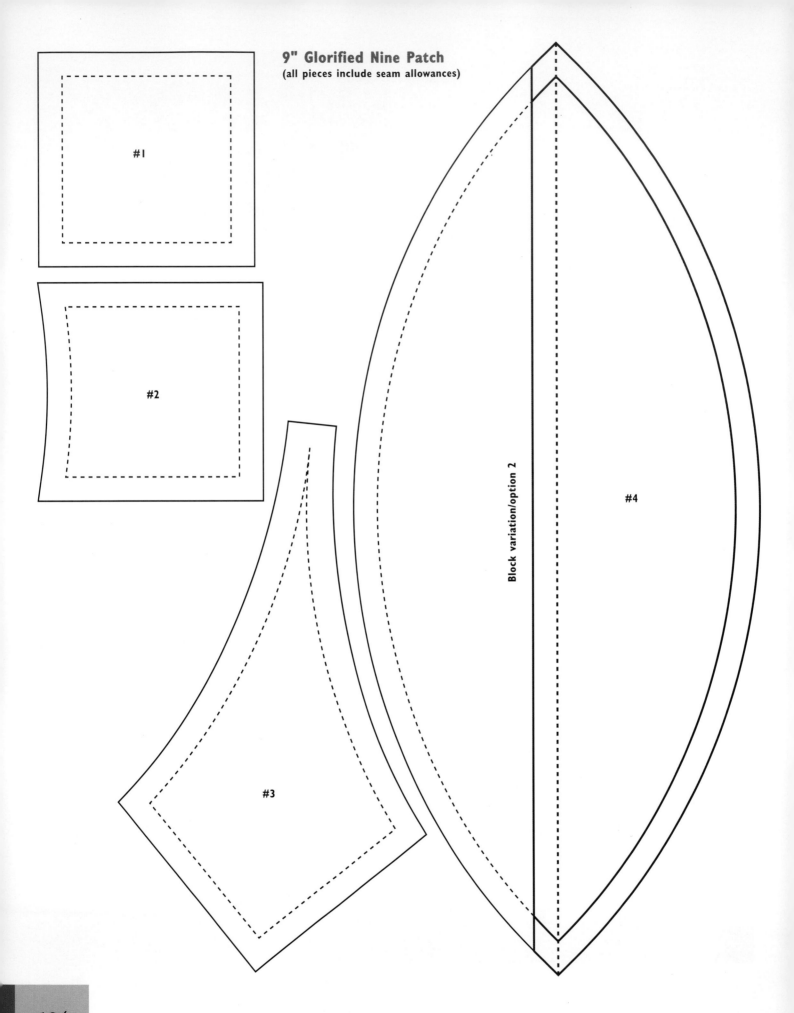

9" Glorified Nine Patch
(all pieces include seam allowances)

#1

#2

#3

Block variation/option 2

#4

Stars on the Half-Shell,
1998, 35" x 35".
Designed, pieced, and
quilted by Laurine Leeke.

Drunkard's Path,
1996, 54" x 55".
Designed, pieced,
and quilted by
Harriet Hargrave.

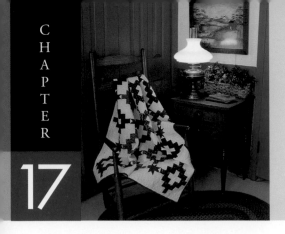

Piecing Strategies

Every block has a piecing strategy. Every quilt has a piecing strategy. Two different quilters will not necessarily use the same system to piece a block or make a quilt. The important thing is for you to learn to think logically. When selecting a block that you've never sewn before, you may need to experiment with different methods before deciding which one is going to be the best.

Many different factors influence your decision about which method to use when. Your skill level, the complexity of the block, and the fabric color "recipe" are three very important things to keep in mind when deciding how to tackle a new project.

If you've chosen a block that has many pieces and is complex, a larger grid will be easier to piece. Larger blocks will have a different presence in a quilt than smaller blocks. On the other hand, complex small pieces may not be a problem for you to piece, and smaller blocks may be needed to achieve your desired finished look. The same block in different sizes can have two totally different impacts on the quilt.

If you're making a scrappy sampler quilt, strip piecing may not be advisable. On the other hand, if you decide on a two fabric quilt using only Ohio Star blocks then some of the assembly line techniques covered in the earlier chapters may be an excellent choice.

We always recommend making a trial block before cutting all the blocks for an entire quilt. This trial block may be in the same fabrics or they can be practice fabrics. What you don't want to do is cut blocks for an entire quilt and then learn that one of your calculations was wrong! The trial block can also be a way to explore different construction approaches. A simple 4-patch unit will not have nearly as many elements to take into consideration as a more complicated block such as Aunt Sukey's Choice.

AUNT SUKEY'S CHOICE
Let's look at and analyze the Aunt Sukey's Choice block.

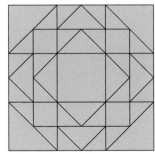

Aunt Sukey's Choice

There are corner units that have sub-units that must be sewn before you can add the corner triangles.

Piecing order

Next there are the central side "geese" sub-units to construct before sewing two of them together to make the final unit.

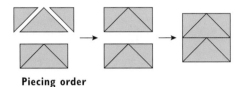

Piecing order

When you have four corner units and four side units, you can begin sewing the final block together.

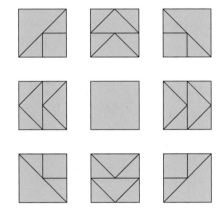

Putting the block together

How will you cut the pieces for this block? Will you cut all individual pieces without templates? Will you cut all pieces with templates? Will you cut some with and some without templates? What about constructing the geese units? Perhaps you'd rather use one of the geese methods described in Chapter 14 (page 165). These are all decisions you need to make before charging into the entire quilt. The longer you

Jacob's Ladder à la Scraps, 1998, 50" x 50". Designed, pieced, and quilted by Harriet Hargrave.

quilt, the easier these decisions become because you have experience behind you to influence the decisions. That doesn't mean that you'll always make the same decisions. It just means you'll have more experience in different methods to aid the process of making decisions.

JACOB'S LADDER

Jacob's Ladder is another lovely old pattern that has a lot of design impact in a fairly simple block. Let's look at it.

The block consists of 4-patch blocks and half-square triangles.

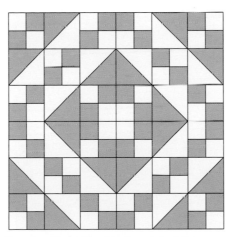

Four Jacob's Ladder blocks set together

Four of these blocks together create the quilt's interesting pattern.

When beginning the process, you need to determine the size of the

finished block. Divide the block size by six to get the grid. Is it a friendly number? The quilt in the photo has a 9" finished block. $9 \div 6 = 1\frac{1}{2}$". In other words, our base grid is $1\frac{1}{2}$". So the 4-patch and the half-square triangles would be 3" finished units. What size block would it be if the grid were 2"? 2" x 6 = 12" With a 2" base grid the 4-patch and half-square triangles would each be 4" finished units. Once you've determined the size, how do you want to cut and piece the units? Will you use strip piecing for the 4-patches, or cut individual squares? Which of the triangle methods would you like to work with?

Jacob's Ladder block

Pinwheel Chain, 1998, 60" x 74½". Designed and pieced by Sharyn Craig.
Quilted by Barbara Ford.

In the previous examples we've assumed you had the block pattern to begin the process. But, what if you had a picture of an entire quilt? You may have taken a picture at a quilt show, torn it from a magazine, or flagged it in a favorite book. You have no set of instructions guiding you through the process. How do you get started? Follow along as we work through the *Pinwheel Chain* quilt.

PINWHEEL CHAIN

First you need to find the block units that comprise the quilt. Look for any straight grid lines that can divide the quilt into workable units.

What you discover is that it's a two-block set up needed to make this quilt. First the Chain block, then the Pinwheel block. How would you divide the Chain and the Pinwheel for piecing?

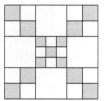

Chain block

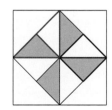

Pinwheel block

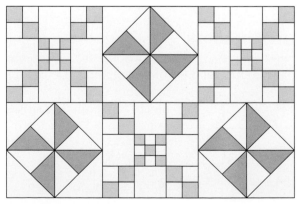

Pinwheel Chain units

Next we need to determine the size of these two blocks. It will probably be easier to begin with the Chain block. The Chain block has three equal divisions. The center square is a 9-patch and the four corners are 4-patches. If we're going to have to divide the 9-patch into 3 equal divisions, it's important that when you pick a size, you start with the smallest element that you are willing to work with. For our example we'll assume a 3" finished 9-patch, which means that each of our small squares will be 1" finished size. If the 9-patch is 3" finished, then the 4-patches will also be 3" finished, which means those squares are 1½" finished. This also means that the solid squares between the 4-patches and 9-patch will be finished 3" squares. These are all nice numbers, so it looks like we made a good choice.

Now let's look at the Pinwheel block. It too is 9" finished, so the four corner triangles must be 4½" half-square triangles. What do we know about the inside Pinwheel? We know that, corner to corner, it measures 9". That must mean that one of the triangles that makes the pinwheel is a 4½" quarter-square triangle. To make the Pinwheel, you need four dark and four light triangles. Let's continue on to the method for making these units. First, you need to determine your fabric recipe. If you want totally scrappy chain pieces, as in the quilt shown here, then you probably aren't going to opt for a strip piecing technique to make the 4- and 9-patches. It may seem like a lot of work to cut and individually sew the squares together, but that will assure you of random color placement. The Pinwheel blocks were all made from two solids, one green and one white. Two fabrics might be the perfect opportunity to select a speed technique, but which one?

Remember that the basic unit is a 4½" quarter-square triangle. Do we want to treat it as a quarter-square triangle?

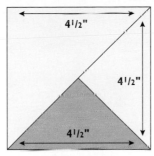

Quarter-square triangles

If you look at the pattern, you'll see that four half-square triangle units can be used also.

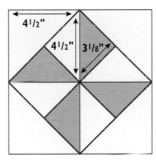

Half-square triangles

But what would they measure? The numbers don't turn out as nicely as the quarter-square units, but this could be an easier way for you to piece. To determine this, draw out the 9" block on graph paper and measure each unit. Once you see the numbers, determine which unit you'll work with. Then consider where you want the straight of grain. Positioning it on the two short sides of the triangle will give straight grain all the way around the outside edge of the inner Pinwheel block.

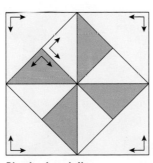

Pinwheel grainline

Shall we make templates, use paper piecing, or perhaps a sheeting technique? We can do any of the above, depending on whether we make half-square units or quarter-square units. Harriet would opt to make half-square units with the "sheeting up technique". No commercial product exists for this size unit (3⅛"), but she can draw a 4" grid on fabric to accommodate this size.

There are some of you who will decide not to make the block if you have to use templates, so what might another approach be that would allow you to cut the pieces without templates?

You may want to review Chapter 5 (page 51) for more detail here, but in a nutshell, if you find the short side of the triangle (by dividing 4.5 by 1.414), you will learn that the short side is actually 3.182, which quilters will round off to 3⅛". Now you can cut it without templates by adding ⅞" to 3⅛" and cutting a 4" square, slicing once corner to corner. Because you learned about drafting in Chapter 5 you have the tools that make having options possible. Remember, it is about having choices!

Ready for some fun? Let's do a bit of "What If"-ing with this quilt. "What if I substitute a different block for the Pinwheel?" Any block that would look good on point can replace the Pinwheel in the center of this block. The only problem is the block would have to be a 6¼" finished block. Or would it? 6¼" is not a common size, but 6" is. If the new block were 6", what will that do to the other pieces needed? Six ÷ 1.414 = 4.243 (or 4¼"). The corner triangles will be 4¼" half-square triangles. That means the block is now a finished 8½". Okay, now, back to the Chain block. We now have 8 ½" to work with. 8½" does not divide "nicely" by 3.

What other option is open to us that would give us the same visual effect? What if we made the center 9-patch a finished 3", which would leave 5½" to divide in half for each 4-patch? $5\frac{1}{2} \div 2 = 2\frac{3}{4}"$. This works. Half of $2\frac{3}{4}$ is $1\frac{3}{8}$. The little squares in the 4-patches would be $1\frac{3}{8}"$ finished, the little squares in the 9-patch would each be 1" finished, and the solid squares would finish 3" x $2\frac{3}{4}"$. These are now "nice" numbers.

Sharyn's *Peony Chain* was made in exactly this way. She had the 6" Peony blocks that she had made several years earlier, but nothing excited her for a setting until she saw a 1930s Pinwheel Chain quilt. She was inspired by the palette and feel of the quilt, but definitely did not want to make a reproduction 1930s quilt. She also decided to replace the 9-patch in the center of the chain with a solid square so the chain would be less predictable. Now, what other design options can you come up with?

ALBUM STAR

For our next example, let's look at the *Album Star* quilt. (If you're interested you can find the original inspiration for this quilt on page 59 in the book *Quilts, An American Tradition*.) Now, we will grant you that the original quilt had a few more blocks than the Album quilt that Sharyn made, but it's the same block, setting, and color recipe.

Compare the Album quilt to the *Aunt Sukey's Delight* quilt pictured on page 201. Would you believe that the same photo inspired Sharyn to make both of these quilts?

Aunt Sukey's Delight started with the same basic fabric recipe, but quickly changed. She decided to use a different light background for each block (so she wouldn't have to worry about how much fabric she would need).

Peony Chain, 1998, 56 x 56". Designed, pieced, and quilted by Sharyn Craig.

Album Star, 1998, 39" x 51". Pieced by Sharyn Craig. Quilted by Joanie Keith.

She selected the Aunt Sukey's Choice block to replace the Album block. She wanted another block that can effectively be constructed in two fabrics and has no dark that touches the outer edge of the block. Even the basic setting of the two quilts is the same. The album quilt features the blocks on point, while the Aunt Sukey's Delight sets the blocks straight. Both have the Sawtooth Star sashing like the original. With all the different light backgrounds, the blocks are made more effective with dark sashing strips, rather than a light value fabric. After auditioning several different colors, green was chosen. Instead of using all one fabric, Sharyn selected several different green fabrics for sashing. The same is true of the cheddar-gold stars. Why should she use one fabric when each one could be different?

These are two totally different quilts. One is not better than the other. Neither approach is right or wrong. The two quilts have been presented here to illustrate a point. Sometime you may want to reproduce an antique quilt; another time you may just want to pull elements of the original to use. What's stopping you?

ALBUM

The Album block, also known as Roman Cross, Album Patch, Friendship Chain, and Courthouse Square, has been popular with quilters since the late 1800s. Let's look at the construction of the block itself.

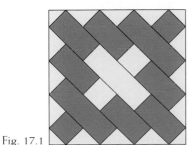

Fig. 17.1

Album block. Diagonal appearance when set straight.

Aunt Sukey's Delight, 1998, 59½" x 70½". Designed and pieced by Sharyn Craig. Machine quilted by Joanie Keith.

As you can see in Figure 17.1, the block has a diagonal appearance when set straight, but if turned on point it appears straight. Look at the construction of the block. There are numerous pieces and triangles along the edges. Sharyn would approach this block with templates (given on page 204). But what if we looked at the block differently? What if we wanted to eliminate the triangle templates and that type of piecing, and wanted to work in only strips? It can be done if we sew accurately and carefully. Examine Figure 17.2. If all the rows were made into strip units and the ends were cut to create the triangles along the edge, would this block be more appealing to you to make?

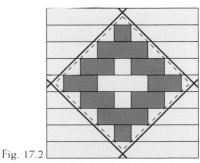

Fig. 17.2

Straight appearance when set on point

For those of you that really dislike all the math, this method keeps everything simple. There are no diagonal measurements, and you can see that there are only four different strip lengths needed. *Album Quilt* was made by Harriet's daughter, Carrie. It was one of her first pieced quilts, and she chose to use this technique because the original block totally intimidated her as a new quilter.

Mary Ellen Hopkins has been noted for having an ingenious eye for spotting different approaches to piecing solutions. She created a thought process called sharing the corner. For another really exciting way to piece the album quilt, refer to her book *Connecting Up*.

One last challenge before we leave this chapter. We found this block in the *Nebraska Quilts* book and loved the way it brought all the elements we've been covering in this book into one place at once. We call this the Ultimate quilt block. Where else can you find 9-patches, geese units, fence units, half-square triangle units, and a star in the same block?

The chart on the next page will help you get started. It provides three different finished sizes for the block. In calculating the sizes, we started with the individual square of the 9-patch and assigned $1/2$", $3/4$", or 1" to the finished piece. If you want yet a different size from these, you know what to do!

As you can see, we also give you a plain line drawing of the block. Feel free to reproduce this drawing and color it different ways. You should also feel free to substitute different stars or blocks in the center of the block. Our example quilt uses a Sawtooth Star, but you can use a LeMoyne Star, or any other block instead! As the saying goes, the ball is now in your court. What are you going to do with it?

Album Quilt, 1998, $46^{1}/_{2}$" x $46^{1}/_{2}$". Designed and pieced by Carrie Hargrave. Quilted by Harriet Hargrave.

Album Variation, 1998, 39" x 47", 1998. Pieced and quilted by Harriet Hargrave.

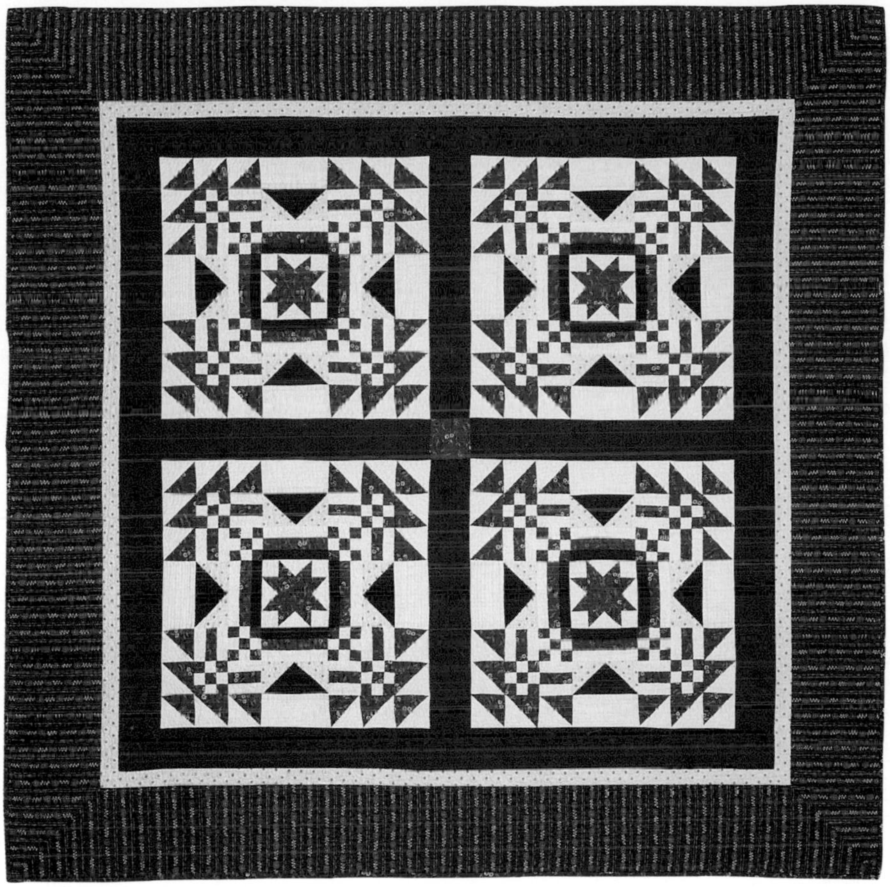

The Ultimate Quilt, 1998, 51½" x 51½". Pieced by Sharyn Craig. Quilted by Joanie Keith.

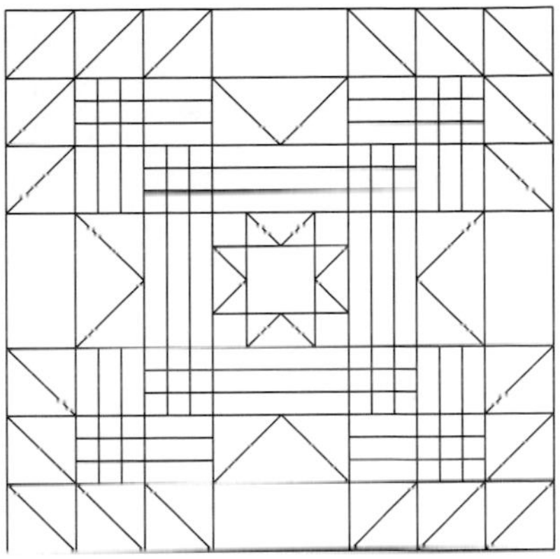

Sawtooth Star center

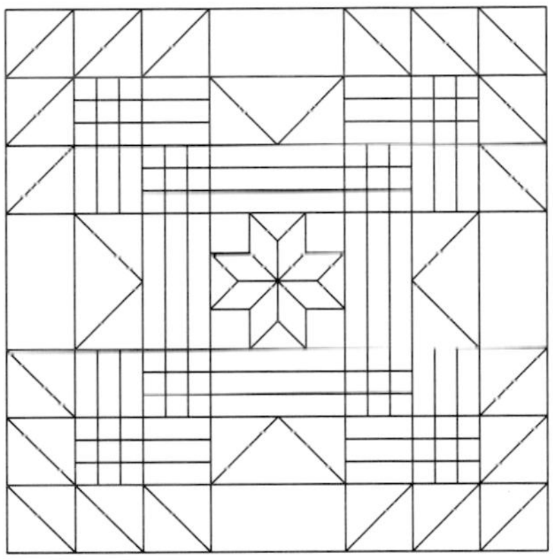

LeMoyne Star center

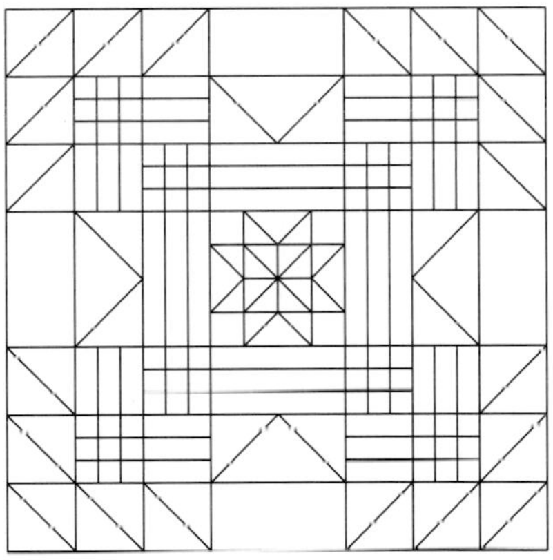

Barbara Frietchie Star center

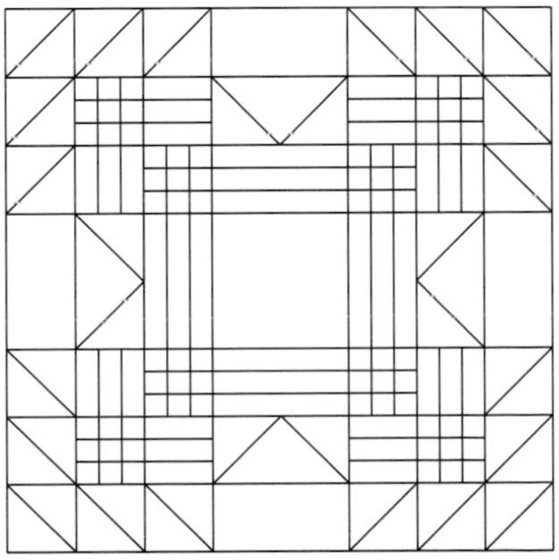

What other block or design might you put in the center?

Sizes of Units Needed for the Ultimate Quilt Block

Size Units Needed	Finished Block Size 12"	16"	18"	24"
	1 1/2"	2"	2 1/4"	3"
	1 1/2" / 3"	2" / 4"	2 1/4" / 4 1/2"	3" / 6"
	1 1/2"	2"	2 1/4"	3"
	1 1/2"	2"	2 1/4"	3"
	1 1/2" / 3"	2" / 4"	2 1/4" / 4 1/2"	3" / 6"
	1 1/2" / 3"	2" / 4"	2 1/4" / 4 1/2"	3" / 6"
	3"	4"	4 1/2"	6"

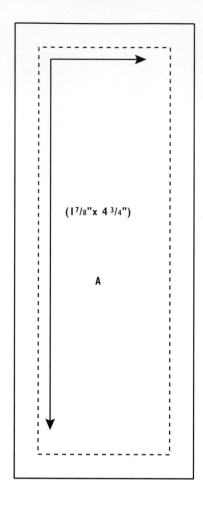

$(1^7/_8" \times 4^3/_4")$

A

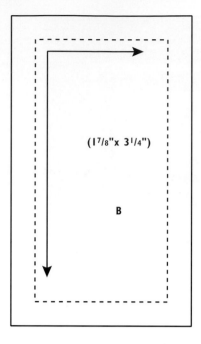

$(1^7/_8" \times 3^1/_4")$

B

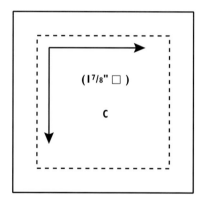

$(1^7/_8" \; \square \;)$

C

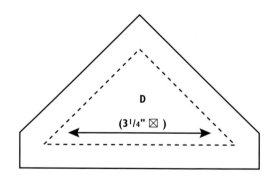

D

$(3^1/_4" \; \boxtimes \;)$

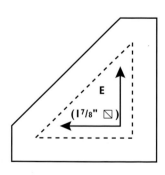

E

$(1^7/_8" \; \boxtimes \;)$

CHAPTER 18

Borders

The body of your quilt top is done. Now it's time to look at the possibility of adding borders. Borders are the final touch—the frame for your work of art. They are meant to set off or complement the quilt top. You need to approach borders in exactly the same way you would a painting you want to frame. Some paintings need elaborate frames, tinged with gold leaf. They need multiple layers of matting to add texture and color. Other paintings are perfectly finished with nothing added. They might simply be completed with a plexi-box. We all know that there are many steps between extremely elaborate and very plain. Your quilt top is absolutely no different.

Two people can purchase the same print from an artist and frame it differently due to personal taste, how they decorate, or need it to fill a particular space. This is going to be true with a quilt too, so don't get too hung up on looking for the "right answer." There are no rules, only guidelines, when it comes to deciding how to border your quilt.

Some all over patterns, such as Log Cabin and Drunkard's Path, often utilize the entire size of the quilt top, eliminating borders altogether. The binding is used to frame the top and stop the eye. Other times, you see fewer blocks used so that a wide, plain border can be added to show off extensive quilting. You can have multiple borders, borders that repeat an element of the block design, stripes, or any number of other possibilities. Whatever you choose, remember that a border can draw the eye inward and reinforce the design of the overall quilt top. Your preference is part of the quilt design process, which can be approached in different ways. One is to totally plan out the quilt on paper, including the borders. The design, width, and number of fabrics are determined before cutting and sewing.

Another method is to design and sew the center of the quilt top and then design the border treatment. This way, you get a real feeling for the effects of the color, pattern, and placement of the fabrics on the overall look of the quilt. Often what looks great on paper does not play out the same in cloth.

If you choose to put a very simple border of one to three fabrics in strips around the center, a fun way to design is to "audition" fabrics. It's a mistake to think that only the fabrics already used in the quilt top can be used in the border. Adding a totally new fabric can really pull the project together and add spark. Take the quilt center and lay it on many different fabrics to determine the ones you like. This also helps you get an idea of how wide to cut the borders of each fabric. Position the audition fabrics at different widths next to the center. Stand back and let them speak to you. You will most often know when it's too wide or too narrow. Before picking up the fabric, measure the width that "feels" best; that will be the width cut for the borders.

Half Log Cabin quilt top before borders

Sharyn auditioned various pieced borders for her Half Log Cabin quilt top. She had the body of the quilt together and was trying to decide how to finish it. It could have been considered finished just as it appears on page 205. But before automatically quitting, it's sometimes fun to play first. We are going to walk you through her auditioning process. She is allowing various options to "try out" for the part.

First she tried some simple strips: a narrow band of light followed by a wider strip of a dark brown fabric. Fabric can be folded and placed on the flannel wall flanking the quilt. Occasionally, you might need to pin the border fabric to the flannel, but it isn't necessary to actually cut the fabric into strips for this initial audition.

She wondered what it would look like if something extra was added just in the corners of the dark border. A stray LeMoyne star was called into action. She put one block in the corner, stood back, and looked at it.

Next, she decided to try repeating the dark triangles to create a zigzag effect followed by a floating border of light. Immediately she knew that she had found her answer. However, one doesn't always know immediately. Sometimes you have to let the top "mull" (like aging wine or cheese). It is important that you give the quilt a chance to "talk to you." This can be loud and clear or it can be a soft whisper. When you doubt your own judgment, remember what we said in the beginning of this chapter. There are no wrong decisions, just personal taste, which affects what each individual decides to do. Some of you may be looking at the border options for this quilt and think, "Gee, I would have liked it better if she had selected the plain strip borders."

AUDITIONING VARIOUS PIECED BORDERS

Auditioning simple strip borders

Simple strip borders with LeMoyne Star in corners

Auditioning with zigzag border

Simple Borders

When deciding to go with simple borders, you need to keep scale in mind. Remember, these aren't rules but guidelines. Normally, the last border added is the widest. Usually the last border is a darker value. Using a dark binding next to a light strip can also create a stopping place for the eye. If you decide to go with more than one strip of fabric around the quilt, the various strips are usually of different widths and values. Often three strips are used to frame a quilt. When using three, the strips may follow the pattern of medium, narrow, wide, with the narrow strip being lighter or brighter in color and value. If you use one strip around the quilt, it's important that it be wide enough so that the viewer doesn't think you ran out of fabric but not so wide as to overpower the rest of the design. Again, audition the fabrics. Their value and intensity will determine what width they should be better than any rule.

It is strongly recommended that you spend time looking at a lot of quilts, both in books and at quilt shows. Study the way quilts are bordered. When you go to a quilt show (if they allow photography), take pictures of quilts with borders that intrigue you. You don't have to find a Lone Star quilt to determine how to border your Lone Star. If you do find one, however, it can be fun to see how someone else resolved that challenge. Don't get caught up in the feeling as you gain experience as a quiltmaker that using a simple band border is "copping out" or letting the quilt down. Actually, simple borders can often be the best solution. The busier or more involved the inside of the quilt is, the more likely it's going to be that a simple border will enhance the quilt and allow some breathing space. If you look at the *Ohio Stars* quilt on page 163, you'll see that

Sharyn added a very simple dogtooth border that merged the brown and black plain strips. This blending of colors through triangles adds an elegant but soft touch around the outer edge. The design doesn't compete with the simplicity of the stars, but instead creates additional visual impact.

Look at the *Pinwheel Chain* quilt on page 198. The playful and whimsical touch added by the reverse sawtooth border in bright colors definitely finishes the design. The reverse sawtooth shape repeats the line of the original Pinwheel block. Borders can often pull out elements and pattern shapes from the body of the quilt. This reverse sawtooth border on the *Peony Chain* quilt found on page 200 wouldn't have been nearly as successful, because that shape is not found in the Peony blocks. Sharyn auditioned several different pieced borders before determining that this quilt was going to be happiest with simple plain strips.

It is not our intent to get involved with designing borders for your quilts in this chapter. There are several excellent books on this subject, and it's too large a topic to cover in this small space. We have listed several at the end of the book (page 234). Instead, we are more concerned about your quilts laying flat and hanging straight. How often have you walked through quilt shows and noticed many quilts that do not hang straight? It is very disturbing and detracting from the quilt when this happens, and it can be avoided.

The basic truth about this is that it has to be thought about right from the beginning of the piecing process. We have suggested over and over that you really take the time to experiment with all the different techniques in this book and find what works best for you and what

gives you the greatest accuracy. That is the key—accuracy in straightening the grain of your fabric, measuring, cutting, sewing, and pressing. Measuring is probably the single thing that rewards you with the most successful results. It applies to almost every step in quiltmaking. If the measuring is off anywhere along the line, there is little chance that your quilt top will lay flat and square.

MEASURING YOUR QUILT TOP FOR BORDERS

Once the quilt top is completed and well pressed, you need to measure the top to determine the length needed for the borders.

The first step is to fold the quilt top in several places to determine if the top and bottom are the same width as the center and the two sides are the same length. To do this, fold one end of the top over to the center as shown in Figure 18.1. Are they the same width? Repeat with the other end. Do the same with the sides, one side at a time. Are they the same length?

> *Tip* When measuring, do not measure along the actual outside edge, since it's easy to stretch that edge as you measure.

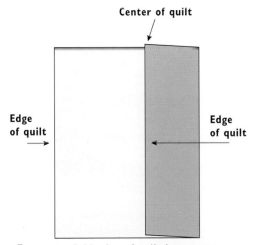

Fig. 18.1 **Fold edge of quilt into center**

If everything is perfectly even, you're ready to measure and cut the border strips. But what if things don't come out evenly? Now is the time to make corrections. Harriet does this by examining the piecing of the seams where the rows are joined. It is a common problem for the fabric to pivot slightly as you're nearing the end of any seam. If this has happened, then it's possible that a slightly larger or smaller seam was taken at the edge, making that side of the quilt shorter or narrower than the opposite side where the seam started. If this is the case, release the stitches and restitch, being very careful to not let it happen a second time. Just one or two threads' difference per seam can throw off the measurements dramatically. Seams can be checked within the blocks also. Whatever you determine, attempt to make corrections until you're within ¼" or so of being even when the top is folded and measured.

Next, use a 16" or larger square ruler or a carpenter's or dressmaker's square and check all four corners. Are they perfectly square? If not, shave away any little bits that are causing the problem. If it's really out of square, look at the internal piecing of the block in the corner. If the corner is not square when the first border is sewn on, the border cannot lay flat.

Square corner with ruler

Once the quilt top is even on top and bottom with the center (the same length as the center on both sides) and the corners are square, you're ready to measure for and design or cut your borders.

Begin by measuring through the center lengthwise to determine the actual length. The side borders are determined by the length of the quilt.

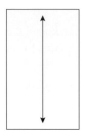
Measure through center of quilt

The top and bottom borders are cut the width of the top through the center, plus the width of the two side borders. It is best to attach the side borders first, then measure the width from the raw edge of one border through the center to the opposite raw edge.

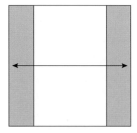
Measure border to border

If you need borders longer than you can cut a strip, you'll need to piece it. The angle of the seam is a personal preference. Harriet prefers a 45° angle, Sharyn likes her border strips pieced straight across. If the fabric is a busy print, chances are the seams will never show. But if it's a solid, it will be obvious on many quilts. Look at the illustration above right and get a feel for what your eye prefers.

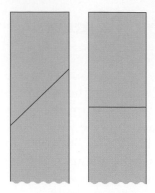
Two ways to splice a border seam

Plain Strip Borders

Some quilters feel that strips for borders absolutely must be cut parallel to the selvages, taking advantage of the no-stretch lengthwise straight of grain. Others use strips cut selvage to selvage, using the crossgrain of the fabric. It is definitely true that the lengthwise grain will stretch less than the crosswise grain, but if you're careful in handling the crosswise strips, you can have success both ways. The important thing is strategic pinning before sewing strips onto the top.

If you're using a directional print or stripe for the border, let the direction of the stripe or print make the decision as to which grain to use.

To piece strips on an angle, overlap them into an L, draw a line corner to corner, if necessary, and stitch from the outside edge.

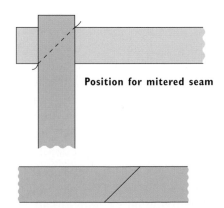
Position for mitered seam

Strip Borders with Corner Blocks

Corner blocks are a nice addition to a plain strip border. This block can be one of the design blocks from the top, a new design block, a different color, a place for special quilting, or any number of other ideas.

You need the measurement for both the length and width of the top. Cut borders to these measurements for all four sides. Attach the side borders first, measuring and pinmarking as discussed below. Press seam toward border.

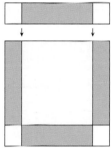

Attaching a border with corner blocks

Cut or piece the blocks needed for the corners. Sew a corner square onto each end of both the top and bottom border strips. Press the seams toward the border strip.

Attach top and bottom borders to the quilt top, pinning carefully to match the seam of the corner block and the side border seams. Press seams toward borders.

Sewing Plain Strips to the Body of the Quilt

You've measured your quilt top. You've cut and, where necessary, seamed your strips together to create the border lengths. Now you're ready to attach those strips to the body of the quilt. Never just take the strips and quilt top to the sewing machine and start feeding them through the machine. Always carefully pin the strips to the quilt top prior to sewing. We don't care if you do have a walking foot on your machine; this is one of the only firm rules in quiltmaking. *Always pin borders to the quilt top prior to sewing.*

Make placement marks on the strips before pinning them onto the edge of the quilt top. Fold each border in half lengthwise to find its center and mark with a pin. Place a pin at the edge measurements if you're cutting the border longer than the actual measurement. If it's a very large quilt, find the midway point between the center and edge and place a pin at this position on both sides of the center. Repeat process for quilt top.

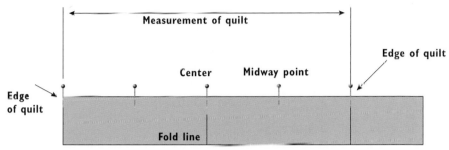

Measuring and marking center points

When pinning the border strips to the quilt top, we recommend that you work at the ironing board or on a large table. Lay your quilt top on the surface face up. Start at the center. Place the center pin on the border at the center of the top. Pin in place. Line up the edge pins on the border with the edges of the top, then position the midway pins at the midway measurement of the top. Now you can pin the border securely to the top between these marker pins. Take the top to the sewing machine and sew with the border strip on top, removing pins as you go. Don't sew over pins if you can avoid it. Go to the ironing board and press the strip in the closed position, then fold the strip over and glide the iron from the quilt top across the seam allowance, gently pushing the seam allowance toward the border strip. Repeat this process for the opposite side, then attach the top and bottom borders. Once all four borders are attached, measure each corner with the square again and check for squareness. Make any corrections that are necessary before adding the next round of strips.

> ## Note
>
> **ORDER TO ATTACH STRIPS**
> There are no solid rules about what borders go on first, whether it's sides then top and bottom, or top and bottom then sides. It depends on what appeals to you. Look at the illustrations below and notice your first reaction to each. If you feel like the first one is balanced and the second is not, you'll probably prefer to attach your border in that order, and vice versa. It's recommended, however, that you be consistent when you're adding several plain strip borders to the same quilt.
>
>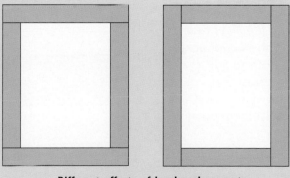
>
> **Different effects of border placement**

Pieced Borders

Pieced borders can take some additional work. Suppose you've decided you want a particular pieced border for your quilt. Once you've measured your quilt top, you need to determine what size the pieces are going to be. Let's assume that our quilt measures 60½" (this is 60" finished, which is the number we use next). For our example, let's say we are putting a 3" sawtooth border on the quilt. 60 ÷ 3 = 20. That tells us we would need 20 triangles to fit along the outer edge of the quilt. We are always hoping for "nice" numbers. The previous example was definitely a nice number. But, what if your quilt top had measured 59½". 59" ÷ 3" = 19.66666666 triangles per side. "I don't think so." So then what? We could take 59 and divide it by 20 triangles per side to find out the size of the single triangle. 59 ÷ 20 = 2.95". Again, that is not a nice number to work with. So, what other solutions can we find? Depending on the quilt, it's often possible to shave a bit from the edges to make the quilt a new "nice" size. Look at the pink and blue *Half Log Cabin* quilt with the flying geese border (page 174). In order to make the geese fit the Log Cabin blocks perfectly, Sharyn had to cut approximately ½" from each side of the quilt. Now the geese fit perfectly with no fudging, easing, or stretching.

Another possibility is to add framing, or coping strips, to the body of the quilt first. *The Pinwheel Chain* quilt (page 198) shows coping strips that were added both to add visual space and to make sure that the new finished size of the quilt was a size that can be successfully divided into "nice" numbers.

Butted or Mitered Corners

It is truly a personal choice as to whether mitered or butted corners are best on a quilt, unless you're using a stripe or other directional print. Stripes really frame the quilt nicely when mitered. Mitered corners do take more fabric and more time, but the results can be well worth it. If you're sewing multiple strips next to one another for the border, miter them after sewing strips together. You only miter each corner once this way. The seams will miter like a stripe in the corners, and you'll have the total width of the border measurement to work with.

The first step in mitering is to measure the length of the quilt top. To that measurement, add two times the width of your border, plus 5". This is the length you need to cut or piece the side borders. For example, if the quilt top is 60" long and the borders are 6" wide, you'll need border strips that are 77" long (60" + 6" + 6" + 5" = 77"). Cut or piece two border strips this length. Pin securely and stitch the strips to the sides of the quilt top. Do not stitch off the edge of the quilt top. Stop and backstitch at the seam allowance line, ¼" in from the edge. The excess length will extend beyond each edge. Press seams toward border.

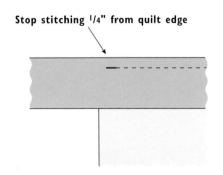

Stop stitching ¼" from quilt edge

Determine the length needed for the top and bottom border the same way, measuring through the center of the quilt to the raw edges of each border. Add 5" to this measurement. Cut or piece these border strips. Again, pin, stitch up to the ¼" seam line, and back-stitch. Each corner seam should be stitched just to one another so that the border strips extend beyond each end.

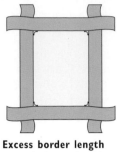

Excess border length extends beyond each end

To create the miter, lay the corner on the ironing board, supporting it so that it doesn't drag and distort the corner. Working with the quilt right side up, open and press one border. Open and press the adjacent border, laying it on top of the first one.

Position border strips for mitering

Fold the top border strip under so that it meets the edge of the bottom border and forms a 45° angle. If the border is a plaid or stripe, make sure that the patterns match along the folded edge. Press the fold in place.

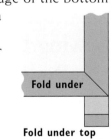

Fold under

Fold under top border strip 45°

Pin the fold in place. Position a 90° angle ruler over the corner to check that the corner is flat and square. When everything is in place, remove the pins and press the fold firmly.

Square corner

Carefully center a strip of masking tape over the mitered fold and secure firmly. Turn the quilt top over. On the wrong side of the border, draw a line slightly outside of the crease created when the fold was pressed. This will be your stitching line.

Hint: If you stitch right on the crease, you might catch the masking tape. Fold the center section of the top diagonally from the corner, right sides together, and align the long edges of the border strips.

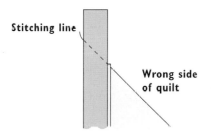

Beginning at the inside corner, backstitch and stitch on the line toward the outside point, being careful not to allow any stretching to occur. Backstitch at the end. Turn the quilt top over and remove tape, checking to see that the corner lies flat. Trim the excess border fabric to ¼" seam allowance. Press the seam open.

Harriet has always had difficulty getting mitered corners to lie perfectly flat, so she handles the corners a bit differently. Instead of sewing on the back side on the line, she stitches from the front.

Once the fold is in position, she carefully pins it in place on the top side. Using either a hand blind stitch or a mock hand appliqué stitch on the machine with nylon thread, she stitches the fold down to the bottom piece, making very small invisible stitches. Once the fold is totally stitched down, trim the excess border fabric to a ¼" seam allowance. This method is extremely successful, especially when working with multiple pieced strips and stripes.

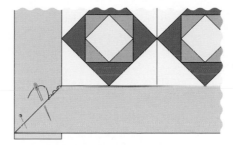

Hand stitching on top of miter

Working with Border Stripes

Border stripes can produce dramatic results when used for the borders of a quilt, but they can be a bit tricky in positioning and getting the corners to turn properly. The method given here was in *American Quilter*, spring, 1988. Jeanne Riley shared a very accurate method for foolproof border stripes.

When measuring the lengths needed for the borders, be sure to add at least two additional design elements to these measurements to assure you have enough length to properly place the design in the stripe. There are generally at least four stripes across the width of the fabric, so you only need to buy one length of fabric, the length of the longest border measurement you calculate.

First, decide what part of the border design to use in the mitered corner. You are striving to have all four corners be the same or at least have matched pairs.

To find the mitering point: Fold the stripe right sides together, matching the printed designs.

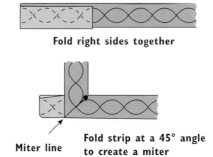

Fold right sides together

Fold strip at a 45° angle to create a miter

Miter line

Lay the strip back at a 45° angle until you find a design that you like. Trace the design from the mitered corner onto a piece of tracing paper. Mark the miter seam line and place a dot at the point where the corner will turn. (Put this dot on the seam line, not on the raw edge.) This is the mitering point.

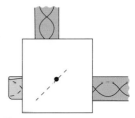

Trace corner onto paper

Trace a few of the design elements of the stripe to the right of the mitered seam line. Draw the cutting lines along the edge of the stripe. Label the paper "C side."

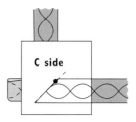

Trace design onto paper

Flip the paper over and see if the design is the same. If it is, label this side "D side." If it's not, trace the other side of the miter with another piece of tracing paper and label it "D side."

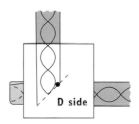

Flip over paper to trace other side

Lay the stripe out straight, right side up. Identify the design repeat. You'll see that the repeat allows you to position the dot any number of places.

Your miter could start here, or here, or here, etc.

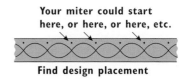

Find design placement

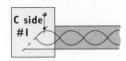

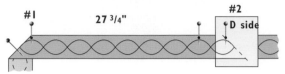

Use paper to find miter position

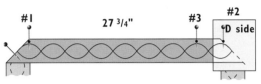

Measure length to other miter

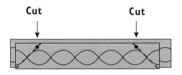

Adjust for pattern repeat

Cut miters after placement

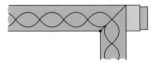

Take tucks for fit

Sew corners and align design

Position a dot as close to the left end of the stripe as possible and pin (#1) the paper tracing there. Mark the dot placement with a pin. Fold the stripe to form the miter seam line and pin. Do not cut.

Starting at the dot, measure down the length of the stripe and pin $\frac{1}{4}$" short of the raw edge. Line up the dot with the "D side" of the paper with a pin (#2).

You will find that the design lines will probably not match up. The D side may need to be moved farther to the right to make the design line up. Do not move it to the left. Place another pin (#3) where the D side design lines up with the stripe. Fold the stripe to form the other miter line and pin. Cut off most of the excess. Press both miter seam lines.

Unfold the mitered corners. This stripe is now the pattern with which to cut the opposite side border. Lay the right sides together with the uncut stripe and match the design elements along the stripe. Cut and fold under the miter lines on the second stripe as you did the first. Press both ends.

Measure the distance between pins #2 and #3. This is the amount that needs to be taken out of the length to have the corners turn and match properly. A tuck may have to be taken in the center of the stripe. The tuck is one half the distance between the two pins. If this measurement is large enough to be obvious in the design of the stripe, take several tiny tucks along the length. This will be less disturbing to the pattern repeat.

To make a tuck, fold the strip in half, right sides together. If the tucks are tiny, use an edge-stitching foot and change the needle position to the correct bite to keep the tuck perfectly straight and even. Open and check for accuracy. Repeat for the other border. Stitch the borders onto the quilt.

To add the remaining two borders, you will repeat the above process. Measure across the center of the quilt and cut the stripes. Mark and make any necessary tucks. These may be different, as these borders are shorter.

Attach stripes to the top and bottom edges of the quilt, pinning closely along the length of the stripe. Stop at the miter point dot and backstitch at the beginning and end of each seam. Turn the stripe out and press. Leave the miter creases unfolded. Lay the side miters over the bottom stripes and line up the designs in the corners.

Stitch in place, then trim the excess strip to a $\frac{1}{4}$" seam allowance. Repeat for the remaining corners.

This is just the beginning of what can be done with borders. There are numerous books on the market that can take you to the steps beyond basic. See Recommended Reading on page 234 for a few preferred titles.

Quilting Ideas & Suggestions

Congratulations! Your quilt top is finished and you're ready to go on to the next step—quilting. Quilting is a funny word, used very generically in the quilt world. We call ourselves quilters, whether or not we have ever actually quilted a top, batting, and backing together. In reality, we are toppers until we complete this stage of the process.

This is not a chapter about the technicalities of "how" to quilt, but rather about choosing "what" to quilt on the surface of your new tops. There are many books on the market that will instruct you on the actual quilting, and we do not have the space here to do it justice. Instead, we have chosen to walk you through the designing process that goes beyond fabric, color, and pattern.

If you haven't already decided on a quilting pattern for the top, now is the time to decide how you'd like the finished quilt to look. This is a part of quiltmaking that most quilters find extremely difficult. There are no right or wrong ways to quilt a top and no rules about design or pattern. If you're unsure about what you like, start looking at the quilting on quilts. It seems that today's quilters get overly involved with the fabric, pattern, and color of the top, but do not think through the whole process of turning the top into a quilt. Quilting is not even a passing thought as the top is being made,

and we discover that when it's done we have no idea what to do with it.

Harriet found years ago that the quilting was her favorite part of the quiltmaking experience, but that she needed ideas and inspiration to get the ideas generated. Here are some things that might help you.

■ **The next time you go to a quilt show or quilt shop, look at only the quilting on quilts,** not the color and fabric. See how the quilting enhances or detracts from the overall appearance of the quilt.

■ **Take pictures of quilting,** whether you like the quilt or not. If you see a border treatment you like or a block pattern, photograph it and start an idea file.

■ **Cut out pictures from magazines of quilts** that have quilting ideas you might like to use.

■ **Buy every quilt design book you can find.** These are loaded with border, sashing, and block designs that can be copied, enlarged, or reduced to fit your needs. Many have coordinating border and block patterns.

■ **Buy precut stencils of designs you like.** Don't worry about the size, just look for pattern and design. Don't overlook the complex ones that you really like. Even if your quilting skills are not there yet, they soon will be. The stencil might not.

■ **Sketch quilting designs from antique quilts.** You might not like the colors or the block, but the

quilting pattern can be adapted to many other blocks.

■ **Really study antique quilts.** Try to collect as many books with photos of antique quilts as you can, if you like the quilting style. Quilters of long ago put much work into and emphasis on the quilting, and many ideas can come from just one quilt.

Once you have an idea file started, you'll find yourself looking for quilting ideas as well as color and pattern ideas on all the quilts you view. Your focus begins to broaden. When you start to plan the quilting design, you might consider doing what Harriet does.

Hang the quilt top on the design wall, and sit on the floor or at a table in front of it, surrounding yourself with every picture, stencil, and design book you have. Look at the quilt. Does it have large blank areas that will let quilting really stand out, or is it very busy with fabric and piecing, meaning that quilting should mainly be used to support the layers? Does the quilt have an era it's replicating? A style? Is it an Amish quilt? Is it a reproduction of the 1800s? Does it feel structured and organized or more casual? These questions will direct your search. As you are looking at the top, consider your quilting ability, as well as time and your enjoyment of quilting. If you love to quilt and have time to put into it, elaborate feathers and background fill-in stitching will be welcome. But if you're new to quilting, limited in time, or really don't care for the process that much, a simpler design will be in order. Be realistic about your ability to actually finish the quilt in a reasonable time, given your schedule and life.

Start looking through designs until you start to get a feel for what might work on your particular quilt top. Make a separate pile of the pictures and designs that seem to work.

Once you've narrowed the field, you can begin to audition the designs. There are a couple of ways to do this. One is to simply place the stencil or design on top of the quilt top, stand back, and see how it "feels." You will find that your eye will pick up whether the design blends, fits, fights, is the wrong angle, and so forth, and the elimination process continues. If you have difficulty working this way, try the second method. Purchase a quantity of clear plastic sheets. These can be stiff acrylic from the art supply store or even clear tablecloth plastic from the hardware store. You will also need dry marking board markers or overhead transparency markers like Vis-à-Vis®. Just make sure that they erase (either wet or dry) off the plastic. Draw the design(s) you're considering onto the plastic with the marker, then position it on the quilt top.

This allows you to get a better idea of what the design looks like quilted. With a large enough sheet of plastic, a combination of designs can be viewed at once, allowing you to plan the entire quilting pattern before marking anything onto the fabric.

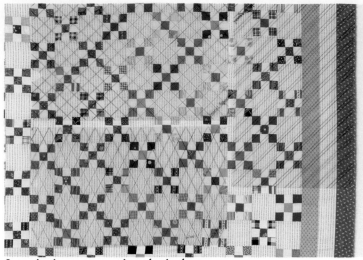
Interviewing process using plastic sheets

As you proceed through these exercises, you'll start to develop your own style.
■ How far apart do you like line spacing?
■ Do you like double lines or single lines of quilting?
■ Do you like the background filled in with stippling or echoing or just left unquilted?
■ Do you love feathers, or are they too fussy for your quilts?
■ How do you like to quilt pieces of the block? In the ditch or 1/4" from the seam?
There are just as many decisions to be made about the quilting as the fabric selection, and it can be just as exciting.

When looking at the borders, think about keeping the quilting density the same as in the body of the quilt. Often borders have less quilting, causing the batting to distort slightly. The borders can offer a space to really show off quilting, or they can simply have lines in them that continue from the body of the top.

We cannot even begin to approach the vast subject of quilting designs in this chapter. There are excellent books that give explicit detail about quilting designs, drafting quilting patterns, making patterns fit given

areas, and a host of other related topics. For some of Harriet's favorite titles, see Recommended Reading on page 234. Following are illustrations of the quilting designs that Harriet and Sharyn used on the some of the quilts presented in this book. We realize that one of the problems with quilt books is that the quilting is very difficult to make out in a photograph, so we have provided you with this idea section so you have a starting place for your developing quilt collection.

As for the actual act of making stencils, selecting marking tools, marking the top, and quilting the quilt itself, there are many excellent books on the market that will give you detailed instructions for both hand and machine quilting. We did not feel it necessary to take the space in this book to cover this topic in detail, especially since Harriet has already written a book on machine quilting, *Heirloom Machine Quilting*. Once you're ready for this step, study and choose a quilting instruction book that meets your needs. For additional titles on hand and machine quilting, see Recommended Reading on page 234.

Fence Post (page 97)

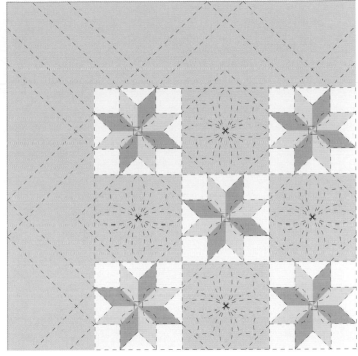

LeMoyne Star (page 177)

Glorified Nine Patch (page 193)

The Colors of Fall (page 136)

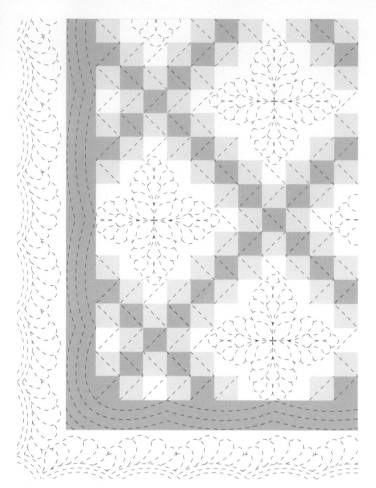

Christmas Double Irish Chain (page 113)

Quilting variation shown on Triple Irish Chain (page 113)

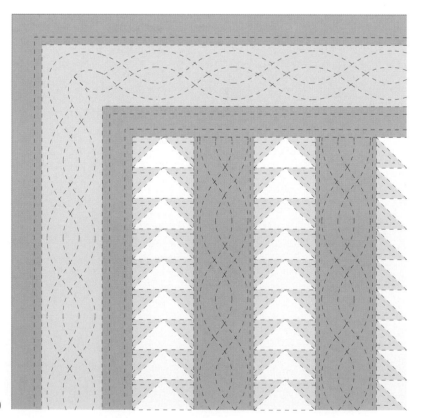

Migration (page 165)

Barnraising Log Cabin (page 123)

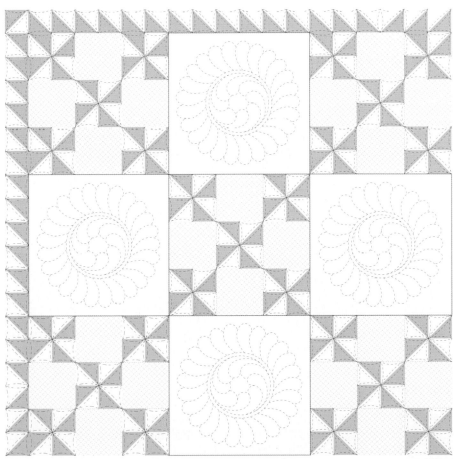

Double 9-Patch Pinwheel (page 145)

Battings, Backings & Bindings

Once the quilt top is finished, take some time and examine it. Turn it to the back side and clip away any thread tails that were missed in the piecing process. Also clip any raveling threads from the seam allowances. These threads have a tendency to show under light areas of the block from the front side after quilting. If the seam allowances are not even, with the darker seam allowance being wider, grade (trim) the seam so that the darker seam allowance does not shadow through to the front of the quilt. Try to have the back of the quilt top as neat as possible. Do a final pressing of the top. Check the back for twisted seams or seams that are not laying flat. Repress if necessary. Check that the front seams are laying flat with no pleats pressed in.

If you thought all the decision making was over when you decided on the fabric, quilt pattern, color placement, and size of the quilt top, guess what? There is more! Now you're ready to decide on a backing fabric, batting choice, and type of binding. Again, we are not here to make these decisions for you, but to assist in learning how to make wise decisions based on your taste, style, and desired finished look for your quilt.

Batting

Harriet has written and lectured extensively about batting. It is one of her passions in her quilt-making career. Seems like a strange passion, doesn't it? But when you think of a quilt, isn't it the batting that really makes it a quilt? Without batting the top is still just fabric, not a quilt. Once you know more about batting, you'll get excited about all the choices that are now available and how wonderfully different your quilts can be through wise choices.

No one batting is appropriate for every quilt. Quilters need to consider things such as desired surface texture, weight, warmth, loft, drape, shrinkage, fiber content, washability and wearability, bearding properties, and ease of needling. All of these factors play as important a role in the quilt's overall appearance as do fabric choices and pattern selection. Remember, a top is not a quilt until it's quilted, and it is batting that turns the top into a quilt.

Instead of relying on the opinion of others as to which batting to use in your new tops, we are going to suggest that you continue with the exploration of quiltmaking by learning to choose your battings wisely and with direct consideration of the quilt top it's going into.

When deciding on an appropriate batt for a quilt top, ask yourself these questions:
■ Do I want a natural, synthetic, or blended fiber batt?
■ Do I want the quilt thick or thin?
■ Do I want the quilt to look flat or fluffy?

■ Do I want to hand or machine quilt it?
■ How close do I want to quilt this top?
■ Do I like to quilt?
■ Do I need this quilt for warmth, or do I want a "cooler" quilt? Is it for summer, spring, fall, or winter temperatures?
■ Is the finished quilt going to be washed a lot, or is it just for show?
■ Did I prewash my fabrics or not? Do I want shrinkage to give me an "older" look?
■ Is the quilt going to hang on the wall or lay on a bed?
■ Do I want the quilt to look antique or contemporary?
Let's examine this list and see how these answers can lead you to a batting choice.

The fiber content of the batting can affect the overall appearance of the quilt. Battings are made of cotton, cotton/polyester blends, wool, silk, and polyester. Below is a generalized listing of different styles of batting.

COTTON
Whether you desire a batting that reacts like those products available in the 1800s or 1930s, or you want the more contemporary look of the newer products, it's available.

Vintage style cotton batts require closer quilting (1" and closer) and will have a higher percentage of shrinkage than the "new generation" batts. In recent years, batting companies have started to needlepunch the fibers together, claiming that these cotton batts can be quilted up to 3" apart. With the addition of a scrim binder, claims are made that quilting distances can go up to 8" apart! Battings are also available that are made from blending fibers. They are 80% cotton/20% polyester.

Some General Characteristics About Cotton

■ Cotton sticks to the fabric, making it easy to machine quilt, but it can be more difficult for some hand quilters to needle. Bleaching cotton makes the fiber drier, causing more drag on the thread when hand quilting. The natural, unbleached battings tend to be easier for hand quilters to use.

■ Cotton shrinks, giving an older or antique look to quilts where the batting and fabrics have not been prewashed.

■ Cotton is a very comfortable fiber. It breathes, allowing excess heat to escape and keeping you from getting too warm under cotton quilts. It is one of the best fibers for baby quilts.

■ Cotton endures. Even with hard use, cotton ages gracefully, becoming softer and more cuddly with age if quilted adequately.

WOOL

Wool batting is starting to enjoy a revived interest from quiltmakers. Wool is a preferred fiber when warmth and durability are needed. We use it as a substitute for polyester when natural fibers are desirable. The comfort of wool is universally recognized as superior to that of man-made (thermo-plastic) fibers.

Wool has some very desirable characteristics that no other fiber provides.

■ Wool is very warm and lofty without being heavy. It has the ability to retain its loft and recover from compression better than any other fiber. This resiliency offers long-lasting beauty and warmth. Wool quilts and comforters can be aired twice a year to reinstate loft and fullness to the fiber.

■ Wool breathes, keeping it from getting hot and keeping our skin warm yet dry. It moderates temperature, so that you never get overly hot or overly cold sleeping under it.

■ Wool can also absorb up to 33% of its own weight in moisture without feeling damp, as opposed to 4% for synthetics. It diffuses that moisture into the atmosphere. This makes it a perfect quilt to be used in a damp, cold climate. Polyester tends to get clammy as it gets damp.

Tip A note about bearding of wool and silk: Bearding is when little tufts of batting fiber work their way to the surface of the outer fabric. If this occurs with wool or silk batts, very carefully clip away the strands as close to the surface of the fabric as possible. Separate and fluff the layers apart if possible, allowing the strands to pull back inside. Never pull the fibers, as the problems only worsen.

■ Wool is naturally flame-resistant. When it's exposed to fire it smolders at a low temperature and self-extinguishes with a cool ash, making it an extremely safe fiber to use for small children.

■ The new wool batts are washable, with little or no shrinkage.

■ Wool is extremely easy to hand quilt, often referred to as "quilting through butter."

Tip Many batting brands suggest that they can be quilted up to 10" apart. We would like you to be aware of a basic problem with this misleading claim. What is being said is that the batting will not fall apart if quilted up to 10" apart. But they are not taking into consideration the weight and wear and tear on the limited number of quilting stitches that are expected to hold everything together. Quilts are heavy and even heavier when wet during washing and drying. When a quilt is quilted farther apart than 3", there are not enough quilting lines to support this weight. This causes broken stitches and quilts that wear quickly and look less than healthy in a very short period of time. We would like you to consider keeping your quilting lines no farther apart than 3" when planning your quilting design. If you look at the beautiful antique quilts that have survived for the past 150 years or more, you'll notice that they are heavily quilted, especially compared to many of the quilts being produced in our era of quiltmaking. If you want your labor of love to last through years and years of use, try to avoid the temptation of taking the easy way out and doing minimal quilting on your tops. With good batting choices and adequate quilting, your quilts should look lovely for a long, long time.

SILK

Silk is a fiber that we seldom see used in quilts. It is used more for garments, as it's extremely light-weight and warm but very expensive. Today's silk battings can be hand washed in cold water, drip dried, and air fluffed, using no heat at any time. It can be made thin or thick depending on how much you stretch and feather the fibers onto the project. It is recommended that stitching lines be within 1½" minimum and that you avoid excess handling of the batting.

POLYESTER

Manufacturers have really worked to improve the quality of polyester batting over the past few years. The new polyesters have a lovely soft hand, less bearding, and longer loft retention than in years past. Polyester battings can give you the loft that is lacking in cottons, as well as more warmth. However, for some, it's a fairly hot fiber to sleep under, as it does not have the ability to breath and keeps the heat and moisture from dissipating. Polyester batts tend to be very stretchy and are not the best choice for a quilt that is going to hang on a wall for any period of time. They need to be quilted evenly over the entire surface of the quilt. Distortion is a problem when some areas are quilted heavily and others lightly. It is one of the most difficult battings to machine quilt, but hand quilters tend to get very small stitches in the new soft products. Polyester does not shrink, so an antique appearance is not possible, but if loft and a smooth look is what you want, it does a nice job.

Are you confused? When you start to shop for batting and encounter all the different types, and diverse opinions of people concerning batting, you may become overwhelmed in a hurry. We do not have the

space in this book to explore this topic thoroughly, so we are going to suggest that you refer to Harriet's books *Heirloom Machine Quilting* and *From Fiber to Fabric,* for the most complete information on making test samples of various battings as well as detailed information on various brands.

Other Suggestions for Working with Battings

SPLICING

Battings come in various sizes, but often you need a larger size than is available in a particular brand. This is when you need to splice two batts together to get the needed size. Frequently, two even straight edges are butted and whip-stitched together. However, the problem with this method is that the splice appears as a 'break line' through the quilt. Instead of butting two straight edges together, Harriet suggests overlapping the two pieces of batting 6" to 8". Cut a serpentine line through both layers. The gradual undulating curves will butt together perfectly once the end of each layer is removed.

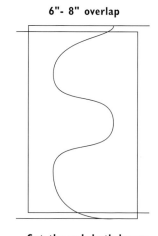

6"- 8" overlap

Cut through both layers

Hand stitch the batting together using ½"-long loose herringbone stitches. This serpentine-stitched splice will eliminate any unsightly evidence of where you made the splice.

Herringbone stitch

BATTING GRAINLINE

Many battings have a grainline. Some are more prevalent than others. To find the grainline of the batt, gently pull on it from both directions. Like fabric, the length of some batts is stronger and less able to stretch than the crossgrain. This grain needs to be taken into consideration when layering a quilt, as it can determine which direction you machine quilt first. Most polyester and wool batts do not have a recognizable grainline. They tend to stretch evenly in both directions.

Another consideration is how a quilt hangs on a wall. Always make sure that the lengthwise grains of both the batting and backing is going the length of the quilt as it hangs on the wall. Gravity can pull and stretch the fabric, especially the batting, until it sags and distorts terribly. If the stretchy grainline is being pulled constantly by gravity, you can imagine the damage and appearance. On the other hand, the lack of stretch in the lengthwise grain will slow this problem considerably. Because many polyesters and wools stretch both directions, it might be wise to not consider them for use in a hanging quilt.

We hope you're getting excited about batting and recognize that there is a lot to learn about it before you put it randomly into your favorite quilt. Many of the problems that occur in finished quilts are simply caused by using a batting that's wrong for a particular quilt.

Backings

When choosing a backing (also known as lining) for your quilt, think about letting it compliment the front. It used to be that most backings were solids or muslin, but backings have gotten a lot of attention over the past years and are now made from prints or even pieced units. If you're an excellent quilter, a solid fabric will really show off your quilting. If you're new to quilting, however, a print will camouflage any uneven stitches or contrasting threads.

The backing fabric needs to be the same fiber content, quality of cloth, weight, and thread count as the fabrics used for the top. A limited number of prints, as well as muslin, are available in 90" widths or wider for backings, though the majority of fabrics used for backings are 45" wide. Avoid using bed sheets, as they have a higher thread count and are hard to needle.

To determine the yardage needed for a backing, be sure to add 2" to 3" to the size of the quilt top on all four sides. It is helpful to make a sketch of the quilt-top measurements to help you determine any seams that might be needed and

> **Tip** An easy formula for yardage calculation is to divide the width of the quilt top by the width of the fabric (minus selvages) and round up to the nearest whole number. This gives you the number of lengths of backing you need. Multiply the length of the top in inches by the number of lengths you need, then divide by 36" to determine the number of yards you'll need to purchase.

whether to make the seams horizontal or vertical for the best usage of the yardage. See Figure 20.1 for various seam configurations to use in calculations. When figuring yardage, don't forget to subtract the width of the selvages, as they need to be removed before piecing the lengths together. 42" is the standard width used to figure yardage.

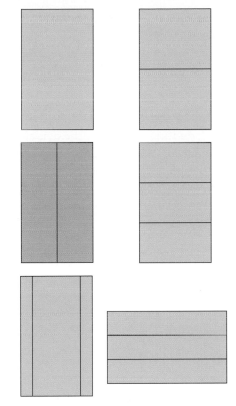

Fig. 20-1 **Backing seam placement options**

Quilts that are 42" wide or narrower need only one length of fabric (plus 4" to 5"), as the width of the fabric is wide enough to accommodate the width of the quilt top. If the top is 42" or wider, you need to seam two pieces together. If you buy two lengths of fabric for the backing for a quilt 60" long, you need 3½ yards (64" x 2 ÷ 36" = 3.56 = 3½ yards). If the seams are run horizontally, and the quilt is 44" wide, you would need only 2⅔ yards (48" x 2 ÷ 36" = 2.67 = 2⅔ yards). Quite a savings. Horizontal seams utilize the width of the fabric with the least left over.

Twin- and throw-sized quilts are generally around 72" wide or square. Using the formula, we find that two widths of fabric are needed. If the quilt is 72" x 90" and the seams are vertical, you need 5¼ yards. Horizontal seams would require three widths, needing 6 yards. Vertical seams would be the best choice.

Full sized quilts average 81" x 96" finished. Again, 2 widths will just be wide enough, needing 5⅓ yards. Horizontal seams would require 8 yards.

Queen quilts average 90" x 108" finished. Now 3 widths of fabric are required. 9⅓ yards are needed for vertical seams, but only 8 yards for horizontal. Note: If you choose to use vertical seams, they appear the most balanced if you keep one full width in the center and divide the remaining width equally between the remaining two lengths and join them on either side of the center panel.

King quilts are generally 120" x 120". A full three widths are needed for the backing, each being 3½ yards long, needing a total of 10½ yards for the backing, regardless of which direction the seams are going, as the quilt is square.

The listed yardages are just examples based on the specific quilt sizes given. It is easy to figure backing yardage if you simply plug your quilt top sizes into the formula.

Preparing the Quilt Backing and Batting

If you've prewashed your fabrics, Harriet recommends that you lightly starch the backing fabrics if you're planning to machine quilt. (If you're hand quilting, you would not need to do this.) Starching gives the fabric body, so there is a slimmer chance of getting tucks and puckers on the backing during the quilting process. It also makes gliding the fabric under the needle easier.

Often batting is wrinkled and distorted when you take it from the package. Cotton battings can be lightly steamed with your steam iron to soften and remove the wrinkles. Polyester and wool can easily be stretched out of shape during the packaging process. Placing the batt in a warm dryer with a damp washcloth and tumbling for about 10 minutes will help this problem. You may have to work a distorted area into submission while layering if it's too badly stretched.

At this point, we are going to direct you to any of the numerous books that will walk you through preparing the layers for quilting, as well as the actual quilting itself. Whether you are planning to hand or machine quilt, there is not enough space here to even begin to cover the topic. Machine quilting is covered thoroughly from this point on in *Heirloom Machine Quilting* by Harriet. Several excellent books are available for those of you who prefer hand quilting. See Recommended Reading on page 234 for a list of these titles.

Preparing the Quilt for Binding

Once the layers are quilted, you are now ready to prepare the edges for binding. You will need to first remove the excess batting and backing from the edges, square the corners, and straighten the edges.

Use a long ruler and a large square to trim the edges. Starting in the corner, check for squareness with a square ruler and trim the edges. Repeat for all corners. Next, trim the sides, keeping the border width accurate and aligning with the corner cuts. Repeat this for all four sides.

Fold the quilt ends into the center to make sure that all the widths are the same. Repeat for the sides. If the quilting runs right up to the raw edge, you won't have to add additional stabilization. If the edges are loose, we suggest that you baste (either by machine or by hand) the edges together to eliminate the possibility of distortion when sewing on the binding. Note: If you're basting by machine, be very careful not to stretch the edges as they pass under the foot. A walking foot is a great help in this process.

Binding

The quilt top has been pieced, layered, and quilted. All that now remains is to close up the edges, and at long last your quilt will be finished. Done. Ready to use. It is an exciting step ahead, and one you must not rush through. All too often, quiltmakers get to this point, then hurriedly, and without much effort, do "something" to close up those edges. Over and over at judged quilt shows, bindings are the biggest negative that a judge will find in a quilt. It's important that the way you finish your quilt looks as nice as the rest of your quilt.

You have several alternatives about how to give closure to the quilt. The most common method is an applied binding. The binding can be straight grain or bias. Fabric has three grains: straight, cross, and bias. Straight grain runs parallel to the selvages, cross grain is perpendicular to the selvages, and bias is at a 45° angle to the straight and cross.

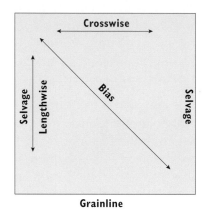

It is thought that bias grain makes a stronger edge and will last longer, especially on a bed quilt, because the wear and tear is spread over a diagonal web of threads rather than being positioned along only one or two threads as it is in straight grain. On the other hand, bias grain on a straight edge is stretchy and, if care is not taken, can stretch when applied and cause rippling along the edge. This decision becomes a personal preference as you gain experience with both.

If you're binding a quilt with straight edges you can use either. If you're binding a quilt with curves or scallops, or even if just the corners are rounded, then it will have to be bias grain in order to work. Harriet is a bit unorthodox when it comes to binding grainline. She uses neither straight nor true bias but instead a bit of both. When fabric is taken from the bolt, it's generally not on grain without some straightening. Instead of straightening the grain, Harriet cuts her strips from the off-grain fabric. This provides strips that are not perfectly on grain yet not true bias. This gives her the best of both methods, since the grain is slightly off, allowing more threads to take the wear, but not nearly as stretchy as bias.

Bias can be purchased as binding tape, or you can make your own from either grain choice. Most quiltmakers today prefer to make their own binding, as it gives them more options for print and color. Probably the easiest to make and apply is called a French Fold binding. For French Fold binding, you typically cut strips up to 2½" wide. The width you cut the strip is dependent upon how thick the batting that you've used is and how wide you want the finished binding to be. If you're reproducing a quilt from the 1800s, you'll want your binding to be as narrow as you can possibly work with—generally ¼" wide finished. These strips would be cut 1½". Regardless of the width of the binding you choose, remember that it should not be empty, but rather be totally filled with the batting and quilt layers.

STRAIGHT GRAIN DOUBLE FOLD BINDING (French Fold)

To determine how much binding you need, calculate the perimeter (distance around) of your quilt. 2 x the length + 2 x the width = the total inches of binding needed. A quilt 60" x 80" would require 280" of binding. It is recommended that you add a minimum of 10" to this sum to allow for turning corners and piecing strips together. So, how many strips is this? If you do the figuring based on 42" strips (selvage to selvage), then 290 ÷ 42 = 6.90 strips. Round up to 7, and you would need to cut 7 strips across the width of your fabric.

If the idea of doing all this math drives you crazy (after all, you just need to know how many strips to cut), then you can always do what Sharyn does. She starts by cutting one strip and laying it down along one edge of the quilt, she then "guesstimates" how many strips are needed for that side. If the quilt is square, she multiplies that number by four. If a quilt is rectangular, she does the strip test once for the short side and once for the long side, then doubles each of those numbers. Add those two numbers together and you know your needs.

See the chart below which gives you an estimate of the yardage needed to bind various size quilts with straight-grain binding. These measurements are based on ½" finished binding.

BIAS GRAIN DOUBLE FOLD BINDING

Stripes and plaids can make fun-looking bias edges, because there is an extra element of design created by the new pattern. A stripe actually makes a candy-cane look if cut on the bias.

Typically, bias strips are cut from a square. Lay your ruler corner to corner across the diagonal of the square and slice.

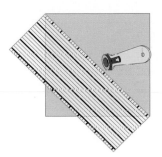

Slice the square in half

Position the two triangles one on top of the other, lining up the diagonal slice. Measure from this edge and cut them into the desired width strips.

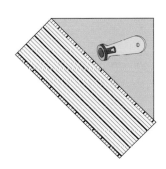

Cut bias strips

When you work with a large square of fabric, you may find it helpful to fold the stacked triangles in half as illustrated before cutting.

Cut folded stacks

Estimated Yardage for ½" Wide Straight Grain Binding			
Quilt Size	# of 2½" Wide Strips	Inches of Fabric	Yards of Fabric
Wallhanging (36" x 36")	5	12½	⅜
Twin (54" x 90")	8	20	⅝
Double (72" x 90")	8	20	⅝
Queen (90" x 108")	10	25	¾
King (120" x 120")	12	30	⅞

A similar method, continuous bias, involves using the same square sliced in half diagonally but sewing the triangles together so that you continuously cut the marked strips. (1) Cut a square of fabric the size needed (see chart). Cut the square in half diagonally, creating two triangles.

(2) Sew these triangles together as shown, using a ¼" seam allowance.

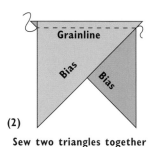

(2)

Sew two triangles together

(3) After sewing, open the triangles and press the seam open. This will give you a parallelogram. Using a ruler, mark the entire back side with lines spaced the width you need to cut your bias. Cut along the first line about 5".

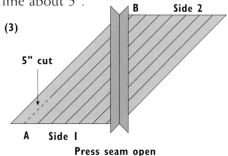

(3)

5" cut

Press seam open

(4) Connect A and B and Side 1 and Side 2 to form a tube. (The cut edge on the first line will line up with the raw edge at B. This will allow the first line to be offset by one line.) Pin the raw ends together, making sure that the lines match. Sew with a ¼" seam allowance.

(4)

Offset by one line and sew tube

Estimated Yardage for ½" Bias Binding		
Quilt Size	Bias Needed	Fabric Needed
Wallhanging (36" x 36")	4½ yards	22" square
Twin (54" x 90")	8½ yards	28" square
Double (72" x 90")	9½ yards	30" square
Queen (90" x 108")	11½ yards	33" square
King (120" x 120")	14½ yards	38" square

If you've aligned the seam properly, you'll have an extra strip at each end. Continue cutting on the line you started in Step 3. As you cut on the line, the tube will become one long piece of bias.

You're probably wondering how big a square to begin with and how many strips you need to cut. Here is an easy formula you can use to figure out the yield of running inches in bias strips that you can get from a square: **side x side ÷ the width of strips to be cut. Example: 22 x 22 = 484 ÷ 2 ¼" (binding size) = 215".**

Another easy way to calculate the amount of bias you can get from a square is to divide the square size by the width of bias needed, then multiply only the whole number portion of the answer by the square size again. Example: a 22" square ÷ 2¼" (width of bias) = 9.78. Multiply 9.78 by 22 = 215" of bias yielded.

Here's a chart you might like to keep handy that tells you the yield of bias strips per square when cut 2" or at 2¼".

Yielded Bias Strips per Square		
Fabric Square	Yield in Inches (2" Strip)	Yield in Inches (2¼" Strip)
12" x 12" (144 sq. in.)	72"	64"
18" x 18" (324 sq. in.)	162"	144"
22" x 22" (484 sq. in.)	242"	215"
36" x 36" (1296 sq. in.)	648"	576"

APPLYING DOUBLE FOLD BINDING

First you must join the strips together. If you're using bias strips, they are already angle cut. If you've cut straight grain strips, you first want to cut the ends at a 45° angle. To do this easily, fold your cross grain strips in half to match the selvages. Position the 45° angle of the ruler on the edge of the strip as shown, then cut. Repeat with the remainder of your strips.

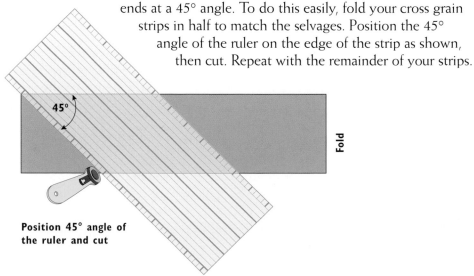

45°

Fold

Position 45° angle of the ruler and cut

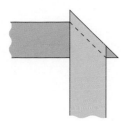

Join strip ends together

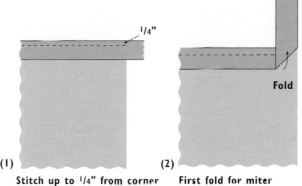
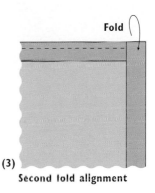

(1) **Stitch up to ¼" from corner**   (2) **First fold for miter**   (3) **Second fold alignment**

To join the strips together, line up the edges, offsetting by ¼" and sew with a ¼" seam allowance. Continue joining all the strips together into one continuous length.

Your next step is to press the strip. Begin by first opening up the seams and pressing. Next, fold the strip in half lengthwise, wrong sides together, and press the entire length.

(1) To attach the binding to the quilt, begin by positioning the raw edges of the binding with the raw edges of the quilt. You want to begin not at the corner of the quilt, but rather somewhere inconspicuous along one side. Start sewing approximately 5" from the end of the binding. Using a ¼" seam allowance, stitch in place, stopping ¼" from the corner, and either lock the stitches or turn the quilt and backstitch off the back edge.

(2) Turn your quilt so that you're lined up to sew the next side. Fold the binding straight up toward the side you just sewed, then refold toward the new edge, lining up the second fold with the outer edge of the quilt, and the raw edges of the binding with the raw edges of the quilt.

(3) Begin sewing at the outer edge of the quilt; sew through all layers at the corner. Continue down the edge, repeating the corner treatment.

To join the pieces together, you have two choices. One is to seam them together following Method 1; the other is simply to lay the end inside the start as described in Method 2.

Harriet's favorite is Method 1, because she likes that all the seams are finished on the bias and that you cannot tell where you start and stop. Sharyn always uses Method 2 because, try as she will, she cannot get those pieces exact when she tries to seam them together.

METHOD ONE: SEAMING THE ENDS TOGETHER

As you approach the end of the binding where you started, stop about 16" from the beginning stitches. This allows for plenty of room in which to join the ends on the bias. Overlap the loose ends of binding where they meet. Lay the ends of the Side 2 binding strip flat. Lay the beginning end of Side 1 on top of Side 2, keeping both binding strips folded.

(1) **Label side 1**

(1) Label the long point of Side 1 "A." Label the short point of Side 1 "B."

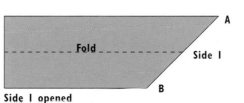

Side 1 opened

(2) Mark dot A onto the top layer of Side 2. Mark dot B onto the bottom layer of Side 2.

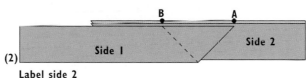

(2) **Label side 2**

(3) Open Side 2 and measure ½" to the left of these dots. This provides seam allowances. Cut on this line.

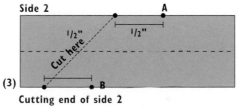

(3) **Cutting end of side 2**

(4) Open Side 1. With right sides together, stitch Side 1 to Side 2 using a ¼" seam allowance.

Press the seam open. Fold the joined strip in half and press. The binding should be a perfect fit.

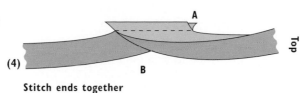

(4) **Stitch ends together**

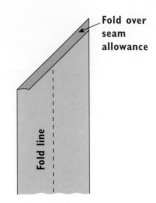

(I) Fold ¹/₄" seam allowance on 45° angle

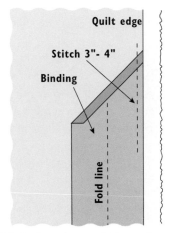

(2) Stitch through one thickness from point

Quilt edge

Stitch 3"- 4"

Binding

Fold line

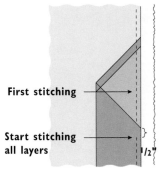

(3) Fold binding over to double

First stitching

Start stitching all layers

¹/₂"

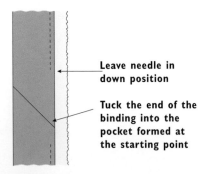

(4) Tuck in end and close stitching

Leave needle in down position

Tuck the end of the binding into the pocket formed at the starting point

Fold over seam allowance

Fold line

METHOD TWO: LAY IT INSIDE

(I) Cut and join strips as in Applying Double Fold Binding, page 224. Fold the entire length of strip in half, wrong sides together, and press. At one end of the strip fold a ¹/₄" seam allowance over to the wrong side and press.

(2) With the long fold open, position the binding on top of the quilt top. Start stitching the binding at the point, stitching through only one thickness of the binding. Stitch for about four inches.

(3) Lift the presser foot and cut the threads. Fold the binding over to double. Start stitching about ¹/₂" below the short edge of the point and continue around the entire quilt as in Applying Double Fold Binding, page 224.

(4) Once you've arrived back to the beginning, tuck the end of the binding into the pocket. Lower the needle into the fabric. Lay the end of the binding strip over the point and single thickness that was the starting point. Cut off the end just before the stitching that started going through all layers. Tuck the end into the pocket and finish closing the seam.

FINAL SEWING OF BINDING

Wrap the binding around to the back of the quilt, placing the folded edge of the binding on top of the stitching line, and blind stitch by hand. Begin the blind stitch by inserting the needle under the edge of the binding right at the fold edge of the binding. Next, put the needle into the quilt immediately across from where it is in the binding. You don't want to stitch through to the front, just into the batting. Let your needle travel approximately ¹/₄" through the inside of the quilt. Emerge and travel into the binding, again right at the edge. Continue in this manner.

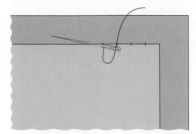

Finish edge with blind stitching

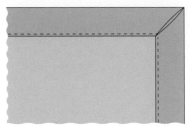

Binding machine straight stitched

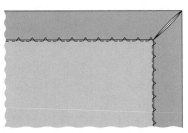

Binding machine blind stitched

When you get to the corners, you'll find that the corner is already formed on the top of the quilt, but you'll need to coax the miter on the back with your fingers. Fold one side down, then the other, creating a neat miter. The fold should be opposite that on the front side, distributing the bulk evenly for both sides. This gives a flat corner.

You might prefer to do the second side of the binding by machine. Both Sharyn and Harriet enjoy performing the binding process by hand. It is one time that you can snuggle up with the quilt and relax with the stitching. However, we know that not everyone finds this a relaxing experience. The binding can be machine stitched down, using either a straight stitch or a blind hem stitch.

The easiest way to achieve a nice machine-applied binding is to stitch the binding to the back of the quilt first, then bring it around to the front and either straight or blind stitch it in place.

We suggest using an edge-stitch foot to achieve the neatest and most accurate straight stitch. Change the needle position on your machine to the right. The guide on the foot will run right in the ditch of the binding seam, and the needle will stitch just on the folded edge of the binding.

When using the blind stitch, use invisible thread; you'll be stitching in the ditch as well as on the binding, and the thread will show on the quilt top. The blind stitch setting on most machines has three to five straight stitches, then a single zigzag. Set the machine to a narrow stitch width (the narrower it is, the less noticeable it will be) and a stitch length of no more than $^1/_4$" between the zigzag. If your machine zigzags to the right, the bulk of the quilt will be on your left. If it doesn't and you have a mirror image feature on the machine, engage it so that it zigzags to the right. If this is not possible, the bulk of the quilt will be inside the arm of the machine.

OTHER BINDING OPTIONS
1" Border Binding
The 1"-wide border binding is fun and fast. The wide-finished binding also serves as a small border or frame for the quilt.

Cut strips $5^1/_2$" wide. If you need additional length to make the border for one side of the quilt, join the strips on the bias as described with double folded binding. Do not join all the strips together this time as you did for $^1/_2$" binding. The strips need to be 5" to 6" longer than each side of the quilt. Fold the strips in half lengthwise, making them $2^3/_4$" wide, and press.

To prepare the quilt top, trim the backing and batting to $^3/_4$" beyond the edge of the quilt top. This extension will be enclosed within the binding. Sew the binding onto one top side of the quilt top, starting and stopping $^1/_4$" from the raw edge (the seam line) that is perpendicular to the edge you are sewing.

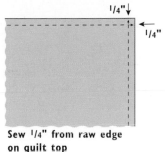

Sew $^1/_4$" from raw edge on quilt top

A $2^1/_2$" to 3"-wide tail of binding has been left at each end of each border strip. Join these tails at the corners to make perfect miters by folding one edge's tail back so that it lies exactly on the binding (see Figure 20-2). Lay the other side over it. Draw a line on the top piece that extends the seam line of the binding piece that is on the bottom. This is line AB.

Find the measurement that is halfway between the folded edge and the seam line of AB. C is the midpoint of line AB. Draw a line from C perpendicular to AB. On this line, measure a length up from C that is the same length as AC or CB. This point is D. See Figure 20.3.

Example: If AC = $1^1/_4$", CB should = $1^1/_4$" and CD should = $1^1/_4$". Draw in a sewing line that goes from A to D and from D to B.

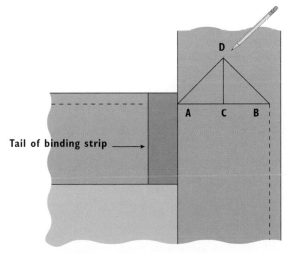

Figure 20.2   **Prepare corner**

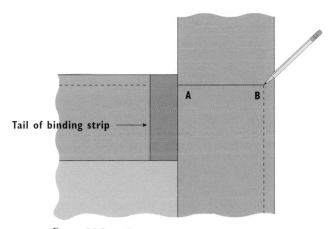

Figure 20.3   **Develop sewing line**

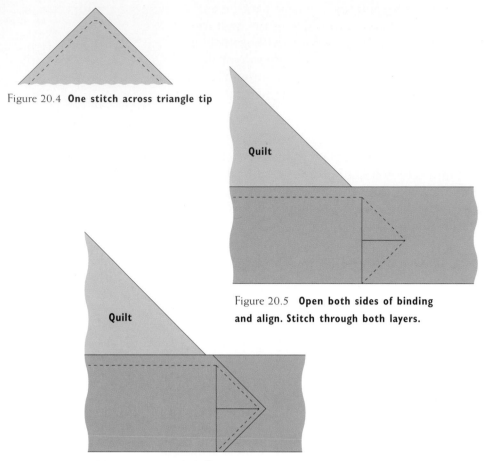

Figure 20.4 **One stitch across triangle tip**

Figure 20.5 **Open both sides of binding and align. Stitch through both layers.**

Trim excess, leaving ¹/₄" seam allowance

Open both sides of the binding and fold the quilt diagonally from the corner. Align both binding strips so that their edges are exactly even and their corners match. Pin in place and sew line ADB. See Figure 20.5. Backstitch at the beginning and end. At the point, you need to take a stitch across the point to keep it perfect. Stop stitching one stitch from the point, take one stitch across to the other side, and continue down line DB. See Figure 20.4.

Trim seam allowance. Use a point turner to straighten the point and roll the binding to the back. The folded edge should align with the seam line on the back, making a perfect mitered corner on the front and back. Stitch in place by hand or machine.

WRAPPED EDGE (BACK TO FRONT)

If your backing fabric compliments the front of the quilt and is big enough, you can elect to simply wrap the back around to the front and finish the edges of your quilt that way. Begin by basting the quilt layers together along the outer seam line. Trim the batting to extend beyond the seam line so that the total measurement includes the width of the binding. The batting should entirely fill the new edge. The backing width beyond the seam line is equal to the binding width x 2, plus ¹/₄". Working on a large table or ironing board, lay the quilt out flat, right side up. This edge can be stitched using the same blind stitch as for the Double Fold Binding, page 226 or you can use a running stitch through all layers.

Mitered Corners for Wrapped Edge Binding

You will miter the four corners first. Press each corner of the backing over the quilt top, making sure that the tip meets the corner seam line.

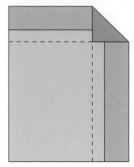

Press each corner of backing

Trim away the tip of the corner and press backing edges ¹/₄" to the front.

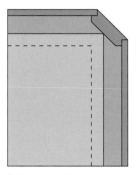

Trim tip and press

Fold one edge over the quilt top, covering the seam line. Fold the opposite edge, forming a mitered corner. Pin and blind stitch.

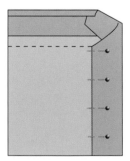

Fold over edges

Butted Corners for Wrapped Edge Binding

Press one pair of opposite backing edges $1/4$" to front. Fold backing to front again, covering the seam line. Pin and stitch.

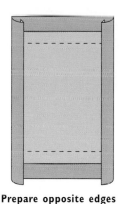

Prepare opposite edges

Press and pin the remaining sides of the backing edges in the same manner. Pin and stitch.

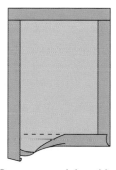

Prepare remaining sides

INSERTED EDGES

An inserted edge can include prairie points, scallops, ruffles, or piping. To create the inserted edge, attach the insertion to the front and batting and sew through all layers all the way around the quilt. Next, fold the back of the quilt over the seam allowance and blind stitch in place.

To Make Prairie Points

Prairie points are a fun way to add interest to the edge of a quilt. They can be added after the quilt top is quilted—especially if the quilting extends to the edges of the quilt top or before the quilting is done.

The points are made by cutting $3\frac{1}{2}$" squares of the chosen fabric or fabrics. Each point will cover about $2\frac{1}{2}$" to 3" along the quilts edge. Divide the total perimeter of the quilt top by $2\frac{1}{2}$ or 3 to find out how many points are needed.

Fold each square in half diagonally, right side out. Fold in half again, forming a small triangle. Press.

Folding a prairie point

Working from the quilt top front, align the long side of the folded triangle to the raw edge of the quilt top. Begin at the center of one side of the quilt. The points will lap over one another. Adjust this along the side to fit evenly. Stitch onto the quilt top and batting.

Trim the batting and backing to be even with the top. Trim out as much of the batting from this seam as possible. This will eliminate the bulk caused by the extra fabric from the triangles. Turn the prairie points so that they face out from the quilt top. The raw edge of the quilt top will be inside. Turn under $1/4$" of the backing. Blind stitch the folded edge of the backing to the prairie point edges, completely covering the seam.

A very slick way of making continuous-band prairie points has been floating around since before 1989, but the name of the inventor and where the technique came from seem to have been lost. It has been in magazines, given out as free hand-outs by sewing machine companies, and offered in guild newsletters. Whoever came up with this great idea, please come forward!

There are fewer possibilities for variation in color and fabrics with this method than with the individual squares, but it's certainly faster and easier. Because they are not made individually, they are always the same size and evenly spaced.

Our example here will produce an edging with triangles that finish to $1^{3}/_{4}$" high and $3^{1}/_{2}$" wide along the straight edge. As always, we recommend that you make a sample to experience the technique and determine what your measurements will be.

1) Start by cutting an 8"-wide strip of fabric the same length as one edge of the quilt, plus about 6" extra. If necessary, piece strips together to get this needed length.
2) Place wrong sides of the strips together and fold the strip in half lengthwise. Press well.
3) Place the fabric strip wrong side up, opened to the 8" width. Beginning at one end, start marking off 4" segments on one side of the band. On the opposite side, begin 2" in from the end and again mark off 4" segments. The 2" portion will be on opposite ends and opposite sides and will be cut away, as will as any extra fabric not included in the 4" segments. It makes no difference if one side is longer or has one more square than the other.
4) Cut the squares on the marked lines from the outer edge to the center pressed fold.

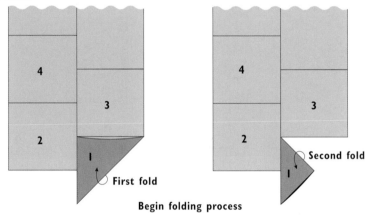
Begin folding process

Prepare 4" segments on strip

You will be pressing as you go, so work at the ironing board. Begin by turning the fabric wrong side up and fold the points as follows:
(a) Beginning with Point #1, place it nearest to you and make the first fold as shown. Next, turn the top corner down for the second fold.
(b) Move to Point #2 and make the first fold. Next, fold Point #1 across the bottom part of Point #2. Make the second fold of Point #2. This will enclose half of the base of Point #1. Pin in place.

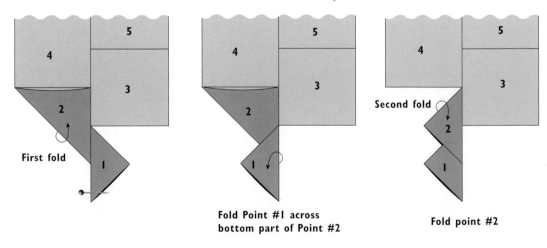
Fold Point #1 across bottom part of Point #2

Fold point #2

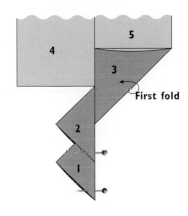

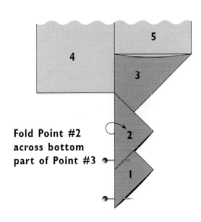

First fold

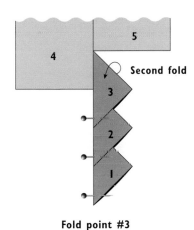

Fold Point #2 across bottom part of Point #3

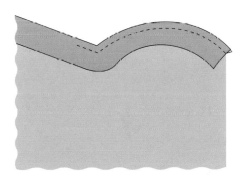

Second fold

Fold point #3

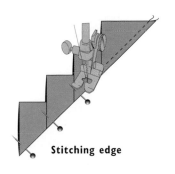

Stitching edge

(c) Next, make the first fold of Point #3. Now fold points #1 and #2 over and make the last fold on Point #3. This will enclose half of the base of Point #2. Pin in place. (d) Continue in this manner, alternating from side to side, until all the points are folded and pinned.

5) Once the entire strip has been folded and pinned, machine stitch ⅛" from the raw edge, removing pins as you go. Press.

6) Repeat this process for each side of the quilt.

7) Pin the prairie points in position on the right side of the quilt top, keeping the backing fabric out of the way. If there are any extra complete points beyond the edge of the quilt, cut them off. Do not cut through a point. Ease if necessary to make it fit perfectly.

8) Sew a ¼" seam allowance through all the layers except the backing. Trim any excess batting close to the stitching.

9) Once the prairie points have been sewn, fold them away from the quilt top and stitch the backing in place along the seam line on the back.

Scallops

Single thickness binding is the easiest to work with when applying it to inside corners. Cut bias strips 1¼" wide. After trimming the quilt layers, pin the edge of the binding to the edge of the quilt top. As you stitch, ease the binding around the outer curves, being careful not to stretch it in the process. At the inside point of the curve, lift the presser foot and pivot, taking care that no pleats or puckers are formed in the binding. Once stitched, clip the seam allowance at inner points to the stitching.

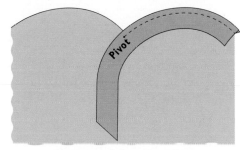

Stitching and pivoting at point

Turn under raw edge ¼" and fold binding over quilt edges to backing and pin. Blind stitch, folding miters at inner points.

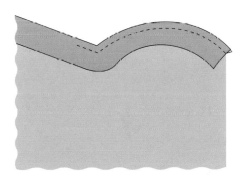

Folded miter

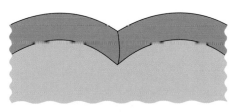

Turn binding over

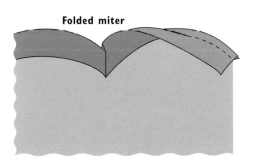

Piping

Piping is made from strips cut ³/₄" wide across the width of the fabric. Piece the strips together with 45° angle seams. Join enough strips to make a length about 3" longer than each side of the quilt. Press the strips in half lengthwise, right side out. Pin the piping strips to the right side of each quilt edge. Overlap the strip ends at the corners. Next, place the binding on top of the piping strips, keeping the edges even. Pin and stitch through all layers, following the above instructions for applying bindings. Take extra care to keep the seams even, as this determines the finished width of the piping.

BLOCKING THE FINISHED QUILT

Blocking may not be necessary for bed quilts and throws; however, wall quilts may require this technique to ensure that they hang straight. Begin by laying the quilt flat on a floor and see how flat it lies. You are checking to make sure the layers did not stretch and distort through the quilting and binding process. If you see that there is waviness in the borders or along the edge, you may need to block and steam the quilt into shape.

Start by pinning a string the length of the quilt in a straight line parallel to the floor or wall. Next, drop a plumb line from the corner (if the string is on a wall), using a weight to make it hang straight. If the string is on the floor, use a carpenter's square. The strings will give you straight lines to work off of. Position the quilt, aligning one corner with the strings, stretching slightly if necessary. Pin in place just inside the binding, using as many pins as necessary. This will keep the edge straight. Measuring diagonally corner to corner in both directions, as well as side to side and top to bottom along several points, do your best to pin the quilt into a carpet (small quilts can be done on a design wall), so it is as straight and square as

possible. If you're working on the wall, work with a dampened press cloth. Place it over a section, then use your iron on a wool setting and press the cloth until it's almost dry. The layers of the quilt will absorb the moisture and then dry to shape. If you're working on the floor, spray-dampen the entire surface of the quilt and leave it pinned to the floor until it is dry. Working on the floor with an iron can be tricky with synthetic carpet.

Hanging Methods

The most common method used to hang a quilt is to attach a sleeve to the back top edge of the quilt. To make a sleeve, cut a strip the width of the quilt by 8". Hem each of the short edges. Fold the strip in half lengthwise, wrong sides together, and press. If using an applied binding, the raw edges of the sleeve can be positioned with the outer edge of the quilt and stitched at the same time that the binding is applied. The bottom edge of the sleeve, the fold edge, is then whip stitched by hand through the backing and batting, but not through to the front of the quilt.

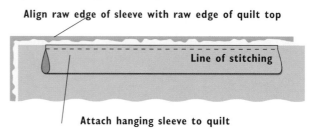

Align raw edge of sleeve with raw edge of quilt top

Line of stitching

Attach hanging sleeve to quilt

If you're making a temporary hanging sleeve, both long edges of the sleeve need to be whip stitched by hand. Start by hemming the ends of the sleeve. Next, fold the strip in half, wrong sides together. Do not press, but rather sew the raw edges together. Then go to the ironing board and iron the strip so that the seam is in the center of one of the sides. Position the pressed sleeve with the seamed side toward the quilt. Whip stitch by hand.

If you have a very large quilt, or one that doesn't quite want to hang flat, you might want to try placing one sleeve at the top and one at the bottom. A wooden rod at the bottom will weight the quilt and help it hang smoother.

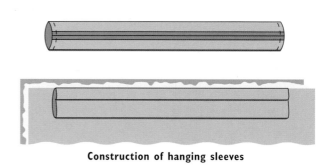

Construction of hanging sleeves

A rod can be inserted into the opening of the sleeve pocket (between the two sleeve layers, not actually touching the quilt). Depending on the size of your quilt, select a wood piece strong enough not to bow while hanging. ¹/₄" x 3" wood molding works well for even a very large quilt.

Method One for hanging is to insert the wooden rod into the sleeve so that it extends approximately ¹/₂" on each end. Use nails with ¹/₄" heads upon which the rod can sit.

Method Two for hanging is to insert the wooden rod into the sleeve so that it extends approximately ¹/₄" on each end. Insert a screw eye into the rod at each end. A tiny nail through the screw eye assures that the quilt won't fall off.

For more ideas and instructions on different edge finishes, see Recommended Reading on page 234.

Recommended Reading

COLOR
Color and Cloth, Mary Coyne Penders,
     The Quilt Digest Press

Color Confidence for Quilters, by Jinny Beyer

Creative Ideas for Color and Fabric, Susan McKelvey

The Magical Effects of Color, by Joen Wolfrom

WORKSPACE
*Dream Sewing Spaces: Design and Organization for Spaces
     Large and Small*, by Lynette Ranney Black

*Setting up your Sewing Space: From Small Areas to Complete
     Workshops*, by Myrna Giesbrecht

Sew Organized!, by Michelé Shoesmith

ROTARY CUTTING
Judy Martin's Ultimate Rotary Cutting Reference by Judy Matin

Measure the Possibilities with Omnigrid
     by Nancy Johnson-Srebro

The Quilter's Guide to Rotary Cutting by Donna Poster

Timeless Treasures: The Complete Book on Rotary Cutting
     by Nancy Johnson-Srebro

PRESSING IDEAS
Press For Success, Secrets for Precise and Speedy Quiltmaking
     by Myrna Giesbrecht

LOG CABIN
#5 A Log Cabin Notebook by Mary Ellen Hopkins

Classic American Quilt Collection, Log Cabin (Rodale Press)

Design Challenge: Half Log Cabin PLUS by Sharyn Craig

Design Challenge: Half Log Cabin Quilts by Sharyn Craig

Log Cabin Design Workbook by Christal Carter

Log Cabins: New Techniques for Traditional Quilts
     by Janet Kime

BORDERS AND SETTINGS
Borders by Design by Paulette Peters

Pieced Borders by Judy Martin and Marsha McCloskey

Sensational Sets & Borders (Rodale Press)

Sensational Settings by Joan Hanson

Sets and Borders by Gwen Marston and Joe Cunningham

Surprising Designs from Traditional Quilt Blocks by Carole Fure

Borders and Finishing Touches by Bonnie Browning

MACHINE QUILTING
Exploring Machine Trapunto by Hari Walner

Fast & Fun Machine Quilting (Rodale Press)

Heirloom Machine Quilting by Harriet Hargrave

Machine Quilting with Decorative Threads by Maurine Noble

Trapunto by Machine by Hari Walner

HAND QUILTING
Hand Quilting with Alex Anderson by Alex Anderson

How to Improve Your Quilting Stitch by Ami Simms

Learn to do Hand Quilting in Just One Day
     by Nancy Brenan Daniel

Loving Stitches by Jeanna Kimball

The Perfect Stitch by Roxanne McElroy

Surface Textures by Anita Shackelford

DESIGNING QUILTING PATTERNS
Encyclopedia of Designs for Quilting by Phyllis Miller

The Essential Quilter by Barbara Chainey

Mastering Quilt Marking by Pepper Cory

Quilt It by Barbara Chaney

Quilting Makes the Quilt by Lee Cleland

Quilting with Style by Gwen Marston and Joe Cunningham

EDGE FINISHES
A Fine Finish by Cody Mazuran

Fantastic Finishes (Rodale Press publication)

Happy Endings by Mimi Dietrich

Resources

GRAPH PAPER
Chitra Publications
Public Avenue
Montrose, Pennsylvania 18801
(800) 628-8244
chitra@epix.net

TEMPLATE KIT MATERIAL
John Flynn
Flynn Quilt Frame Company
Shiloh Overpass Road
Billings, Montana 59106-3905
(800) 745-3596
www.flynnquilt.com

About the Authors

Both Harriet Hargrave and Sharyn Craig have Home Economics degrees with an emphasis in clothing and textiles. They share a love of fabric and its texture and color. They both started sewing at very early ages, progressing from doll clothes, to their own clothes, their families' clothes, to home decorations and crafts.

Harriet started quilting seriously in 1974, working alongside her mom. Her early quilting career included producing baby quilts for craft shows and teaching adult education classes. In 1980, Harriet opened her quilt shop, Harriet's Treadle Arts. The adult ed. students followed Harriet into her shop and continued investigating the various machine arts in her shop classroom. Her specialty at that time was free motion machine embroidery, machine arts, and machine quilting. In 1982, Harriet attended one of Mary Ellen Hopkins's seminars. Mary Ellen's method of working with patchwork blocks opened a whole new way of thinking for Harriet. This led Harriet into teaching strictly quilting and forgoing the machine arts. Today she is best known as the pioneer of machine quilting and appliqué.

Sharyn started quilting in 1978, when she took an adult education class. By 1980, her enthusiasm for making quilts led her into teaching the classes themselves: first one, then two, finally four classes a week, averaging 50 students per class. She taught within the adult ed. system for 11 years. In 1991, Sharyn began to teach internationally. One of her strongest talents is the ability to come up with efficient, organized sewing systems that relate to traditional blocks. She is also known as an inspiring teacher who encourages her students to be creative in their own work.

Between the two of them, they have accumulated over 40 years of teaching experience, completed hundreds of quilts, and taught thousands of students.

Index

Other Fine Books by Harriet Hargrave

An American Quilt Retailer
Classics Award winner
—Best Instructional Book for
Machine Quilting

**Mastering Machine
Appliqué**

*The Satin Stitch, Mock
Hand Appliqué and Other
Techniques*
by Harriet Hargrave

From Fiber to Fabric

*The Essential Guide to
Quiltmaking Textiles*
by Harriet Hargrave

**Heirloom Machine
Quilting**

*A Comprehensive Guide to
Hand Quilted Effects Using
Your Sewing Machine,
Third Edition*
by Harriet Hargrave

**Quick-Look
Guide: Choosing
Batting**

**Take this handy guide
with you to shop for bat-
ting! Filled with valuable
tips and charts in an
easy-to-use format.**

by Harriet Hargrave

**Quick-Look
Guide: Caring for
Fabric & Quilts**

**Keep this handy guide
near your laundry area!
Packed with valuable tips
and charts in an easy-to-
use format.**

by Harriet Hargrave

Other Fine Books from C&T Publishing

An Amish Adventure: 2nd Edition, Roberta Horton
The Best of Baltimore Beauties, Elly Sienkiewicz
Curves in Motion: Quilt Designs & Techniques,
     Judy B. Dales
*Fabric Shopping with Alex Anderson, Seven Projects to Help
     You: Make Successful Choices, Build Your
     Confidence, Add to Your Fabric Stash,* Alex Anderson
Fancy Appliqué: 12 Lessons to Enhance Your Skills,
     Elly Sienkiewicz
Fantastic Fabric Folding: Innovative Quilting Projects,
     Rebecca Wat
Free Stuff for Collectors on the Internet, Judy Heim and
     Gloria Hansen
Free Stuff for Gardeners on the Internet, Judy Heim and
     Gloria Hansen
*Hand Quilting with Alex Anderson: Six Projects for Hand
     Quilters,* Alex Anderson
*The New England Quilt Museum Quilts: Featuring the
     Story of the Mill Girls. With Instructions for 5 Heirloom
     Quilts,* Jennifer Gilbert
Pieced Flowers, Ruth B. McDowell
*Pieced Roman Shades: Turn Your Favorite Quilt Patterns
     into Window Hangings,* Terrell Sundermann
Piecing: Expanding the Basics, Ruth B. McDowell
*Quilt It for Kids; 11 Projects, Sports, Fantasy & Animal
     Themes, Quilts for Children of All Ages,* Pam Bono
Quilts from Europe, Projects and Inspiration, Gül Laporte
*Quilts from the Civil War: Nine Projects, Historical Notes,
     Diary Entries,* Barbara Brackman

Rx for Quilters: Stitcher-Friendly Advice for Every Body,
     Susan Delaney Mech, M.D.
Scrap Quilts: The Art of Making Do, Roberta Horton
Shadow Quilts: Easy-to-Design Multiple Image Quilts,
     Patricia Magaret and Donna Slusser
Special Delivery Quilts, Patrick Lose
Tradition with a Twist: Variations on Your Favorite Quilts,
     Blanche Young and Dalene Young Stone
Wild Birds: Designs for Appliqué & Quilting,
     Carol Armstrong

For more information write for a free catalog:
C&T Publishing, Inc.
P.O. Box 1456
Lafayette, CA 94549
(800) 284-1114
e-mail: ctinfo@ctpub.com
http://www.ctpub.com

For quilting supplies:
Cotton Patch Mail Order
3405 Brown Avenue, Dept. CTB
Lafayette, CA 94549
e-mail: quiltusa@yahoo.com
http://www.quiltusa.com
(800) 835-4418
(925) 283-7883